Third Edition

Workbook in Everyday Spanish

Book 1

Elementary/Intermediate

Julio I. Andújar

Robert J. Dixson

Prentice Hall

Upper Saddle River, New Jersey 07458

Editor-in-Chief: *Rosemary Bradley*
Associate Editor: *María F. García*
Senior Managing Editor: *Deborah Brennan*
Cover & Interior Design: *Ximena Piedra Tamvakopoulos*
Senior Marketing Manager: *Christopher Johnson*
Manufacturing Buyer: *Tricia Kenny*

©1997, 1991, 1958 by R. J. Dixon Associates
Published by Prentice Hall, Inc. A Viacom Company
Upper Saddle River, New Jersey 07458

Printed in the United States of America
10 9 8 7 6 5 4 3 2 1

ISBN   0-13-432774-8

Prentice Hall International (UK) Limited, *London*
Prentice Hall of Australia Pty. Limited, *Sydney*
Prentice Hall Canada Inc., *Toronto*
Prentice Hall Hispanoamericana, S.A., *México*
Prentice Hall of India Private Limited, *New Delhi*
Prentice Hall of Japan, Inc. *Tokyo*
Prentice Hall of Southeast Asia Pte. Ltd, *Singapore*

Contents

Preface

Workbook in Everyday Spanish is a two-volume program offering a tried and true approach to reviewing grammar and vocabulary. The program is intended as a supplement to your main classroom text, for homework assignments and self-study. Both volumes offer a systematic, graded presentation and practice of Spanish grammar, vocabulary and sentence structure.

As in previous editions, the third edition is organized into one- or two-page *Worksheets* that present a topic and provide practice of that topic. The presentations include clear and concise English explanations of key grammatical points followed by straightforward examples that guide students through the accompanying exercises. The topics are then reinforced in self-contained *Review* sections. After most *Review* sections is a **Buscapalabras** or word game that keeps student interest level high.

The convenient format of *Workbook in Everyday Spanish* allows students to write directly in their books, tear out their worksheets, and submit them to their instructors for evaluation. A separate Answer Key is also available free of charge to instructors using *Workbook in Everyday Spanish* and for student purchase.

The *Third Edition* has been enhanced by sequencing topics to correspond to the scope and sequence of most Spanish language texts. This makes the *Workbook in Everyday Spanish* program ideal for use as a supplement to any Spanish language text.

Contents

Worksheet 1.1 Definite articles and gender of nouns

Definite articles **el, la, los, las** (*the*) agree in gender and number with the noun they precede. Generally, nouns ending in -a, -as are feminine and take **la, las.** Nouns ending in -o, -os are usually masculine and take **el, los.** Several exceptions are described on p. 144. The gender of nouns ending in other vowels or in consonants must be memorized.

EXAMPLES:

el gato	*the cat*	**los** estudiantes	*the students*
la gata	*the cat*	**las** vacaciones	*the vacations*
el elefante	*the elephant*	**el** papel	*the paper*

➤ Fill in the correct definite article.

1. ___El___ libro

2. ___Las___ muchachas

3. _____ calles (f)

4. _____ cuaderno

5. _____ mujeres (f)

6. _____ hombres (m)

7. _____ profesor (m)

8. _____ cubanos

9. _____ mexicana

10. _____ señores (m)

11. _____ casa

12. _____ colores (m)

13. _____ manzanas

14. _____ papeles (m)

15. _____ ventanas

16. _____ amigos

17. _____ escuela

18. _____ médico

19. _____ primas

20. _____ hermana

21. _____ enfermera

22. _____ enfermeras

23. _____ cielo

24. _____ español (m)

25. _____ lápices (m)

26. _____ muchacho

27. _____ muchacha

28. _____ puertas

29. _____ plátanos

30. _____ padres (m)

31. _____ ciudad (f)

32. _____ noches (f)

33. _____ madre (f)

34. _____ verduras

35. _____ pan (m)

36. _____ niña

37. _____ ruidos

38. _____ profesora

39. _____ cuchillo

40. _____ cucharas

Worksheet 1.2 Indefinite articles

The indefinite article **un (a)** is used with a masculine noun.

EXAMPLES: **un** lápiz   *a pencil*   **un** niño   *a boy*

The indefinite article **una (a)** is used with a feminine noun.

EXAMPLES: **una** pluma   *a pen*   **una** camisa   *a shirt*

➤ Fill in the correct indefinite article.

1. __Un__ libro
2. __Una__ pluma
3. _____ muchacho
4. _____ cuchillo
5. _____ ejercicio
6. _____ pizarra
7. _____ escuela
8. _____ hermano
9. _____ muchacha
10. _____ amigo
11. _____ amiga
12. _____ manzana
13. _____ cuaderno
14. _____ médico
15. _____ profesora
16. _____ primo
17. _____ cuchara
18. _____ maestro
19. _____ escritorio
20. _____ hermana

21. _____ puerta
22. _____ señora
23. _____ familia
24. _____ zapato
25. _____ camisa
26. _____ corbata
27. _____ ventana
28. _____ silla
29. _____ norteamericano
30. _____ panameño
31. _____ sopa
32. _____ calle (f)
33. _____ papel (m)
34. _____ mujer (f)
35. _____ color (m)
36. _____ señor (m)
37. _____ ciudad (f)
38. _____ padre (m)
39. _____ nación
40. _____ madre (f)

Worksheet 1.3 Plural nouns

Nouns ending in a vowel form their plural by adding -s (except as noted on p. 20).

EXAMPLES:	SINGULAR:	libro	mesa	calle
	PLURAL:	libros	mesas	calles

Nouns ending in a consonant form their plural by adding -es (except as noted on p. 20).

EXAMPLES:	SINGULAR:	papel	color	ciudad
	PLURAL:	papeles	colores	ciudades

➤ Change to the plural.

1. libro _____

2. dólar _____

3. ventana _____

4. silla _____

5. papel _____

6. guitarra _____

7. suramericano _____

8. calle _____

9. mujer _____

10. hombre _____

11. padre _____

12. profesor _____

13. cuaderno _____

14. catedral _____

15. muchacha _____

16. médico _____

17. primo _____

18. venezolano _____

19. tomate _____

20. amiga _____

21. cubana _____

22. motor _____

23. cuarto _____

24. español (m) _____

25. corbata _____

26. señor _____

27. señora _____

28. familia _____

29. zapato _____

30. chaqueta _____

31. flor _____

32. cuchillo _____

33. escuela _____

34. ciudad _____

35. madre _____

36. noche _____

Worksheet 1.4 Descriptive adjectives

Adjectives usually follow the nouns they modify (**un libro** *nuevo*, **una mesa** *redonda*). Most adjectives have a masculine and a feminine form (**rojo, roja**), as well as a singular and a plural form (**rojo, rojos, roja, rojas**). All adjectives agree in number and gender with the nouns they modify.

EXAMPLES: SINGULAR   PLURAL
        MASCULINE: el libro **rojo**   los libros **rojos**
        FEMININE: la mesa **roja**   las mesas **rojas**

➤ Supply the correct form of the adjectives in parentheses.

1. una casa _____ (bonito)
2. el libro _____ (negro)
3. los libros _____ (grueso)
4. una mesa _____ (sucio)
5. un muchacho _____ (alto)
6. una camisa _____ (amarillo)
7. un juego _____ (divertido)
8. una mujer _____ (bonito)
9. una clase _____ (nuevo)
10. un médico _____ (famoso)
11. una muchacha _____ (alto)
12. una flor _____ (blanco)
13. una lección _____ (largo)
14. dos libros _____ (caro)
15. una casa _____ (pequeña)
16. una pluma _____ (nuevo)
17. un hombre _____ (viejo)
18. dos hombres _____ (viejo)
19. una mujer _____ (rubio)
20. dos mujeres _____ (rubio)
21. dos calles _____ (ancho)
22. una profesora _____ (bueno)
23. una chica _____ (mexicano)
24. dos chicas _____ (mexicano)
25. dos ojos _____ (negro)
26. la nariz _____ (largo)
27. dos lecciones _____ (largo)
28. un profesor _____ (cómodo)
29. una silla _____ (cómodo)
30. dos sillas _____ (cómodo)
31. una manzana _____ (rojo)
32. dos camisas _____ (blanco)
33. tres plátanos _____ (amarillo)
34. una noche _____ (frío)
35. un automóvil _____ (moderno)
36. dos señoras _____ (rico)
37. el médico _____ (italiano)
38. la enfermera _____ (cubano)

Worksheet 1.5 More on descriptive adjectives

Some adjectives do not have the **-o** or **-a** ending to indicate masculine or feminine gender. They have the same ending for both genders and agree in number only. These adjectives may end with a vowel (**grande, verde**) or with a consonant (**fácil, popular**). Form the plural of adjectives ending with a vowel by adding **-s** (**grandes, verdes**); form the plural of adjectives ending with a consonant by adding **-es** (**fáciles, populares**).

EXAMPLES: el alumno **inteligente**   los alumnos **inteligentes**
la alumna **inteligente**   las alumnas **inteligentes**
el ejercicio **fácil**   los ejercicios **fáciles**
la tarea **fácil**   las tareas **fáciles**

➤ Change each of the following phrases to the plural.

1. el muchacho popular _____

2. la lección difícil _____

3. el emigrante pobre _____

4. el libro caro _____

5. el hombre italiano _____

6. el ejercicio difícil _____

7. la mujer inteligente _____

8. la flor amarilla _____

9. la comida española _____

10. la criada eficiente _____

11. el gato interesante _____

12. el niño inteligente _____

13. la muchacha baja _____

14. la mesa redonda _____

15. el reloj viejo _____

16. la ciudad grande _____

17. el pueblo grande _____

18. el libro verde _____

19. la pregunta difícil _____

20. la lección nueva _____

21. la profesora nueva _____

22. el soldado norteamericano _____

23. la pared blanca _____

24. el muchacho español _____

25. la clase fácil _____

26. el escritorio gris _____

27. la muchacha pobre _____

28. la pluma verde _____

29. el lápiz verde _____

30. el profesor nuevo _____

31. el reloj interesante _____

32. el suramericano alto _____

33. la norteamericana alta _____

34. la blusa azul _____

Worksheet 1.6 The verb *ser*

The verb **ser** is conjugated as follows:

		ser (*to be*)			
yo	soy	*I am*	nosotros(as)	somos	*we are*
tú*	eres	*you are*	vosotros(as)**	sois	*you are*
usted	es	*you are*	ustedes	son	*you are*
él, ella	es	*he is, she is*	ellos, ellas	son	*they are*

➤ Supply the correct form of **ser**.

1. Nosotros _____ somos _____ estudiantes **de geografía.**

2. El mundo _____ grande e int**eresante.**

3. África y Asia _____ continentes **enormes.**

4. Europa _____ un continente **también.**

5. Abdul, tú, _____ de África.

6. Yo _____ de Europa.

7. España _____ un país europ**eo.**

8. Las tradiciones de España _____ bonitas.

9. Finlandia _____ un país frío.

10. Vosotros _____ de Finlandia.

11. Elena y Carlos _____ de Bogotá.

12. Bogotá _____ la capital de **Colombia.**

13. Los señores Garza _____ venezolanos.

14. Tú _____ de Venezuela **también.**

15. La señora Garza _____ una actriz fa**mosa.**

16. Yo _____ admirador de **ella.**

17. Nosotros _____ de varias ciu**dades.**

18. Alicia, tú _____ de una ciud**ad bonita.**

19. Buenos Aires _____ la capital de **la Argentina.**

20. Dos productos de la Argentina _____ la plata y la **carne.**

21. Ustedes _____ amigos de **varios músicos** puertorriqueños.

22. Ellos _____ populares con **los estudian**tes.

23. Julio Iglesias _____ de España.

24. Usted _____ de Cuba.

25. Puerto Rico y Cuba _____ islas caribes.

26. La geografía _____ muy interes**ante, ¿verdad?**

* The familiar form **tú** is mostly used with peers, family members, pets, and servants. **Usted** is used in all other cases and takes the same verb form as **él** and **ella.**

** **Vosotros** is used only in Spain; all other Spanish-speakers use **ustedes.**

Worksheet 1.7 **Subject pronouns**

Subject pronouns are often omitted from the sentence unless needed for clarification or emphasis. We say **somos amigos** (omitting the subject pronoun **nosotros**) because the verb form clearly indicates that the subject is first person plural. In **es interesante**, however, the subject could be **él, ella, usted, la maestra, el libro,** or anyone or anything that is second or third person singular.

➤ Supply the correct subject pronouns; include all possible choices.

1. _____ soy aficionado al cine.

2. _____ son estrellas de muchas películas.

3. _____ es un buen actor.

4. _____ es una buena actriz.

5. _____ eres admiradora de varios actores.

6. _____ son populares en los teatros.

7. _____ es vendedor de boletos en el teatro.

8. _____ eres dueño de un teatro elegante.

9. _____ somos cancioneros argentinos.

10. _____ eres una cancionera muy buena.

11. _____ soy un cantante muy bueno.

12. _____ es una bailarina muy popular.

13. _____ es un cómico muy gracioso.

14. _____ son payasos del cine mexicano.

15. _____ son amigas de los payasos.

16. _____ somos bailarines y cómicos.

17. _____ son actrices y cancioneras.

18. _____ somos populares en la televisión.

19. _____ es la esposa de un actor famoso.

20. _____ son residentes de Hollywood.

21. _____ somos turistas en Hollywood.

22. _____ es muy simpática.

23. _____ soy amigo de actores de teatro.

24. _____ son amables e interesantes.

Worksheet 1.8 Indefinitive articles with modified nouns

The indefinite article is omitted before an unmodified noun of nationality, occupation, religion or rank that follows **ser**.

EXAMPLES: Elena **es** médico.
             Él **es** italiano.

It is always used, however, when the noun is modified.

EXAMPLES: Elena **es** un buen médico.
             Él **es** un italiano muy simpático.

➤ Supply **un** or **una** if needed.

1. Ella es _____ profesora norteamericana.

2. Pablo es _____ argentino.

3. El* señor Pérez es _____ zapatero muy bueno.

4. La señora Ruiz _____ buena abogada.

5. Yo soy _____ cubano.

6. Ella es _____ española.

7. Jaime es _____ ingeniero.

8. Él es _____ ingeniero mecánico.

9. El señor García es _____ poeta español.

10. El señor Mendoza es _____ arquitecto.

11. Él es _____ arquitecto famoso en Chile.

12. Tú eres _____ muchacho muy cómico.

13. Ella es _____ alumna estudiosa.

14. Él es _____técnico.

15. Isabel es _____ peluquera popular.

16. El doctor Soto _____ chileno.

17. Ella es _____ muchacha muy atractiva.

18. *El diario* es _____ periódico popular.

19. Alberto _____ capitán.

20. Él es _____ muy generoso.

21. Iliana _____ católica.

22. Ella es _____ católica muy ferviente.

23. La maestra es _____ muchacha joven.

24. Ella es _____ puertorriqueña.

25. ¿Tú eres _____ actriz puertorriqueña?

* The definite article is used before all titles, except in direct speech.

Adjectives

➤ Supply the correct form of the adjective in parentheses.

1. La escuela es _____ (nuevo).

2. La directora es muy _____ (joven).

3. El subdirector es un poco _____ (viejo).

4. La biblioteca es _____ (moderno).

5. Los libros son _____ (popular).

6. El auditorio de la escuela es _____ (grande).

7. Los estudiantes son _____ (amable).

8. La maestra de matemáticas es _____ (gordo).

9. Dos maestros son _____ (flaco).

10. María y Elena son _____ (rubio).

11. Muchos estudiantes son _____ (moreno).

12. Los pupitres son _____ (amplio).

13. El escritorio del director es _____ (azul).

14. Las cortinas de los salones son _____ (verde).

15. La lección de biología _____ (interesante).

16. Los libros son _____ (difícil).

17. Una amiga es _____ (panameño).

18. Los centroamericanos son _____ (estudioso).

19. La maestra de gimnasia es muy _____ (simpático).

20. El timbre de la escuela es _____ (eléctrico).

21. Las pizarras son _____ (verde)

22. La tiza es _____ (blanco)

23. Los deportes son _____ (divertido).

24. Las secretarias de la escuela son _____ (cooperativo).

25. El presidente de la clase es _____ (guapo).

26. Muchos graduados son _____ (famoso).

More on the verb *ser* and adjectives

➤ Choose the correct form.

1. Nosotros _____ (son, somos) amigos.

2. La lección de hoy _____ (es, son) difícil.

3. _____ (Los, Las) tareas de hoy también son difíciles.

4. Pepe y María son muy _____ (popular, populares) en la escuela.

5. La profesora de matemáticas es _____ (señora, una señora) alta.

6. Las puertas de la sala son _____ (grande, grandes).

7. El profesor es _____ (ingeniero, un ingeniero).

8. _____ (Nosotros, Nosotras) somos amigas.

9. El lápiz es rojo y la pluma es _____ (amarillo, amarilla).

10. Yo _____ (soy, es) alumno de español.

11. Ella _____ (soy, es) alumna de español.

12. _____ (Los, Las) padres de ella son cubanos.

13. La profesora nueva es _____ (norteamericano, norteamericana).

14. Ellas son _____ (hermanos, hermanas).

15. Nosotros _____ (son, somos) compañeros de clase.

16. _____ (Él, Ella) es la profesora de Elena.

17. Los dos muchachos son fuertes y _____ (altos, altas).

18. María es _____ (rubio, rubia) de ojos azules.

19. Caracas es una ciudad _____ (moderno, moderna).

20. Otras ciudades de Venezuela son muy_____ (antigua, antiguas).

21. Joaquín es _____ (muchacho, un muchacho) muy inteligente.

22. La familia de Enrique es muy _____ (rico, rica).

23. Los ejercicios de hoy son bastante_____(difícil, difíciles).

24. Las tareas de hoy son _____ (fácil, fáciles).

25. Joaquín es _____ (muchacho, un muchacho).

26. _____ (El señor, señor) Ruiz es subdirector de la escuela.

27. Las escuelas de México _____ (es, son) enormes.

28. El peruano es _____ (aficionado, aficionada) a la gimnasia.

Palabras revueltas

➤ Can you circle fourteen descriptive adjectives?

B	B	L	A	N	C	O	I	A	C
X	U	O	H	V	I	E	J	O	D
D	E	N	G	U	A	P	O	U	S
S	N	U	E	V	A	L	O	R	P
R	O	J	O	A	L	I	N	D	A
P	A	Z	U	L	T	T	L	R	N
L	M	B	A	J	O	G	S	U	C
O	F	R	I	O	S	J	A	T	H
S	U	C	I	A	L	A	R	G	O

As you find the words, copy them in the spaces below:

1. _____
2. _____
3. _____
4. _____
5. _____
6. _____
7. _____
8. _____
9. _____
10. _____
11. _____
12. _____
13. _____
14. _____

Part 2

Contents

Worksheet 2.1 **The present tense of regular *-ar* verbs**

Regular **-ar** verbs (**caminar, estudiar**) are conjugated as follows:

The present tense also describes daily or general actions.

hablar (*to speak*)			
yo	hablo	nosotros(as)	hablamos
tú	hablas	vosotros(as)	habláis
él, ella, usted	habla	ellos, ellas, ustedes	hablan

EXAMPLE: El profesor siempre **habla** español en la clase.

➤ Supply the correct form of the vebs in parentheses.

1. Nosotros_____ (estudiar) mucho en la clase de español.

2. La maestra siempre _____ (hablar) español.

3. Tú _____ (mirar) las palabras en la pizarra.

4. Los estudiantes _____ (escuchar) muy bien.

5. Ellos _____ (practicar) mucho la pronunciación.

6. Yo _____ (necesitar) un buen cuaderno.

7. Ella _____ (enseñar) los verbos regulares.

8. Los verbos _____ (cambiar) de una manera interesante.

9. Ella _____ (preguntar) la hora.

10. Nosotros_____ (contestar) la pregunta.

11. Un alumno _____ (ayudar) a otros alumnos.

12. Yo _____ (trabajar) mucho con los verbos regulares.

13. Los alumnos_____ (usar) cada verbo en una frase.

14. Nosotros_____ (tratar) de usar la forma correcta.

15. Tú siempre _____ (comunicar) entusiasmo en español.

16. La maestra _____ (recitar) versos en la clase.

17. Nosotros_____ (desear) cantar cada día.

18. Hoy Catalina_____ (tocar) la guitarra.

19. Otros estudiantes _____ (comprar) discos compactos.

20. El club_____ (gastar) mucho dinero en refrescos.

21. Nosotros_____ (conversar) siempre en español.

22. Ellas _____ (tomar) limonada en cada reunión.

23. Una estudiante peruana _____ (visitar) el club.

24. Nosotros_____ (cantar) una canción para ella.

25. Los muchachos _____ (bailar) con las muchachas.

Worksheet 2.2 Subject pronouns with *-ar* verbs

With the exception of **usted/ustedes**, subject pronouns are usually omitted because the verb ending identifies the subject. The subject pronoun, however, is used for stress or emphasis and precedes the verb.

EXAMPLE: **Yo** canto, pero **ella** baila.

➤ Supply the correct subject pronoun(s); include all possible choices.

1. _____ hablamos muy poco en la biblioteca.

2. _____ busco una mesa grande.

3. _____ necesita un diccionario.

4. _____ miras el mapa de Europa.

5. _____ estudian geografía.

6. _____ preparo un informe para mañana.

7. _____ compras un bolígrafo rojo.

8. _____ usamos papel blanco con líneas azules.

9. _____ hablo muchas veces con la maestra.

10. _____ ayuda a los estudiantes.

11. _____ practican deportes.

12. _____ trato de practicar también.

13. _____ enseña inglés muy bien.

14. _____ cantamos en voz baja.

15. _____ explico la lección a un amigo.

16. _____ escucha muy bien las explicaciones.

17. _____ pasamos dos horas en la biblioteca.

18. _____ presenta una lista de palabras nuevas.

19. _____ copia datos de un libro de referencia.

20. _____ dibujan mapas de las Antillas Mayores.

21. _____ hablan sobre los productos de Chile.

22. _____ contesto una pregunta sobre la Argentina.

23. _____ espero leer una novela interesante.

24. _____ informa sobre la poesía moderna.

25. _____ gastan mucho dinero en libros nuevos.

26. _____ deseamos leer varios libros sobre México.

Worksheet 2.3 Negation

To make a verb negative, simply place **no** to the left of the verb.

EXAMPLE: ¿**No** habla español muy bien Julia?
No, ella **no** habla español muy bien.

➤ Rewrite each sentence, making the verb negative.

1. Yo gasto mucho dinero en las tiendas. _____

2. Tú necesitas una bicicleta nueva. _____

3. Ella compra una bicicleta usada. _____

4. Usted usa un martillo en el trabajo. _____

5. ¿Es ligero ese martillo? _____

6. Nosotros pagamos demasiado aquí. _____

7. ¿Son caros los limones? _____

8. Juan trabaja en el mercado. _____

9. ¿Es moderno ese mercado? _____

10. Las manzanas pesan un kilo. _____

11. El mercado selecciona las verduras frescas. _____

12. Los plátanos son verdes. _____

13. ¿Son baratas las peras? _____

14. El pescado es muy caro. _____

15. El carnicero es excelente. _____

16. Él pesa las chuletas de cerdo. _____

17. El pavo pesa doce libras. _____

18. La gran venta es mañana. _____

19. Ellas buscan precios bajos. _____

20. ¿Aceptas estos dulces? _____

21. Trato de bajar de peso. _____

22. Ella desea comprar un helado. _____

23. Esta tienda es famosa. _____

24. ¿Caminamos al supermercado? _____

25. Yo compro en un mercado cerca. _____

Worksheet 2.4 Interrogative sentences

To form a question, start with an inverted question mark (¿) and place the verb before its subject.

EXAMPLE: Él corre todas las mañanas.
          ¿Corre él todas las mañanas?

➤ Change the following statements to questions.

1. Tú lavas la ropa en el río. _____

2. Ellos nadan en el Lago Superior. _____

3. Luisa mira los barcos en el mar. _____

4. El joven escucha el ruido de las olas. _____

5. Pablo busca una playa tranquila. _____

6. Ustedes pescan en el Océano Pacífico. _____

7. Ellos hablan mucho sobre la pesca. _____

8. Mamá prepara una comida con mariscos. _____

9. Tú cenas cerca del mar. _____

10. Papá habla con los pescadores. _____

11. Ellos tienen barcos muy grandes. _____

12. El capitán saluda a los pasajeros. _____

13. El tío Carlos ayuda a los marineros. _____

14. Los novios pasean en la cubierta. _____

15. Catalina viaja a Puerto Rico. _____

16. Ella llega en un barco lujoso. _____

17. Una amiga acompaña a Catalina. _____

18. Marta compra un traje de baño. _____

19. Catalina usa el traje del año pasado. _____

20. Ellas descansan mucho en la playa. _____

21. Nosotros regresamos a Puerto Rico. _____

22. El enseña a muchos nadadores. _____

23. Ellos necesitan mucha práctica. _____

24. Los campeones ganan medallas de oro. _____

25. La natación atrae a muchas personas. _____

26. Tú trabajas en la tienda. _____

27. El tío Luis es payaso. _____

28. El circo viaja a muchas ciudades. _____

29. Ellos miran los tigres._____

30. Papá compra muchos boletos. _____

31. Los músicos tocan *Sobre las olas*. _____

32. Los caballos bailan cuando escuchan la música._____

_____

33. Los acróbatas entran pronto. _____

34. Los bomberos son muy valientes. _____

35. Usted desea regresar al circo mañana._____

Worksheet 2.5 More on plural nouns

The worksheet on *plural nouns* (page 4) reminded you to pluralize nouns ending in a vowel by adding **-s**, or **-es** if they end in a consonant. These additional rules must also be applied:

	SINGULAR	PLURAL
• Nouns ending in **-z** change **z** to **c** before adding **-es**.	la luz	las lu**ces**
• Nouns ending in **-es** or **-is,** with no accent, are the same in singular and plural.	el lun**es**	los lun**es**
• Nouns ending in **-n** or **-s,** with an accent on the last syllable, drop the accent in the plural.	la lecci**ón**	las lecci**ones**
• Other words that end in **-n** add an accent.	exame**n**	exámen**es**
• Family names never change in the plural.	**Mendoza**	**los Mendoza**
• These same spelling rules apply to adjectives as well as nouns.	capa**z**	capa**ces**

➤ Change to the singular.

1. los lápices _____

2. los franceses _____

3. los lunes_____

4. los ingleses _____

5. los jóvenes _____

6. los árboles _____

7. las mujeres_____

8. los martes _____

9. las veces_____

10. las voces _____

11. las francesas _____

12. los colores _____

13. las naciones _____

14. las narices _____

15. los actores _____

16. las actrices _____

17. las oraciones largas _____

18. los niños inteligentes _____

19. las niñas inteligentes_____

20. los cinturones rojos_____

21. las ciudades pequeñas _____

22. los hermanos Ramírez_____

23. los esposos García _____

24. los cuadernos azules _____

25. las naciones grandes_____

26. las horas felices _____

27. los pescadores japoneses _____

28. los viernes y sábados _____

29. las hermanas Ordaz_____

30. las reuniones familiares_____

➤ Change to the plural.

1. el capitán del barco_____

2. la actriz capaz _____

3. el cocinero portugués_____

4. la cocinera portuguesa _____

5. el ingeniero joven _____

6. el empleado atento_____

7. la voz baja _____

8. el patrón de la fábrica _____

9. la comida costarricense _____

10. la nación europea _____

11. el papel azul_____

12. el examen fácil_____

13. la luz roja _____

14. el médico español _____

15. la dosis correcta_____

Worksheet 2.6 The present tense of regular -er verbs

Regular -er verbs (**comer, aprender**) are conjugated as follows:

comer (*to eat*)			
yo	como	nosotros(as)	comemos
tú	comes	vosotros(as)	coméis
él, ella, usted	come	ellos, ellas, ustedes	comen

➤ Supply the correct form of the verb.

1. Nosotros _____ (toser) de vez en cuando.

2. Los fumadores _____ (toser) con frecuencia.

3. Los hábitos buenos _____ (proteger) la salud.

4. ¿Cómo _____ (proteger) tú la salud?

5. Andrés no _____ (beber) mucha agua.

6. Yo _____ (beber) seis vasos de agua diariamente.

7. Ella camina mucho pero _____ (correr) muy poco.

8. Ellos _____ (correr) todas las mañanas en el parque.

9. Él _____ (aprender) las reglas de seguridad.

10. Ellas _____ (aprender) los primeros auxilios.

11. Yo _____ (prometer) comer más verduras y frutas.

12. ¿ _____ (prometer) tú comer menos dulces y helados?

13. El _____ (meter) refrescos en el refrigerador.

14. Nosotros _____ (meter) leche y jugos en el refrigerador.

15. Los niños _____ (crecer) cuando toman leche.

16. Todos _____ (crecer) mucho entre los diez y quince años de edad.

17. En la escuela tú _____ (leer) mucho sobre la higiene.

18. ¿ _____ (leer) usted artículos sobre las vitaminas?

19. Nosotros _____ (comprender) la importancia de la gimnasia.

20. Yo _____ (comprender) la necesidad de tener un cuerpo sano.

21. Ellos _____ (poseer) una extensa colección de medicinas y vendas.

22. ¿ _____ (poseer) ustedes artículos peligrosos en la casa?

Worksheet 2.7 The present tense of regular *-ir* verbs

Regular **-ir** verbs (**vivir, escribir**) are conjugated as follows:

vivir (*to live*)			
yo	vivo	nosotros(as)	vivimos
tú	vives	vosotros(as)	vivís
él, ella, usted	vive	ellos, ellas, ustedes	viven

➤ Supply the correct form of the verb.

1. Yo _____ (asistir) a muchos conciertos sinfónicos.

2. Ellas _____ (asistir) a conciertos de grupos roqueros.

3. Muchos músicos profesionales _____ (vivir) en Nueva York.

4. El mariachi _____ (vivir) en Guadalajara, México.

5. Tú _____ (escribir) la letra de muchas canciones.

6. Ustedes _____ (escribir) música para guitarra.

7. La música _____ (existir) en todas partes del mundo.

8. Los instrumentos del siglo doce no _____ (existir) hoy.

9. Nosotros _____ (discutir) la importancia de la ópera.

10. El violinista _____ (discutir) con el director.

11. Yo _____ (dividir) la orquesta en tres secciones.

12. Ella _____ (dividir) su tiempo entre Londres y París.

13. El director de la orquesta _____ (subir) la escalera.

14. Nosotros _____ (no subir) al balcón del palacio de Bellas Artes.

15. El concierto _____ (abrir) con una cantata de Mozart.

16. Ellos _____ (abrir) las puertas del teatro a las siete.

17. Los compositores a veces _____ (sufrir) mucha pobreza.

18. El perro _____ (sufrir) cuando tú tocas el violín.

19. Yo me _____ (cubrir) los oídos cuando mi hermana canta.

20. La mano del joven pianista _____ (cubrir) la de la bella soprano.

21. Los músicos _____ (recibir) el aplauso de la audiencia.

22. Nosotros _____ (recibir) el placer de escuchar el concierto.

Verbs

➤ Supply the present tense of the following verbs in parenthe**ses.**

1. En mi casa, nosotros _____ (ayudar) a mamá con el trabajo.

2. Mi hermana _____ (sacudir) los muebles del salón.

3. Yo _____ (limpiar) el suelo y las alfombras.

4. Mi abuela _____ (insistir) en lavar los platos.

5. Yo _____ (secar) los vasos y las tazas.

6. Mamá _____ (enseñar) a mi hermana a lavar la ropa.

7. Ella _____ (coser) y mira la televisión.

8. Los niños _____ (crecer) cada año y necesitan ropa nueva.

9. Mi papá _____ (llevar) a la familia a la zapatería.

10. Nosotros_____ (comprar) varios pares de zapatos.

11. Yo _____ (arreglar) mi cuarto y el cuarto de baño.

12. Mamá _____ (meter) la ropa sucia en la lavadora.

13. Mis hermanas_____ (sacar) la ropa limpia de la secadora.

14. Mi tía _____ (planchar) los manteles y las sábanas.

15. De vez en cuando un niño _____ (romper) un juguete.

16. Papá _____ (reparar) los juguetes y los aparatos eléctricos.

17. Nosotros_____ (dividir) las tareas hogareñas entre todos.

18. Los sábados yo _____ (barrer) el patio y la sala.

19. Mañana mi hermano _____ (deber) arreglar el sótano.

20. Tú _____ (sufrir) cuando trabajas en casa.

21. Ustedes _____ (necesitar) ayudar a sus madres con el trabajo.

22. ¿No _____ (comprender) ustedes que mamá necesita ayuda?

23. Los vecinos ricos _____ (pagar) una criada.

24. En mi casa mamá no _____ (depender) de una criada.

25. Nosotros siempre _____ (cooperar) en limpiar la casa.

Subject pronouns with regular verbs

➤ Supply the subject pronoun(s).

1. _____ patinas en la pista de hielo.

2. _____ esquiamos en las montañas.

3. _____ vende boletos para la carrera de motocicletas.

4. _____ nadan en la piscina olímpica de la universidad.

5. _____ compro una canoa para remar en el lago.

6. _____ andas mucho en bicicleta durante el verano.

7. _____ estudio la historia de las Olimpiadas.

8. _____ apreciamos al entrenador de los futbolistas.

9. _____ recibe muchas cartas de los aficionados.

10. _____ escribo cartas al campeón del boxeo.

11. _____ admiramos mucho al capitán de equipo.

12. _____ lees artículos sobre la corrida de toros.

13. _____ recibe los aplausos del público.

14. _____ no matan al toro en la corrida portuguesa.

15. _____ rompen a veces las banderillas.

16. _____ debemos estudiar las reglas de béisbol.

17. _____ explico a los estudiantes las jugadas de baloncesto.

18. _____ vivimos cerca del Hipódromo del Mar.

19. _____ corren rápidamente todos los caballos.

20. _____ prefieres participar en los deportes.

21. _____ no bebo café durante la temporada de fútbol.

22. _____ prohibimos el uso del tabaco y del alcohol.

23. _____ comes alimentos recomendados por el entrenador.

24. _____ compiten en muchos concursos profesionales.

25. _____ siempre tratamos de ganar.

More on verbs

➤ Change the sentences from **yo** to **tú**. Repeat the exercise for each of the other subjects: **él, ella, usted, nosotros, vosotros** (optional), **ellos**. This may be done orally and in writing by placing a strip of blank paper over the answer column.

1. Yo vivo en Santa Fe.   Tú _____

2. Yo estoy en la escuela secundaria.   Tú _____

3. Yo camino con un amigo.   Tú _____

4. Yo estudio lenguas extranjeras.   Tú _____

5. Yo hablo varios idiomas.   Tú _____

6. Yo aprendo a hablar italiano.   Tú _____

7. Yo necesito más práctica.   Tú _____

8. Yo converso con los italianos.   Tú _____

9. Yo admiro a la maestra.   Tú _____

10. Yo escucho bien su clase.   Tú _____

11. Yo debo aprender más.   Tú _____

12. Yo tengo mucha paciencia.   Tú _____

13. Yo practico la pronunciación.   Tú _____

14. Yo saludo a la maestra.   Tú _____

15. Yo paso a la pizarra.   Tú _____

16. Yo escribo una composición.   Tú _____

17. Yo cometo un error.   Tú _____

18. Yo repito una palabra.   Tú _____

19. Yo contesto una pregunta difícil.   Tú _____

20. Yo regreso a mi casa.   Tú _____

21. Yo debo hacer la tarea.   Tú _____

22. Yo uso un bolígrafo.   Tú _____

23. Yo completo los ejercicios.   Tú _____

24. Yo creo que la vida es interesante.   Tú _____

Buscapalabras bilingüe

➤ Find and circle these eight occupations in both English and Spanish: *actress, doctor, engineer, musician, principal, sailor, soldier, teacher*. Three of the words appear diagonally.

```
D   O   C   T   O   R   I   M   O   A   S   M
A   M   A   R   I   N   E   R   O   C   M   P
S   O   L   D   A   D   O   R   P   T   U   O
O   E   N   G   I   N   E   E   R   R   S   L
L   U   E   C   E   I   T   Z   I   E   I   A
D   R   O   U   N   Z   I   N   M   S   C   P
I   R   L   E   I   R   A   C   U   S   I   I
E   L   G   R   T   I   C   I   S   A   A   C
R   N   T   C   A   Z   H   P   I   I   N   N
I   M   A   E   S   T   R   A   C   L   B   I
I   R   E   H   C   A   E   T   O   O   M   R
A   O   D   I   R   E   C   T   O   R   R   P
```

English

_____

_____

_____

_____

_____

_____

_____

Spanish

_____

_____

_____

_____

_____

_____

_____

Worksheet 2.8 The possessive with *de*

In English we say (a) the boy's father or (b) the father of the boy. Spanish uses only (b) **el padre del muchacho**. The word **de** (*of*) may precede the noun (**el padre de Juan**) or the noun and its article:

EXAMPLES: el padre **del** muchacho (**de** + **el** = **del**)   el padre **de la** muchacha
              el padre **de los** muchachos   el padre **de las** muchachas

➤ Supply **de** plus the article (if required): **de, del, de los, de la, de las**

1. El cuchillo es_____ carnicero.

2. La máquina de escribir _____ secretaria.

3. Los uniformes son _____ enfermeras.

4. Los juguetes son _____ niño.

5. El diccionario es_____ maestra.

6. Los martillos _____ carpinteros son grandes.

7. Las hojas_____ árbol son verdes.

8. El vestido _____ ingeniera es nuevo.

9. Las montañas _____ Asia son grandes.

10. Los países _____ Naciones Unidas son importantes.

11. La pelota es _____ equipo de fútbol.

12. Nosotros hablamos_____ capital de Bolivia.

13. El astro _____ película es Cantinflas.

14. María habla con el director _____ escuela.

15. Sancho Panza es amigo _____ Don Quixote.

16. El coche negro es _____ ella.

17. La casa recién pintada es _____ ellos.

18. Los instrumentos musicales son _____ nosotros.

19. Las maletas grises son _____ él.

20. Las ideas mejores son _____ ustedes.

21. La entrenadora _____ tenistas chilenos es famosa.

22. El padre _____ presidente de la universidad es muy simpático.

23. La reina _____ Inglaterra es popular.

24. El abuelo_____ gemelas es generoso.

25. El inventor _____ luz eléctrica es Tomás Edison.

Worksheet 2.9 *Ser* and *estar*

Ser and **estar** both mean *to be*. **Ser** is a linking verb (see page 8). It links a noun with another noun of similar meaning (**Juan es marinero [Juan = marinero]**), or it links a noun with an adjective that describes it (**Juan es valiente [Juan = valiente]**). **Estar** indicates a temporary or acquired condition (**Juan está enfermo, Juan está en Veracruz**). In a few days, Juan **will still be** (**ser**) a sailor and will still be (**ser**) brave, but he may no longer be (**estar**) sick and may no longer be (**estar**) in Veracruz. Here is the present tense of **estar**:

estar *(to be)*			
yo	estoy	nosotros(as)	estamos
tú	estás	vosotros(as)	estáis
él, ella, usted	está	ellos, ellas, ustedes	están

➤ Supply the correct form of **ser** or **estar**.

1. Yo _____ enfermo.

2. Tú _____ bien.

3. Carlos _____ tenista.

4. Ellos _____ aquí.

5. El café _____ caliente.

6. El perro _____ grande.

7. Los zapatos _____ sucios.

8. Ellas _____ francesas.

9. Nosotros _____ contentos.

10. Mérida _____ en Yucatán.

11. Yo no _____ marinero.

12. Ustedes _____ en Cuba.

13. Luis _____ presente.

14. Tú _____ cansada.

15. La mesa _____ limpia.

16. Nosotros _____ norteamericanos.

17. La carne _____ fría.

18. Mi abuelo _____ viejo.

19. María _____ ausente.

20. El gato _____ negro.

21. El gato _____ enfermo.

22. Las cucharas _____ sucias.

23. Las cucharas _____ de plata.

24. La falda _____ limpia.

25. Nosotros _____ en Roma.

26. Nosotros _____ viajeros.

27. Tú _____ bailarina.

28. Los barcos _____ en el mar.

29. Mi tía _____ de Jalisco.

30. Su casa _____ en Guadalajara.

Worksheet 2.10 More on *ser* and *estar*

➤ Supply the proper form of **ser** or **estar**, and be able to justify your choice, writing "T" for temporary, or "P" for permanent in the right margin.

                                                         T   P

1. Nosotros _____ en un buen restaurante.

2. El restaurante _____ famoso, pero caro.

3. Las selecciones del menú _____ numerosas.

4. Las servilletas y los manteles _____ limpios.

5. Todos los camareros _____ muy corteses.

6. Durante la comida uno de ellos _____ cerca de la mesa.

7. Los platos para ensalada _____ fríos.

8. Los vasos para agua _____ grandes.

9. Una arpa _____ en un rincón del restaurante.

10. La señorita que toca el arpa _____ joven.

11. Tres rosas amarillas _____ en cada mesa.

12. Nosotros _____ lejos de la cocina.

13. Los fumadores _____ en otra sección del restaurante.

14. Las rosas de cada mesa _____ amarillas.

15. Todos los platos _____ en una charola (bandeja).

16. El camarero llena los vasos cuando _____ vacíos.

17. El pescado _____ bastante para dos personas.

18. El sabor del pollo _____ excelente.

19. Las papas (patatas) _____ enormes.

20. Los chícharos (guisantes) _____ en salsa blanca.

21. Yo _____ lleno y muy contento con la comida.

22. La selección de postres _____ difícil.

23. La cuenta _____ en una pequeña charola (bandeja) de plata.

24. Las carteras pronto _____ vacías.

25. Creemos que esta propina _____ bastante.

26. El camarero acepta el dinero y _____ contento.

Worksheet 2.11 **More on *ser* and *estar***

➤ Supply the appropriate subject pronoun(s) for the verb in each of the following sentences. Include all possibilities.

1. _____ somos miembros del club de español.

2. _____ es presidente del club.

3. _____ están aquí por primera vez.

4. _____ eres una secretaria eficiente.

5. _____ soy un tesorero de poca experiencia.

6. _____ estamos en la biblioteca.

7. _____ están sentados alrededor de una mesa grande.

8. _____ estás de pie en frente del grupo de estudiantes.

9. _____ es un miembro muy activo del club.

10. _____ son alumnos muy aplicados en todas sus clases.

11. _____ es la maestra favorita de muchos estudiantes.

12. _____ está presente en cada reunión.

13. _____ estamos aquí para planear varias actividades del club.

14. _____ estás cansado de hablar español toda la tarde.

15. _____ está nerviosa cuando habla con la maestra.

16. _____ son estudiantes de la clase superior.

17. _____ estamos en un club que consideramos importante.

18. _____ es uno de los mejores estudiantes.

19. _____ está en el tercer año de español.

20. _____ estás en el primer año.

21. _____ están en el segundo año.

22. _____ somos buenos amigos.

23. _____ son becados.

24. _____ soy miembro de un club muy activo.

25. ¿Eres _____ miembro de un club de español?

Subject-verb agreement

➤ Practice with the verb forms studied so far, changing the subject of each sentence from **yo** to **él.** Be sure to change the verb to agree with the new subject. For more practice, change the subject to **tú, usted, ella, nosotros, ustedes, ellos,** and **ellas.**

1. Yo estoy en una tienda de ropa. _____

2. Yo compro una camisa nueva. _____

3. Yo miro varias corbatas. _____

4. Yo creo que son rojas. _____

5. Yo sufro de daltonismo. _____

6. Yo pido el color correcto. _____

7. Yo vivo en un clima tropical. _____

8. Yo busco ropa más ligera. _____

9. Yo quiero un traje de algodón. _____

10. Yo necesito zapatos negros. _____

11. Yo subo al primer piso. _____

12. Yo encuentro precios más baratos. _____

13. Yo descanso en un banco. _____

14. Yo hablo con otro cliente. _____

15. Yo soy muy listo para comprar. _____

16. Yo describo la cartera que busco. _____

17. Yo selecciono una cartera buena. _____

18. Yo entro en un ascensor. _____

19. Yo bajo a la planta principal. _____

20. Yo firmo mi nombre. _____

21. Yo cambio un cheque viajero. _____

22. Yo pago la cuenta. _____

23. Yo recibo el cambio. _____

24. Yo llevo las compras al coche. _____

25. Yo gasto mucho en las tiendas. _____

Name: _____ Date: _____

More on subject-verb agreement

➤ Choose the correct form and write it in the blank.

1. Los mexicanos _____ (vive, viven) en un país muy bonito.

2. La capital _____ (es, eres) antigua y grande.

3. Tú _____ (debo, debes) viajar a Guadalajara.

4. Guadalajara _____ (está, estás) en el estado de Jalisco.

5. Nosotros_____ (nadamos, nadan) allí en el lago Chapala.

6. Los mariachis _____ (cantas, cantan) en San Juan de Dios.

7. Yo _____ (escucho, escucha) esta música tradicional.

8. Ellos _____ (comes, comen) en la cafetería.

9. Ella _____ (admira, admiras) la arquitectura de la Catedral.

10. Nosotros _____ (asisto, asistimos) a un drama popular.

11. El título del drama _____ (es, está) Don Juan Tenorio.

12. Los dramas del Palacio de Bellas Artes _____ (están, son) buenos.

13. El charro y la china poblana _____ (baila, bailan) en el parque.

14. Ellos _____ (reciben, recibes) el aplauso de la gente.

15. Yo _____ (aplaudo, aplaude) a los bailarines del jarabe tapatío.

16. Otros charros _____ (montamos, montan) a caballo.

17. El charro_____ (es, está) el mejor jinete de México.

18. Ustedes _____ (vemos, ven) al charro en el desfile.

19. Tú _____ (vas, voy) también a la corrida de toros.

20. El toro _____ (corre, corren) muy rápido hacia el torero.

21. Yo _____ (creemos, creo) que el torero es muy valiente.

22. Nosotros_____ (compramos, compras) en el mercado de abastos.

23. Ella _____ (aprende, aprendes) a regatear con los comerciantes.

24. Mi tío _____ (escoge, escogen) las legumbres y frutas en el mercado.

25. Los muchachos y las muchachas _____ (formas, forman) círculos.

26. Ellos _____ (anda, andan) a la derecha; ellas a la izquierda.

27. Esta costumbre _____ (está, es) popular entre los jóvenes.

28. México _____ (conservan,conserva) tradiciones muy bonitas.

29. Ellos _____ (descansan, descansamos) entre las dos y las cuatro.

30. Yo _____ (regresa, regreso) a México a cada oportunidad.

Part 3

Contents

Worksheet 3.1 **The verb *tener***

The verb **tener** (*to have*) is conjugated in the present tense as follows:

tener *(to have)*			
yo	tengo	nosotros(as)	tenemos
tú	tienes	vosotros(as)	tenéis
él, ella, usted	tiene	ellos, ellas, ustedes	tienen

➤ Supply the correct form of **tener.**

1. Tú _____ un coche nuevo.

2. Tu coche _____ seis cilindros.

3. Las llantas _____ letras blancas.

4. Yo _____ un coche más grande y más viejo.

5. Nosotros _____ coches del mismo color.

6. Creo que el motor _____ un problema muy serio.

7. Algunos mecánicos _____ poco entrenamiento.

8. Yo _____ un mecánico experto y honrado.

9. El dice que el motor _____ dos bujías malas.

10. Ustedes _____ el nombre de mi mecánico.

11. Tú _____ mucha suerte con tu coche.

12. La Ciudad de México _____ mucho tráfico.

13. Algunos chóferes _____ poca paciencia.

14. Nosotros_____ mucha experiencia.

15. Usted _____ un lote de estacionamiento.

16. El lote _____ espacio para cien automóviles.

17. Tú _____ mucha cautela cuando manejas.

18. Los peatones también_____ responsabilidades.

19. Ustedes _____ reglas para manejar y para caminar.

20. Nosotros_____ confianza en los otros chóferes.

21. Yo no _____ paciencia para manejar un taxi.

22. El taxista _____ un trabajo muy peligroso.

23. Los caminos _____ muchos camiones grandes.

24. Cada camino _____ su velocidad máxima.

25. ¿ _____ tu licencia para manejar?

Worksheet 3.2 More on the verb *tener*

Many idioms begin with **tener**. Where English uses *to be + adjective*, Spanish may use **tener** + noun:

EXAMPLE:	ENGLISH	SPANISH	LITERAL TRANSLATION
	I am hungry.	**Tengo hambre.**	*I have hunger.*
	I am thirsty.	**Tengo sed.**	*I have thirst.*
	I am hot.	**Tengo calor.**	*I have heat.*
	I am cold.	**Tengo frío.**	*I have coldness.*
	I am afraid.	**Tengo miedo.**	*I have fear.*
	I am sleepy.	**Tengo sueño.**	*I have fear.*
	I am ashamed.	**Tengo vergüenza.**	*I have shame.*

Other idioms include **tener ganas de** (*to feel like*), **tener 7 años** (*to be 7 years old*), **tener razón** (*to be right*), **tener dolor de** (*to have pain in…*).

➤ Supply the correct form of **tener.**

1. Cuando regreso de la escuela yo _____ mucha hambre.

2. Tú no _____ ganas de viajar durante el invierno.

3. En el invierno, nosotros _____ frío.

4. Ellos _____ sed cuando manejan en el desierto.

5. Cuando maneja de noche, él _____ sueño.

6. Usted _____ razón. Manejar demasiado es mala costumbre.

7. Yo_____ ganas de comer más postre.

8. Si comes demasiado, tú _____ dolor de estómago.

9. Mi abuelo _____ setenta y ocho años.

10. Los viejos a veces _____ dolor de garganta.

11. Nosotros _____ calor en la escuela.

12. Ellos_____ ganas de abrir las ventanas.

13. Elena a veces no_____ ganas de asistir a la escuela.

14. Cuando falta a clase, ella _____ vergüenza.

15. Yo creo que las gemelas _____ catorce años.

16. Hoy es mi cumpleaños. _____ veinte años.

17. Nosotros _____ ganas de conocer a los toreros.

18. Los toreros no_____ miedo de los toros.

Worksheet 3.3 *Tener que*

Tener + **que** + *infinitive* is similar to **to have** + *infinitive* in English:

EXAMPLES: Yo **tengo que** estudiar mucho.   *I have to study a lot.*
Tú **tienes que** comer menos.   *You have to eat less.*

Deber and **tener que** are close in meaning, although **deber** implies a stronger obligation:

EXAMPLES: Él **tiene que** hablar.   *He has to talk.*
Él **debe** hablar.   *He must talk.*

➤ Rewrite the following sentences, changing **deber** to **tener que.**

1. El carpintero debe comprar un martillo nuevo.

_____

2. Los zapateros deben hacer zapatos bonitos y modernos.

_____

3. La maestra debe preparar lecciones sobre la Guerra Mundial.

_____

4. Yo debo practicar el piano por muchas horas.

_____

5. Tú debes cantar en voz más alta.

_____

6. El taxista debe conocer las calles de la ciudad.

_____

7. Nosotros debemos ayudar a los niños.

_____

8. Los cazadores deben usar precaución.

_____

9. El candidato debe recibir la mayoría de los votos.

_____

10. Tú debes entrenar a los peloteros.

_____

11. Si yo soy periodista, debo hacer muchas preguntas.

_____

12. Ustedes deben llamar a la policía cuando ven un crimen.

_____

13. Nosotros debemos avisar a los bomberos en caso de fuego.

_____

14. Los anunciadores de radio deben pronunciar cada sílaba claramente.

_____

15. Para tener éxito en su carrera, usted debe estudiar mucho.

_____

16. ¿Qué debes aprender tú para tener éxito en tu carrera o profesión?

_____

Worksheet 3.4 *Tener que* + infinitive

➤ Rewrite each of the following sentences, replacing the italicized verb with the proper form of **tener que** + *infinitive*. If you are not certain whether a verb is **-ar, -er,** or **-ir,** check the verb in the vocabulary of this workbook.

1. Nosotros *protegemos* la salud.

   _____

2. Tú *tomas* vitaminas diariamente.

   _____

3. El señor Ruiz *camina* todas las mañanas.

   _____

4. Ellas *comen* menos postres.

   _____

5. Nosotros *dormimos* ocho horas todas las noches.

   _____

6. Yo *tomo* la medicina en la dosis correcta.

   _____

7. Usted *guarda* cama cuando está enfermo.

   _____

8. Ella *llama* al médico cuando está enferma.

   _____

9. Ustedes *estudian* primeros auxilios.

   _____

10. Tú *bebes* seis vasos de agua todos los días.

    _____

11. Ellos *toman* más jugos y menos refrescos.

    _____

12. Yo *evito* la sal, el azúcar y el colesterol.

    _____

13. Nosotros *aprendemos* el número de emergencia.

    _____

14. Juanito *va* al dentista cada seis meses.

_____

15. Tú *lees* artículos sobre la nutrición y el ejercicio físico.

_____

16. El *practica* la prevención de accidentes y enfermedades.

_____

17. Ella *observa* las reglas de seguridad en el hogar.

_____

18. Yo *uso* ropa protectora en el trabajo.

_____

19. El carnicero *afila* los cuchillos para que corten bien.

_____

20. Ustedes *llevan* salvavidas en sus barcos.

_____

21. ¿Qué *haces* tú para cuidar tu salud?

_____

Worksheet 3.5 More on adjectives

Descriptive adjectives (**rojo, alto, bello**) usually follow the noun they modify. Indefinite or limiting adjectives (**mucho, poco, otro, cuanto, mismo**) always precede the noun:

EXAMPLES: ropa verde   mucha ropa   azúcar blanco   mucho azúcar
            casas nuevas   otras casas   libros grandes   pocos libros

Special cases: **Cada**, regardless of the gender of the noun it modifies, remains unchanged (**cada muchacho, cada muchacha**). **Todo** always precedes both the noun and its definite article (**toda la leche, todos los días**).

➤ In the blanks, supply the correct form of the adjectives in parentheses.

1. Raquel tiene _____ (mucho) amigos en la escuela.

2. Mi hermano gasta _____ (poco) dinero en el almuerzo.

3. Nosotros asistimos a la _____ (mismo) escuela.

4. ¿_____ (Cuánto) hermanos tienes tú?

5. Yo practico la música _____ (todo) la tarde.

6. ¿Lee usted _____ (otro) periódicos también?

7. Marca _____ (cada) número otra vez con cuidado.

8. Los veinte estudiantes tienen sus _____ (propio) pupitres.

9. _____ (Todo) los estudiantes tienen lápices nuevos.

10. Llevo mi cuaderno a _____ (varios) clases.

11. Yo no deseo bailar con mi _____ (propio) hermana.

12. Tengo ganas de bailar con _____ (otro) chicas.

13. La maestra planea _____ (mucho) actividades de recreo.

14. _____ (Varios) maestros participan en los juegos.

15. Mi _____ (segundo) clase del día es de matemáticas.

16. Tengo que pasar un examen _____ (cada) semestre.

17. Estamos en la _____ (último) semana del año.

18. Mi _____ (próximo) clase es la ciencia.

19. _____ (Poco) miembros del coro cantan en voz baja.

20. Mi vecino y yo asistimos a la _____ (mismo) clase.

21. ¿_____ (Cuánto) muchachas participan en los deportes?

22. El _____ (segundo) año de español es muy divertido.

23. Las _____ (último) páginas del libro tienen el vocabulario.

24. Usted no sabe cuánto espero de los _____ (próximo) años.

Worksheet 3.6 Possessive adjectives

Like the adjectives in the previous exercise, possessive adjectives precede the nouns that they modify and agree with their nouns in number and gender. Only **nuestro** and **vuestro** have separate feminine forms (**nuestra, vuestra**), but all plural forms add **-s**.

ENGLISH (SINGULAR)	SPANISH (SINGULAR)	ENGLISH (PLURAL)	SPANISH (PLURAL)
my	**mi(s)**	*our*	**nuestro(s), -a(s)**
your (familiar)	**tu(s)**	*your* (familiar)	**vuestro(s), -a(s)**
your (polite), *his, her*	**su(s)**	*your* (polite), *their*	**su(s)**

➤ In the blanks, supply the possessive adjective which corresponds to the subject of the sentence.

1. Yo ahorro la mitad de _____ sueldo.

2. Yo siempre pago _____ deudas.

3. Yo uso muy poco _____ tarjetas de crédito.

4. Tú respetas a _____ vecinos.

5. Tú acompañas _____ primas.

6. Tú escuchas a _____ padre.

7. Usted trae _____ guitarra a la fiesta.

8. Usted saluda a _____ amigos.

9. Usted canta _____ canciones favoritas.

10. Él necesita _____ pluma de fuente.

11. Él tiene que usar _____ bolígrafo.

12. Él firma _____ cheques en el banco.

13. Ella abre _____ cuaderno.

14. Ella lee _____ poesías nuevas.

15. Ella memoriza _____ poema favorito.

16. Nosotros devolvemos _____ libros a la biblioteca.

17. Nosotros pagamos _____ multas.

18. Nosotros volvemos a casa en _____ camioneta.

19. Ustedes desean vender _____ bicicletas.

20. Ustedes piden permiso a _____ padre.

21. Ustedes ahorran _____ dinero para comprar un coche.

22. Ellas llevan _____ zapatos nuevos.

23. Ellas escogen _____ ropa más bonita.

24. Ellos llegan en _____ coches recién lavados.

Worksheet 3.7 More on possessive adjectives

➤ For further practice with possessive adjectives, plus a general review of plural forms, change each of the *italicized* words below to the plural. Make whatever changes are necessary in the rest of the sentence. Write the entire sentence in the space to the right.

1. Mi *libro* es nuevo. _____

2. Su *tía* es joven. _____

3. Tu *primo* es guapo. _____

4. Mi *hermana* es alta. _____

5. Nuestra *clase* es buena. _____

6. Nuestro *profesor* es simpático. _____

7. Tu *hermano* está enfermo. _____

8. Su *vecino* está enojado. _____

9. Su *jardín* es bello. _____

10. Nuestro *cuarto* es pequeño. _____

11. Mi *primo* es ingeniero. _____

12. Mi *prima* es profesora. _____

13. Su *muñeca* es bonita. _____

14. Tu *hermano* es abogado. _____

15. Su *profesor* es bueno. _____

16. Nuestra *profesora* es buena. _____

17. Mi *compañera* es inteligente. _____

18. Su *amigo* es muy fiel. _____

19. Su *reloj* es de oro. _____

20. Su *vestido* es elegante. _____

21. Su *sombrero* es moderno. _____

22. Su *diamante* es grande. _____

23. Tu *pluma* es nueva. _____

24. Mi *lección* es interesante. _____

Buscapalabras

Palabras revueltas

➤ Here are ten nine-letter words recently used in exercises. Before you can identify them, you will have to unscramble them:

T	A	C	A	M	I	O	N	E
S	O	N	C	A	U	D	E	R
E	N	T	T	I	V	I	A	S
R	A	Z	O	M	I	M	E	R
F	O	L	I	B	A	R	G	O
V	A	S	O	F	R	I	T	O
L	I	M	O	T	U	A	V	O
R	O	S	A	F	R	E	P	O
R	E	M	A	F	R	E	N	E
D	I	O	P	R	E	C	I	O

Solutions

_____ _____ _____ _____ _____ _____ _____ _____ _____

_____ _____ _____ _____ _____ _____ _____ _____ _____

_____ _____ _____ _____ _____ _____ _____ _____ _____

_____ _____ _____ _____ _____ _____ _____ _____ _____

_____ _____ _____ _____ _____ _____ _____ _____ _____

_____ _____ _____ _____ _____ _____ _____ _____ _____

_____ _____ _____ _____ _____ _____ _____ _____ _____

_____ _____ _____ _____ _____ _____ _____ _____ _____

_____ _____ _____ _____ _____ _____ _____ _____ _____

_____ _____ _____ _____ _____ _____ _____ _____ _____

Note: These same ten words will be used in the Laberinto de Palabras on p. 61.

Worksheet 3.8 Irregular verbs *ir* and *ver*

Irregular verbs have one or more forms that differ from the patterns learned for conjugating regular -**ar**, -**er**, -**ir** verbs. Note the differences in **ir** and **ver**:

ir			
yo	voy	nosotros(as)	vamos
tú	vas	vosotros(as)	vais
él, ella, usted	va	ellos, ellas, ustedes	van

ver			
yo	veo	nosotros(as)	vemos
tú	ves	vosotros(as)	veis
él, ella, usted	ve	ellos, ellas, ustedes	ven

➤ **In the** blanks to the right supply the correct form of the verb in parentheses.

1. Yo _____ (ir) al teatro.

2. Yo _____ (ver) un drama.

3. Ellos _____ (ir) a Nueva York.

4. Ellos_____ (ver) una ópera italiana.

5. Usted_____ (ir) a mi casa.

6. Usted_____ (ver) a mis padres.

7. Tú _____ (ir) al museo.

8. Tú _____ (ver) esculturas de piedra.

9. Ellas _____ (ir) al zoológico.

10. Ellas _____ (ver) elefantes y girafas.

11. Nosotros _____ (ir) a España.

12. Nosotros _____ (ver) la Alhambra.

13. Ella _____ (ir) a la iglesia.

14. Ella _____ (ver) al sacerdote.

15. Ellos _____ (ir) al cine.

16. Ellos _____ (ver) muchos payasos.

17. Él_____ (ir) a Brasil.

18. Él_____ (ver) una playa bonita.

19. Ustedes _____ (ir) a un restaurante mexicano.

20. Ustedes _____ (ver) a los mariachis.

21. La señora Pérez _____ (ir) a la casa de su hija.

22. La señora Pérez _____ (ver) a sus nietos.

23. ¿Cuándo _____ (ir) tú al cine?

24. ¿Qué _____ (ver) tú cuando vas al cine?

Worksheet 3.9 *Ir a* + infinitive

Ir a + infinitive is used to express intention or future action. It resembles *to be* + *going to* in English.

EXAMPLES: SPANISH
                Ellos **van a** viajar en Chile.
                Juan **va a** estudiar francés.

            ENGLISH
                They are going to travel in Chile.
                John is going to study French.

➤ In the blank to the right, supply the correct form of **ir a** + *infinitive*.

1. Juanito _____ preparar su lista.

2. ¿Cuándo _____ ser el Día de los Reyes Magos?

3. Ellos_____ traer juguetes y dulces.

4. Yo _____ recibir regalos el 25 de diciembre.

5. Tú _____ esperar hasta el 6 de enero.

6. Nosotros no _____ celebrar la misma fecha.

7. En los Estados Unidos, Santa Claus _____ venir.

8. En España, Melchor, Gaspar, y Baltasar _____ llegar.

9. En ambos países, la gente _____ ir a la iglesia.

10. En esta temporada, muchos parientes_____ visitarnos.

11. Ustedes _____ preparar una comida grande.

12. Tú _____ tener un pastel muy sabroso.

13. Nosotros_____ a intercambiar regalos.

14. Ustedes _____ cantar las Posadas en México.

15. En Michigan yo _____ soñar con una Navidad blanca.

16. Nosotros_____ adornar el árbol navideño.

17. Tú y tus vecinos _____ decorar toda la calle.

18. Ellos_____ usar cien luces eléctricas.

19. Todos los familiares_____ estar juntos este año.

20. Nosotros_____ saludar a muchos vecinos también.

21. Mi tío Pepe_____ llevar su disfraz de Santa Claus.

22. Para nosotros, la Navidad _____ ser inolvidable.

23. ¿Cómo _____ celebrar tú la Navidad?

Worksheet 3.10 Demonstrative adjetives — *este* and *ese*

Este (*this*) and **ese** (*that*) are demonstrative adjectives. Like other adjectives, they agree in number and gender with the nouns they modify:

EXAMPLES:

THIS	THESE	THAT	THOSE
este libro	**estos** libros	**ese** libro	**esos** libros
esta mesa	**estas** mesas	**esa** mesa	**esas** mesas

➤ Supply the correct form of **este** in the blanks.

1. _____ pluma
2. _____ libros
3. _____ ventana
4. _____ puertas
5. _____ zapatos
6. _____ silla
7. _____ cuchillo
8. _____ cuchillos
9. _____ árbol
10. _____ país
11. _____ papel
12. _____ papeles
13. _____ mesa
14. _____ ciudad
15. _____ alumnos
16. _____ corbatas
17. _____ pedazo
18. _____ color
19. _____ ruido
20. _____ niñas

➤ Supply the correct form of **ese** in the blanks.

1. _____ dinero
2. _____ noche
3. _____ página
4. _____ casas
5. _____ manzanas
6. _____ sabor
7. _____ puerta
8. _____ ruido
9. _____ lección
10. _____ lápices
11. _____ clase
12. _____ flores
13. _____ taza
14. _____ muchachas
15. _____ escritorio
16. _____ hombre
17. _____ ejercicios
18. _____ ciudades
19. _____ alumnos
20. _____ montañas

Worksheet 3.11 *Este, ese, aquel*

Aquel is a third demonstrative adjective. Its feminine form is **aquella**, and its plural forms are **aquellos** and **aquellas**. While it is translated the same as **ese** (*that*), there is an important difference: **ese** refers to something near the person addressed by the speaker; **aquel** refers to something far from the speaker and the person addressed by the speaker, but possibly near a third person who is being spoken about:

EXAMPLES:

ENGLISH	SPANISH
near me; near us	**este, esta, estos, estas**
near you	**ese, esa, esos, esas**
near him or her; near them	**aquel, aquella, aquellos, aquellas**

➤ Change each of the following to the plural form.

1. ese libro _____

2. esta mesa _____

3. aquel libro _____

4. esa pluma _____

5. aquella revista _____

6. esa pizarra _____

7. esta ciudad _____

8. aquel escritorio _____

9. ese lápiz _____

10. ese gato _____

11. esa perra _____

12. esta semana _____

13. este mes _____

14. aquel año _____

15. ese muchacho _____

16. esa rosa _____

17. ese clavel _____

18. aquella montaña _____

19. esa lección _____

20. aquel día _____

21. aquel automóvil _____

22. aquella flor _____

23. esa tienda _____

24. ese loro _____

25. aquella jaula _____

26. ese señor _____

27. esa niña _____

28. aquella casa _____

29. esta carta _____

30. esa familia _____

31. este niño _____

32. aquel soldado _____

33. aquella compañía _____

34. esa escuela _____

35. aquella clase _____

36. este refrigerador _____

37. esa librería _____

38. esta palabra _____

39. ese árbol _____

40. esa biblioteca _____

41. esa estufa _____

42. ese árbol _____

Worksheet 3.12 Irregular verbs *hacer* and *poner*

Many irregular verbs are irregular only in the first person singular (**yo**) form. **Hacer** (*to do, to make*) and **poner** (*to put*) are good examples:

hacer			
yo	hago	nosotros(as)	hacemos
tú	haces	vosotros(as)	hacéis
el, ella, usted	hace	ellos, ellas, ustedes	hacen

poner			
yo	pongo	nosotros(as)	ponemos
tú	pones	vosotros(as)	ponéis
el, ella, usted	pone	ellos, ellas, ustedes	ponen

➤ Supply the correct form of the verbs in parentheses.

1. Yo _____ (hacer) la comida.

2. Yo _____ (poner) la comida en la mesa.

3. Ellas _____ (hacer) la tarea.

4. Ellas _____ (poner) la tarea en el escritorio.

5. Nosotros _____ (hacer) galletas.

6. Nosotros _____ (poner) las galletas en una bolsa.

7. Tú _____ (hacer) tu trabajo en la fábrica.

8. Tú_____ (poner) los transistores en las radios.

9. Mi mamá _____ (hacer) un vestido nuevo.

10. Mi mamá _____ (poner) alfileres en la tela.

11. Ellos _____ (hacer) refrescos para todos.

12. Ellos _____ (poner) cubitos de hielo en cada refresco.

13. Yo_____ (hacer) mi tarea de matemáticas.

14. Yo _____ (poner) los problemas en dos columnas.

15. Ustedes _____ (hacer) un mapa de California.

16. Ustedes _____ (poner) los ríos en el mapa.

17. La enfermera _____ (hacer) más cómodo al paciente.

18. La enfermera _____ (poner) sábanas limpias en la cama.

19. Tú _____ (hacer) mucho ruido con tu coche.

20. Tú _____ (poner) un silenciador nuevo en tu coche.

21. Los panaderos _____ (hacer) panecillos.

22. Los panaderos _____ (poner) los panecillos en el horno.

23. ¿Qué _____ (hacer) usted para ganar dinero?

24. ¿Cuánto dinero _____ (poner) usted en el banco?

Worksheet 3.13 Irregular verbs *saber* and *traer*

As with many other irregular verbs, **saber** (*to know, to know how*) and **traer** (*to bring*) are irregular in the first person singular (**yo**) form:

saber			
yo	sé	nosotros(as)	sabemos
tú	sabes	vosotros(as)	sabéis
él, ella, usted	sabe	ellos, ellas, ustedes	saben

traer			
yo	traigo	nosotros(as)	traemos
tú	traes	vosotros(as)	traéis
él, ella, usted	trae	ellos, ellas, ustedes	traen

➤ Supply the correct form of the verbs in parentheses.

1. Tú _____ (saber) la receta para hacer arroz con pollo.

2. Tú _____ (traer) los ingredientes de la receta.

3. Él _____ (saber) limpiar la alfombra.

4. Él _____ (traer) la aspiradora.

5. Nosotros _____ (saber) sacar fotos.

6. Nosotros _____ (traer) nuestra cámara.

7. Andrés _____ (saber) cantar canciones rancheras.

8. Andrés _____ (traer) su guitarra.

9. Yo _____ (saber) abrir una cuenta en el banco.

10. Yo _____ (traer) mis ahorros.

11. Ustedes _____ (saber) patinar.

12. Ustedes _____ (traer) los patines.

13. Ella _____ (saber) construir un estante.

14. Ella _____ (traer) la tabla y los clavos.

15. Usted _____ (saber) plantar los árboles.

16. Usted _____ (traer) sus palas.

17. Las señoritas _____ (saber) montar a caballo.

18. Las señoritas _____ (traer) su caballo favorito.

19. Ellos _____ (saber) hacer muñecas de papel.

20. Ellos _____ (traer) las tijeras.

21. Nosotros _____ (saber) cocinar.

22. Nosotros _____ (traer) los productos químicos.

23. ¿Qué _____ (saber) tú hacer para divertir a tus amigos?

24. ¿Qué _____ (traer) tú a las fiestas?

Worksheet 3.14 Irregular verbs *dar* and *salir*

Dar (*to give*) and **salir** (*to leave, to go out*) are also irregular in the first person singular (**yo**) form only:

dar			
yo	doy	nosotros(as)	damos
tú	das	vosotros	dais
él, ella, ustedes	da	ellos, ellas, ustedes	dan

salir			
yo	salgo	nosotros(as)	salimos
tú	sales	vosotros(as)	salís
él, ella, usted	sale	ellos, ellas ustedes	salen

➤ Supply the correct form of the verbs in parentheses.

1. El profesor _____ (salir) de la universidad.

2. El profesor _____ (dar) lecciones particulares.

3. Nosotros _____ (salir) del teatro.

4. Nosotros _____ (dar) nuestra opinión sobre la película.

5. Tú _____ (salir) de la iglesia.

6. Tú les _____ (dar) dinero a los pobres.

7. Yo _____ (salir) de la escuela.

8. Yo le _____ (dar) una moneda al chófer del autobús escolar.

9. El payaso _____ (salir) del circo.

10. El payaso les _____ (dar) boletos gratis a algunos niños.

11. Ustedes _____ (salir) de la selva de India.

12. Ustedes _____ (dar) un reporte sobre los tigres.

13. Mi mamá _____ (salir) de la cocina.

14. Mi mamá le_____ (dar) galletas a toda la familia.

15. Los turistas _____ (salir) del hotel.

16. Los turistas le _____ (dar) instrucciones al taxista.

17. Usted _____ (salir) del hospital.

18. Usted les_____ (dar) las gracias al cirujano y a las enfermeras.

19. Yo _____ (salir) del taxi.

20. Yo le _____ (dar) una buena propina al taxista.

21. La actriz _____ (salir) del avión.

22. La actriz les_____ (dar) entrevistas a los periodistas.

23. ¿Estás contento cuando tú _____ (salir) de un restaurante?

24. ¿Cuánto le_____ (dar) de propina al camarero?

Worksheet 3.15 Use of the *a personal*

When a human being is the direct object of a verb, the direct object must be preceded by the word **a**. This **a**, which is not strictly a preposition, is known as the personal **a** or **a personal**:

EXAMPLES: HUMAN BEING AS DIRECT OBJECT   NONHUMAN AS DIRECT OBJECT
            Yo veo a Juan.   Yo veo el perro.
            Tú ves al doctor.   Tú ves el coche del doctor.

➤ In the blanks, supply, as needed, the **a personal**, together with the definite or indefinite article, when used: **a, al (a + el = el), a la, a los, a las, a un, a una.** Place an X in the space if no words are required.

1. Yo veo _____ Beatriz muchas veces en el supermercado.

2. Yo veo _____ alcachofas muchas veces en el supermercado.

3. Nosotros escribimos _____ nuestros senadores.

4. Nosotros escribimos _____ cartas para los senadores.

5. El policía ayuda _____ los perros enfermos.

6. El policía ayuda _____ los niños.

7. Tú escuchas _____ tus padres.

8. Tú escuchas _____ el consejo de tus padres.

9. Ellos conocen _____ el gobernador de Utah.

10. Ellos conocen _____ el estado de Utah.

11. Carlos trae _____ María en el coche.

12. Carlos trae _____ el coche de María.

13. Mi vecino enseña _____ mi loro a cantar.

14. Mi vecino enseña _____ mi hijo a cantar.

15. Yo miro _____ una revista bonita en la biblioteca.

16. Yo miro _____ una mujer bonita en la biblioteca.

17. Un chico imita _____ un chimpancé en el zoológico.

18. Un chimpancé imita _____ un chico en el zoológico.

19. Nosotros contestamos _____ los alemanes en alemán.

20. Nosotros hablamos _____ alemán con los alemanes.

21. ¿Invitas tú _____ los mariachis a cantar?

22. ¿Cantan los mariachis _____ canciones rancheras?

Worksheet 3.16 Formation of adverbs

Many adverbs are formed by adding the suffix -**mente** to the feminine singular form of the adjective:

EXAMPLES:

ADJECTIVE	FEMININE SINGULAR	ADVERB
correcto	correcta	correcta**mente**
fácil	fácil	fácil**mente**
claro	clara	clara**mente**

When two or more adverbs modify the same word, -**mente** is added only to the last one:

EXAMPLE: Él habla clara y correcta**mente**.

➤ In the blanks, supply the adverbial form of the adjectives in parentheses.

1. Cristóbal Colón piensa _____ (serio) en la redondez del mundo.

2. Mucha gente escucha _____ (sospechoso) las ideas de Colón.

3. Colón no vive _____ (tranquilo) en Italia.

4. _____ (Difícil), viaja con su hijo a España.

5. La reina Isabel recibe_____ (cordial) al italiano.

6. Ella le dice _____ (triste) que le hace falta dinero.

7. _____ (Bondadoso) y generosamente, ella vende sus joyas.

8. Colón acepta _____ (emocionado) el regalo de tres barcos.

9. El sale _____ (respetuoso) de la corte de los reyes.

10. El almirante cree _____ (sincero) que navega hacia el Oriente.

11. Los barcos llegan_____ (desdichado) a otro continente.

12. El cree _____ (incorrecto) que los habitantes son de la India.

13. Nosotros_____ (curioso) los llamamos todavía indios.

14. Hoy mencionamos _____ (respetuoso) el nombre de Colón.

15. El gran descubridor,_____ (afortunado), hace varios viajes.

16. Un viaje,_____ (desafortunado), resulta en una catástrofe.

17. En La Española él destruye_____ (completo) su barco.

18. El hermano de Colón _____ (heróico) funda un pueblo en la isla.

19. La historia de Cristóbal Colón es _____ (especial) interesante.

20. Otros descubridores contribuyen _____ (histórico) a América.

21. Ponce de León explora _____ (considerable) la Florida.

22. Balboa _____ (increíble) descubre el océano Pacífico.

Irregular verbs

➤ In the blanks, supply the correct form of the verb in parentheses.

1. Tú estás en la cocina, y yo _____ (estar) en la sala.

2. Él sale a las seis, y yo _____ (salir) a las seis y media.

3. Ustedes le dan dinero a la Cruz Roja, y yo le _____ (dar) a la iglesia.

4. Ella sabe bailar bien, pero yo _____ (saber) bailar mejor.

5. Enrique hace poco ruido, pero yo _____ (hacer) mucho.

6. Ellos ponen mucha atención pero yo _____ (poner) más.

7. Tú vas a la escuela de día; yo _____ (ir) de noche.

8. Usted tiene frío, pero yo _____ (tener) calor.

9. Ellas ven películas; yo _____ (ver) los deportes.

10. Él es de Tejas, y yo _____ (ser) de Nuevo México.

11. Yo estoy en la plaza, y tú _____ (estar) en el parque.

12. Yo salgo temprano, pero ellos _____ (salir) tarde.

13. Yo doy una propina adecuada; ella _____ (dar) demasiado.

14. Yo sé la verdad; ustedes no _____ (saber) nada.

15. Yo hago naranjada, y tú _____ (hacer) limonada.

16. Yo pongo el café en la mesa; él _____ (poner) el té.

17. Yo voy a Madrid, pero ella _____ (ir) a Valencia.

18. Yo tengo sed, pero usted _____ (tener) hambre.

19. Yo veo dramas, y ustedes_____ (ver) zarzuelas.

20. Yo soy vendedor, y él _____ (ser) gerente.

General review

➤ Choose the correct form and write it in the blank

1. _____ (Nuestro, Nuestra) entretenimiento le debe mucho a Edison.

2. _____ (Estos, Este) científico es maestro de la invención.

3. _____ (La, El) luz eléctrica es su invento más importante.

4. El también es inventor _____ (del, de el) fonógrafo.

5. _____ (Es, Eres) muy agradable tener en casa música grabada.

6. El inventor _____ (hago, hace) preguntas a su maestro.

7. El maestro _____ (es, está) enojado con el joven Tomás.

8. Tomás_____ (tiene, tiene que) salir de la escuela.

9. Él sólo _____ (recibe, recibo) tres meses de educación formal.

10. Su mamá es _____ (maestra, una maestra) increíble.

11. Ella le enseña mucho _____ (Tomás, a Tomás).

12. Cuando es joven hace_____ (su, sus) experimentos en Ohio.

13. Su laboratorio más famoso_____ (es, está) en Nueva Jersey.

14. El inventor es sordo, pero no _____ (completo, completamente).

15. Él también da _____ (el mundo, al mundo) la cinematografía.

16. ¿Qué_____ (hacemos, hacen) nosotros sin películas?

17. Edison perfecciona _____ (los, a los) aparatos de otros inventores.

18. Hoy no tenemos_____ (que, a) gritar en el teléfono.

19. La máquina de escribir es más _____ (rápida, rápidamente).

20. Hoy_____ (nuestra, nuestras) vida es mucho mejor.

21. Yo _____ (sé, sabe) que Edison es «el Sabio del Parque Menlo.»

22. Tú _____(lee, lees) mucho sobre él y ves una película.

23. Dos actores famosos _____ (tiene, tienen) el papel de Edison.

24. Mickey Rooney es Edison _____ (el, al) joven.

25. Edison el hombre _____ (es, está) Spencer Tracy.

26. Voy _____ (ir, a ir) a Nueva Jersey en el verano.

27. Deseo _____ (ver, ver a) su laboratorio en East Orange.

28. Cuando mis problemas son _____ (difícil, difíciles), voy a pensar en las dificultades de Tomás Edison.

Worksheet 3.17 Irregular verbs *decir* and *oír*

Examine carefully the forms of **decir** and **oír,** which are more irregular than other verbs that were recently reviewed:

decir			
yo	digo	nosotros(as)	decimos
tú	dices	vosotros(as)	decís
él, ella, usted	dice	ellos, ellas, ustedes	dicen

oír			
yo	oigo	nosotros(as)	oímos
tú	oyes	vosotros(as)	oís
él, ella, usted	oye	ellos, ellas, ustedes	oyen

➤ Supply the correct form of **decir** in the blanks.

1. Ellos _____ que están muy ocupados hoy.

2. Tú _____ que vamos a tener un examen mañana.

3. Yo siempre _____ la verdad.

4. Rosa y Elena _____ que van a ir al cine esta noche.

5. Ricardo _____ que la película de hoy es muy buena.

6. ¿Por qué _____ usted que nunca va a aprender español?

7. ¡Cuidado! Juan a veces _____ mentiras.

8. ¿Qué _____ Guillermo de su nuevo trabajo?

9. Él _____ que es interesante, pero difícil.

10. ¿Por qué _____ tú que la gramática española es difícil?

11. Nosotros nunca _____ mentiras en la escuela.

12. Pedro _____ que va a estudiar para abogado.

➤ Supply the correct form of **oír** in the blanks.

1. Yo no _____ bien a la profesora desde este asiento.

2. ¿ _____ bien usted a la profesora desde ese asiento?

3. El señor Gómez no _____ bien. Es un poco sordo.

4. Tú _____ los conciertos por radio todas las tardes.

5. Yo _____ a los hijos de mi vecina desde el jardín.

6. Con tanto ruido yo no _____ nada.

7. Nosotros _____ música clásica, nada más.

8. El director _____ las ideas de los alumnos.

9. Él siempre _____ con paciencia nuestras quejas.

10. Los perros _____ a otros perros ladrar desde muy lejos.

11. Nosotros _____ muchas novelas por radio.

12. Tú _____ mucha música popular por discos compactos.

Worksheet 3.18 Irregular verbs *venir* and *querer*

The verbs **venir** and **querer** are stem-changing verbs **e → ie**. **Venir** also has a stem change in the first person singular:

venir			
yo	vengo	nosotros(as)	venimos
tú	vienes	vosotros(as)	venís
él, ella, usted	viene	ellos, ellas, ustedes	vienen

querer			
yo	quiero	nosotros(as)	queremos
tú	quieres	vosotros(as)	queréis
él, ella, usted	quiere	ellos, ellas, ustedes	quieren

➤ Supply the correct form of the verb in parentheses.

1. Lolita _____ (venir) a cenar con nosotros.

2. Lolita _____ (querer) comer a las seis.

3. Yo _____ (venir) a la escuela en autobús.

4. Yo no _____ (querer) andar demasiado.

5. Tú _____ (venir) a estudiar matemáticas.

6. Tú _____ (querer) ser contador.

7. Nosotros _____ (venir) a la panadería del barrio.

8. Nosotros _____ (querer) comprar pan francés.

9. Ellas _____ (venir) al Palacio de Bellas Artes.

10. Ellas _____ (querer) ver el ballet folklórico de México.

11. Raúl _____ (venir) a la pista de hielo.

12. Raúl _____ (querer) patinar con sus compañeros.

13. Ustedes _____ (venir) al Zócalo de México.

14. Ustedes _____ (querer) ver los edificios históricos.

15. Los turistas nunca _____ (venir) a la plaza de toros.

16. Los turistas no _____ (querer) ver una corrida de toros.

17. Estas muchachas _____ (venir) a Nueva York.

18. Estas muchachas _____ (querer) conocer la isla de Manhattan.

19. Gustavo y Esteban _____ (venir) a la biblioteca.

20. Gustavo y Esteban _____ (querer) buscar libros científicos.

21. Yo _____ (venir) de Zacatecas.

22. Yo _____ (querer) vivir en una ciudad más próspera.

23. Tú _____ (venir) muchas veces al museo arqueológico.

24. Tú _____ (querer) conocer la civilización olmeca.

Worksheet 3.19 Auxiliary verb *poder*

As a common helping verb, **poder** normally precedes the infinitive of another verb.

EXAMPLE: Yo **puedo** bailar el tango.   *I can dance the tango.*

Poder is also a stem-changing verb **o → ue**:

poder			
yo	puedo	nosotros(as)	podemos
tú	puedes	vosotros(as)	podéis
él, ella, usted	puede	ellos, ellas, ustedes	pueden

➤ In the following sentences, add the verb **poder** to the infinitive in parentheses. Write both verbs for example, (**puedo ver**) in the space below.

1. Los estudiantes _____
   (hacer) muchas cosas.

2. Yo _____
   (sumar) números rápidamente.

3. Isabel _____
   (hablar) francés e italiano.

4. Tú casi siempre _____
   (ganar) en la lotería.

5. Ricardo _____
   (dibujar) caricaturas chistosas.

6. Ella _____
   (recitar) poesías dramáticas.

7. Nosotros _____
   (escribir) ensayos interesantes.

8. Tú _____
   (memorizar) mucho vocabulario.

9. Las gemelas _____
   (bailar) como profesionales.

10. Concha y yo _____
    (cantar) dúos de operetas.

11. Federico _____
    (resolver) problemas complicados.

12. Luis y Laura _____
    (escribir) canciones patrióticas.

13. Yo _____
    (pintar) escenas pastorales.

14. Anita _____
    (nadar) en competencia estatal.

15. Ustedes _____
    (recibir) muchos trofeos en gimnasia.

16. Los hermanos Lara _____
    (montar) a caballo.

17. Alejandro _____
    (competir) en el boxeo.

18. Mi hermana _____
    (cocinar) mejor que nuestra mamá.

19. Nosotros _____
    (ser) los campeones del año.

20. Tú _____
    (diseñar) vestidos elegantes.

21. Yo _____
    (usar) una máquina de coser para hacer ropa.

22. Sara _____
    (entender) muchas teorías científicas.

23. Ellos _____
    (reparar) televisores.

24. ¿Qué talentos _____
    (demostrar) usted?

Irregular verbs

➤ Change the pronoun of each sentence from **yo** to **él.** Write both the subject and the verb in the spaces to the right. For further practice, make more answer sheets for changes to other subjects: **tú, ella, usted, nosotros, ustedes, ellos.**

1. Yo tengo una vida llena de actividades. _____

2. Yo digo las frases que debo aprender en español. _____

   _____

3. Yo oigo un programa de noticias en la radio. _____

4. Yo tengo que ayudar con las tareas de la casa. _____

5. Yo hago el café para toda la familia. _____

6. Yo sé si quieren el café con o sin leche. _____

7. Yo salgo de mi casa a las ocho menos veinte. _____

   _____

8. Yo estoy en la clase de español. _____

9. Yo veo las palabras nuevas en la pizarra. _____

   _____

10. Yo doy la tarea a la profesora. _____

11. Yo soy un estudiante aplicado. _____

12. Yo tengo notas muy buenas en cada clase. _____

13. Yo vengo a la dirección para ayudar al director. _____

   _____

14. Yo voy a estudiar para maestro. _____

15. Yo digo a todos que estoy contento con la escuela. _____

   _____

16. Yo sé que los maestros trabajan mucho. _____

17. Yo estoy dispuesto a estudiar muchos años. _____

18. Yo soy miembro del equipo de béisbol. _____

19. Yo voy a participar en una competición. _____

20. ¿Es verdad que yo tengo muchas actividades? _____

Vocabulary check-up

➤ In the blanks, write the opposites of the following words. If you do not know the word, look for its meaning in the vocabulary at the end of the book, then try to remember its opposite.

1. fácil _____

2. pequeño _____

3. abrir _____

4. subir _____

5. entrar _____

6. hombre _____

7. madre _____

8. menos _____

9. triste _____

10. nuevo _____

11. blanco _____

12. mucho _____

13. peor _____

14. temprano _____

15. invierno _____

16. mentira _____

17. tomar _____

18. silencio _____

19. barato _____

20. calor _____

21. jugar _____

22. largo _____

23. perder _____

24. preguntar _____

25. rápido _____

26. frío _____

27. joven _____

28. vender _____

29. lejos _____

30. alto _____

31. sucio _____

32. ausente _____

33. antes _____

34. día _____

35. ir _____

36. enemigo _____

37. allí _____

38. feo _____

39. ahorrar _____

40. estos _____

41. rico _____

42. bueno _____

43. comprador _____

44. enseñar _____

45. débil _____

46. paz _____

47. actor _____

48. noche _____

Laberinto

➤ Return to page 44. Did you unscramble all the words? Now, try to fit them into the squares below:

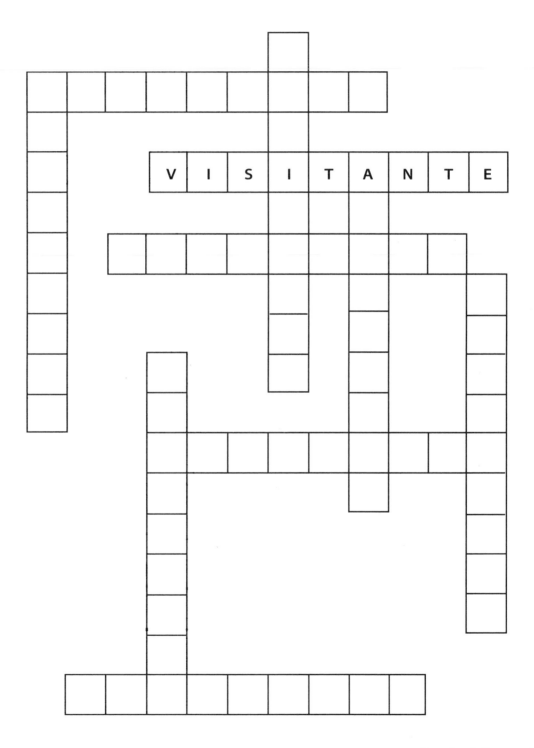

Part 4

Contents

Worksheet 4.1 Preterite tense of -*ar* verbs

The preterite tense (**el pretérito**) is one of the two simple past tenses. It is used to describe an action or event completed in the past. It is not used for repeated actions or actions that continue into the present or future. Regular **-ar** verbs are conjugated as follows in the preterite tense:

hablar			
yo	hablé	nosotros(as)	hablamos
tú	hablaste	vosotros(as)	hablasteis
él, ella, usted	habló	ellos, ellas, ustedes	hablaron

➤ Supply the preterite tense of the verbs in parentheses in the blanks.

1. El señor García, _____ (cruzar) el océano en un barco grande.

2. Los pasajeros _____ (desembarcar) en Portugal.

3. Nosotros _____ (volar) en avión a Madrid.

4. Yo _____ (viajar) con el señor García al sur de España.

5. Él _____ (alquilar) un automóvil para hacer el viaje.

6. Nosotros _____ (manejar) de Madrid a Sevilla.

7. José García me _____ (presentar) a su hermana, Concha.

8. Tú me _____ (saludar) con una sonrisa muy bonita.

9. Los tres _____ (cenar) en un restaurante típico de Sevilla.

10. Un trío gitano nos _____ (cantar) canciones románticas.

11. Una señorita _____ (presentar) un baile flamenco.

12. Los músicos _____ (tocar) guitarras muy finas.

13. Yo _____ (tomar) jugo de manzana con la comida.

14. Tú _____ (bailar) el tango.

15. Nosotros _____ (hablar) español en un restaurante.

16. Concha _____ (charlar) con el camarero.

17. Después, tú nos _____ (llevar) a la cueva de unos gitanos.

18. Yo _____ (encontrar) a unos amigos en la cueva.

19. Los gitanos también _____ (comprar) alfombras elegantes.

20. Tú no _____ (mencionar) que algunos gitanos son ricos.

21. Me _____ (encantar) la semana que pasé con José y Concha.

22. ¿ _____ (Viajar) usted también a alguna parte interesante?

Worksheet 4.2 Preterite tense of *-er, -ir* verbs

In the preterite tense, **-er** and **-ir** verbs share the same endings:

aprender			
yo	aprendí	nosotros(as)	aprendimos
tú	aprendiste	vosotros(as)	aprendisteis
él, ella, usted	aprendió	ellos, ellas, ustedes	aprendieron

vivir			
yo	viví	nosotros(as)	vivimos
tú	viviste	vosotros(as)	vivisteis
él, ella, usted	vivió	ellos, ellas, ustedes	vivieron

➤ Supply the proper form of the verb in parentheses in the blanks.

1. Carolina _____ (cumplir) dieciséis años.

2. Nosotros _____ (asistir) a su fiesta de cumpleaños.

3. Yo _____ (conocer) a Carolina en la escuela.

4. Desafortunadamente, nosotros nunca _____ (salir) juntos.

5. Una muchacha más simpática no _____ (existir).

6. Carolina _____ (recibir) muchos regalos.

7. Ella _____ (abrir) cada paquete con alegría.

8. Nosotros _____ (aplaudir) cada regalo.

9. Sus padres _____ (insistir) en invitar a los parientes.

10. Algunos_____ (escribir) en vez de venir.

11. Yo _____ (beber) tres vasos de agua.

12. Tú _____ (comer) un postre muy sabroso.

13. Los muchachos no _____ (resistir) los dulces.

14. Yo _____ (ver) a muchos compañeros.

15. Alberto _____ (esconder) varios dulces en el bolsillo.

16. Más tarde todos los dulces _____ (desaparecer) misteriosamente.

17. Alberto _____ (salir) temprano para la fiesta.

18. Los mariachis _____ (aparecer) a las ocho en punto.

19. Yo _____ (aprender) a cantar mis canciones favoritas.

20. Carolina les _____ (agradecer) a todos sus regalos.

21. A mí me _____ (parecer) muy divertida la fiesta.

Worksheet 4.3 More on the preterite tense

➤ Supply the preterite tense of the verbs in parentheses in the blanks.

1. Ayer, nosotros _____ (planear) un día de campo.

2. Nosotros _____ (caminar) a lo largo del río.

3. Mis padres y mis hermanos me _____ (acompañar).

4. Tú _____ (llevar) nuestro almuerzo.

5. Yo _____ (escoger) un lugar cerca del río.

6. Mi mamá _____ (colocar) un mantel sobre el césped.

7. Mis padres _____ (descansar) allí.

8. Mis hermanos y yo _____ (jugar) béisbol.

9. Después de una hora, nosotros _____ (desear) almorzar.

10. Tú _____ (ayudar) a mamá con la comida.

11. Yo _____ (abrir) un refresco de limón.

12. Papá _____ (sacar) un termo de café.

13. Yo _____ (comer) jamón y mucha ensalada de papas.

14. Un ejército de insectos _____ (tratar) de comer también.

15. Muy pronto el sol _____ (desaparecer) completamente.

16. Yo _____ (mirar) el cielo lleno de nubes grises.

17. Desgraciadamente, _____ (llover) mucho.

18. Nosotros _____ (empacar) rápidamente la comida.

19. Mi familia y yo _____ (correr) hacia unos árboles.

20. Un árbol muy grande _____ (ofrecer) abrigo por un tiempo.

21. Después de media hora _____ (dejar) de llover.

22. Nosotros _____ (regresar) a casa un poco tristes.

23. El día _____ (empezar) muy bonito, pero terminó mal.

24. Mi padre nos _____ (prometer) otros días de campo.

25. ¿Cómo _____ (resultar) para ustedes ese día?

Worksheet 4.4 More on the preterite tense

➤ Change the following verbs from present tense to preterite tense.

1. Yo estudio _____
2. Él vive _____
3. Ellos compran _____
4. Yo escribo _____
5. Eduardo habla _____
6. Ellos viven _____
7. Elena vende _____
8. Yo espero _____
9. Tú aprendes _____
10. Usted habla _____
11. Él bebe _____
12. Yo como _____
13. Ellos comen _____
14. Tú apareces _____
15. Él sube _____
16. Yo saludo _____
17. Yo camino _____
18. Jorge recibe _____
19. Tú asistes _____
20. Yo abro _____
21. Él ahorra _____
22. Yo pregunto _____
23. Ella escribe _____
24. Ellos comen _____

25. Ellos venden _____
26. Tú vives _____
27. Yo bebo _____
28. Él admira _____
29. Ella gasta _____
30. Usted termina _____
31. Mi tío explica _____
32. Enrique sale _____
33. Tú necesitas _____
34. Él toma _____
35. Yo trato _____
36. María contesta _____
37. Ellos tratan _____
38. Luis trabaja _____
39. Tú llevas _____
40. Nosotros vemos _____
41. Nosotros tomamos _____
42. Tú caminas _____
43. Ellos planean _____
44. Yo salgo _____
45. Él responde _____
46. Yo comprendo _____
47. Tú estudias _____
48. Ella sale _____

Worksheet 4.5 Personal pronouns—prepositional forms

Personal pronouns as objects of prepositions (for *us*, with *them*) follow the patterns below.

EXAMPLES: El regalo es para **mí.**   El regalo es para **nosotros(as)**
           El regalo es para **ti.**   El regalo es para **vosotros(as).**
           El regalo es para **usted.**   El regalo es para **ustedes.**
           El regalo es para **él.**   El regalo es para **ellos.**
           El regalo es para **ella.**   El regalo es para **ellas.**

Note: Except for the first and second persons singular (**mí, ti**), the prepositional forms are identical to the subject pronouns. Note also that these same two pronouns when combined with **con** become **conmigo** and **contigo.**

➤ In the blanks, replace the words in parentheses with the appropriate prepositional pronoun.

1. Yo siempre hablo de _____ (mi hermano).

2. Tú siempre hablas de _____ (tu hermana).

3. Juan estudia con _____ (Felipe, Donato).

4. Elena estudia con _____ (Carmen, Chabela).

5. Él siempre anda entre _____ (Ana, yo).

6. Ella siempre anda detrás de _____ (Pablo, tú).

7. Juan trabaja diariamente con _____ (Carlos, yo).

8. Mario trabaja diariamente con _____ (Alberto, tú).

9. Silvia sale a veces con _____ (tu primo).

10. Tu primo sale a veces con_____ (Silvia).

11. Él dice que tiene buenas noticias para _____ (tú, yo).

12. Yo tengo buenas noticias para_____ (usted, ella).

13. Tus abuelos viven muy lejos de _____ (tus padres).

14. Tu abuelo vive muy lejos de_____ (tu padre).

15. El médico conoce muy bien a _____ (las enfermeras).

16. Los médicos conocen muy bien a _____ (la enfermera).

17. Yo nunca voy al cine sin _____ (mis amigos).

18. Ella nunca va al cine sin _____ (María, yo).

19. ¿Cuándo piensas tú en _____ (tus abuelos)?

20. ¿Por qué visita usted a _____ (esta señora)?

Worksheet 4.6 More on personal pronouns— prepositional forms

REMINDER: **con + mi = conmigo**   **con + ti = contigo**
EXAMPLES: Ella va **conmigo**.   *She goes with me.*   Yo ando **contigo**   *I walk with you.*

➤ Change the following pronouns from singular to plural. Include prepositions.

1. con él _____
2. para usted _____
3. para mí _____
4. hacia mí _____
5. según tú _____
6. conmigo _____
7. sin ti _____
8. sobre él _____
9. lejos de ti _____
10. cerca de mí _____
11. detrás de mí _____
12. en frente de ti _____
13. de él _____
14. con usted _____
15. en él _____
16. sin mí _____
17. para mí _____
18. por mí _____
19. para él _____
20. hacia ti _____

➤ Change the following pronouns from plural to singular. Include prepositions.

1. para nosotros _____
2. con ellos _____
3. para ustedes _____
4. sin nosotros _____
5. con ustedes _____
6. de nosotros _____
7. por ellas _____
8. sin nosotras _____
9. por ustedes _____
10. para ellas _____
11. con ustedes _____
12. sobre ellos _____
13. a nosotros _____
14. de ustedes _____
15. hacia ellas _____
16. a nosotros _____
17. hacia ellos _____
18. según ellas _____
19. en ustedes _____
20. entre ellos _____

Note: After the preposition **según**, the pronouns **tú** and **yo** do not change.

Worksheet 4.7 Direct object pronouns

Direct object pronouns are placed as follows:

EXAMPLES:	ENGLISH (FOLLOW NOUN)	SPANISH (PRECEDE NOUN)	
	He sees me.	Me ve.	
	He sees you.	Te ve.	(familiar)
	He sees you.	Lo (La) ve.	(polite)
	He sees him (her).	Lo (La) ve.	
	He sees us.	Nos ve.	
	He sees you.	Os ve.	(familiar)
	He sees you.	Los (las) ve.	(polite)
	He sees them.	Los (las) ve.	

➤ Supply the direct object pronoun needed to replace the noun in parentheses and rewrite the sentences in the spaces provided.

1. Yo veo (el libro) sobre la mesa. _____

2. Ella necesita (esa pluma). _____

3. El profesor pone (el libro) en su portafolio. _____

4. Ellos practican (los ejercicios) cuidadosamente. _____

5. Tú no necesitas más (este cuaderno). _____

6. Yo veo (al señor García) en la calle con frecuencia. _____

7. Inés trae (a su amiga) a la clase diariamente. _____

8. El profesor busca (sus lentes) por todas partes. _____

9. Yo llamé(a usted y a María) por teléfono ayer. _____

10. Tu escribiste (la carta) por fin. _____

11. Veo (al señor López) casi todos los días. _____

12. También veo (a su esposa) con mucha frecuencia. _____

13. Yo compré (esta pluma) por dos dólares. _____

14. El médico mandó (a Carlos y a Juan) al laboratorio. _____

15. Yo abrí (las ventanas). _____

16. Él siempre prepara (sus tareas) por la noche. _____

17. Yo generalmente vendo (mis libros) al final del curso. _____

18. Alguien compró (el coche de mi tío). _____

19. Ella no tiene (su cartera). _____

20. Veo (a Dolores) de vez en cuando. _____

Worksheet 4.8 Indirect object pronouns

Indirect object pronouns are the same as the direct object pronouns **me, te, nos, os**, except for the third person:

	DIRECT OBJECTS	INDIRECT OBJECTS
SINGULAR:	lo, la	le
PLURAL:	los, las	les

➤ Supply the missing indirect object pronouns in the blanks.

1. Yo _____ vendo mi diccionario (a ti).

2. Tú _____ pagas tres dólares (a mí).

3. Nosotros _____ hablamos (al profesor) en español.

4. El profesor no _____ habla (a nosotros) muy rápido.

5. Juan _____ escribió muchas cartas (a Angélica).

6. Angélica _____ llamó por teléfono (a sus padres).

7. Los artistas _____ cantaron (a nosotros).

8. Yo _____ pedí otra canción (a ellos).

9. Tú _____ sorprendiste (a mí) con el regalo.

10. Yo _____ regalé algo (a ella) también.

11. El maestro _____ explicó (a ti) una regla de gramática.

12. El director _____ explicó un plan (a los maestros).

13. Yo _____ traigo (a ti) todos mis problemas.

14. Tú _____ ayudas (a mi) a resolver mis problemas.

15. El patrón _____ ordena (a nosotros) llegar temprano.

16. Nosotros _____ prometemos (al patrón) llegar a tiempo.

17. Roberto _____ prestó (a Luisa) diez dólares.

18. Ella _____ agradeció (a Roberto) el dinero prestado.

19. La respuesta del estudiante _____ pareció buena (a mí).

20. Los estudiantes _____ parecen buenos (a nosotros).

21. Los veteranos _____ dicen (a mí) que van a desfilar.

22. Yo _____ mencioné (a ti) el desfile de los veteranos.

23. El banco _____ devolvió (a usted) el cheque.

24. (A los bancos) no _____ gustan los fondos insuficientes.

Worksheet 4.9 Redundant personal pronouns

Prepositional pronouns are used with **le**, **les** for emphasis or clarity because **le** and l**es** can refer to you, him, her, or them. The following *redundant* prepositional phrases help to assure clarity:

EXAMPLES: SINGULAR

Le doy el libro a usted *(you).*
Le doy el libro a él *(him).*
Le doy el libro a ella *(her).*

PLURAL

Les doy el libro a ustedes *(you).*
Les doy el libro a ellos *(them).*
Les doy el libro a ellas *(them).*

EXAMPLE: Emphasis: ¡A **mí** no **me** engaña nadie! *Nobody cheats me!*

➤ Supply the indirect object pronoun in the blanks.

1. Él _____ escribió a ella dos cartas ayer.
2. Juan siempre _____ trae a ellas muchas flores.
3. A mí no _____ importa nada su reputación.
4. A Alfredo _____ parece extraño que usted no lo llamó.
5. A ti _____ encanta bailar el salsa.
6. Él siempre _____ manda a nosotros muchos regalos.
7. ¿Quién _____ enseñó a ella a escribir a máquina?
8. A mí _____ encanta estudiar idiomas europeos.
9. A mi esposa _____ encanta el clima de Puerto Rico.
10. A nosotros nos _____ importan las acciones de otros.
11. ¿Qué _____ importa a ti lo que él dice?
12. A mí _____ encanta estudiar idiomas europeos.
13. No _____ importa a Vicente lo que dice el profesor.
14. Él nunca _____ dice a mí lo que va a hacer.
15. A mí _____ desagradan las discusiones.
16. A nosotros _____ agrada mucho la profesora nueva.
17. A Vicente _____ importa lo que dice el profesor.
18. A mí _____ encantan los alumnos recién llegados.
19. Margarita _____ envió un cable a sus padres anoche.
20. A nosotros _____ pareció absurda la actitud de Raquel.
21. ¿Qué _____ parece a usted mi automóvil nuevo?
22. ¿A quién _____ prestó usted el libro de español?
23. Ellos nunca _____ invitan a ti cuando van al campo.
24. A todos ellos _____ encanta nadar en la piscina.
25. ¿A usted _____ parecen fáciles los pronombres personales?

Worksheet 4.10 The verb *gustar*

There is no verb in Spanish that corresponds exactly to *like*. To express this meaning, the verb **gustar** (*to please*) is **used.** In translation, the subject becomes the object, and the object becomes the subject:

EXAMPLES:	ENGLISH	SPANISH	LITERAL TRANSLATION
	I like the story.	Me **gusta** el cuento.	*The story pleases me.*
	I like the stories.	Me **gustan** los cuentos.	*The stories please me.*

➤ Supply the correct form of **gustar** in the blanks.

1. A mí me _____ el color rojo.

2. ¿Cuáles colores les _____ a ustedes?

3. A mis padres les _____ ir al cine.

4. A mi padre le _____ sobre todo las películas históricas.

5. El pescado frito a mí no me _____ .

6. Me _____ mucho más los mariscos.

7. A mis vecinos les _____ las playas de Acapulco.

8. A mi familia nos _____ la playa de San Juan.

9. ¿Les _____ a ustedes las casas de dos pisos?

10. A mí me _____ una casa con muchas habitaciones.

11. ¿Te _____ a ti el chocolate caliente estilo mexicano?

12. No, me _____ más el chocolate caliente sin canela.

13. A los alumnos no les _____ los exámenes difíciles.

14. A otros alumnos no les _____ la tarea diaria.

15. A los argentinos les _____ las carreras de caballos.

16. A los españoles les _____ el jaialai.

17. No me _____ el ruido de los helicópteros.

18. Tampoco me _____ las autopistas ruidosas.

19. A Lucía le _____ los restaurantes.

20. A Antonio le _____ la comida preparada en casa.

21. A los niños les _____ los fuegos artificiales.

22. A mí sólo me _____ los cohetes.

23. ¿Es verdad que no te _____ las espinacas?

24. ¿Cuál verdura te _____ más a ti?

Worksheet 4.11 **More on *gustar***

A number of other verbs follow the pattern of **gustar**:

EXAMPLES: **parecer** *to seem*   **encantar** *to charm, delight*   **fascinar** *to fascinate*
            importar *to matter*   **extrañar** *to seem strange*   **molestar** *to bother*

The verb **disgustar** does not mean *to disgust*; it replaces the English verb *to dislike,* but literally means *to displease.*

➤ Supply the missing indirect object pronoun in the blanks.

1. A mí _____ gusta hablar español con el profesor.

2. A ellos _____ disgusta estar enfermos.

3. No _____ importa a ella el dinero que gasto en ropa.

4. A ti _____ encantan las lenguas extranjeras.

5. A nosotros _____ parece curiosa tu respuesta.

6. A mi hermana _____ fascinan las novelas inglesas.

7. A las mujeres no _____ gusta decir su edad.

8. ¿Qué _____ parece a ti el color de esta corbata?

9. A ti _____ extrañó no ver a Raquel en el baile.

10. A él no _____ importa la opinión de sus abuelos.

11. A los senadores _____ fascinó el plan del presidente.

12. A mí _____ pareció increíble la decisión del juez.

13. A ella _____ encantan las casas viejas de Irlanda.

14. A nosotros _____ extraña la coducta de aquel niño.

15. A la mexicana _____ gustan las tiendas de San Diego.

16. ¿No _____ fascinan a ti aquellos pingüinos?

17. A mí _____ disgustó la neblina de Londres.

18. No _____ importa a ellos la raza del candidato.

19. ¿No _____ pareció hermosa la prima de Arturo?

20. No sabes cuánto _____ gusta a ella la música latina.

21. A Ramón _____ extraña tu falta de entusiasmo.

22. A nosotros _____ fascina la música brasileña.

23. ¿No _____ molesta a ustedes la temporada de las lluvias?

24. ¿Por qué _____ disgusta tanto a ti la televisión?

25. A usted _____ molestan demasiado los mosquitos.

Worksheet 4.12 More on *gustar*

➤ Supply the proper form of the prepositional pronouns in the blanks. Where more than one pronoun may be used, include those possibilities.

1. A _____ nos gusta comer tarde.

2. ¿Cuándo te gusta a _____ comer?

3. ¿A _____ le importa lo que Juan nos trae?

4. Sí, a _____ me gustan los regalos de Juan.

5. A _____ te encanta bailar el tango.

6. A _____ nos gustan los bailes más modernos.

7. A _____ me fascinan los deportes de invierno.

8. A _____ le gustan los deportes acuáticos.

9. A _____ le extrañó ver a Manuel en la playa.

10. A _____ nos gusta ver a Manuel allí.

11. ¿Por qué te parece buena a _____ esta universidad?

12. A _____ me gustan los profesores.

13. A _____ le encantan los perfumes franceses.

14. A _____ no nos gusta el agua de colonia.

15. A _____ te disgusta la fragancia de las camelias.

16. A _____ me gusta oler todas las flores del jardín.

17. ¿Es verdad que a _____ no te gusta el profesor?

18. Al contrario, a _____ me parece excelente.

19. A _____ nos disgustan los perros feroces.

20. A _____ tampoco me gustan los perros tímidos.

21. A _____ no te gustan los precios en Venezuela.

22. A _____ me parecen peores los precios en Brasil.

23. No sabes cuánto me desagrada a _____ el acordeón.

24. ¿A _____ te disgusta ese instrumento también?

25. A _____ les parece increíble el juego.

26. No me importa a _____ la opinión de ellos.

27. A _____ me encanta el juego de tenis.

28. A _____ nos gusta más el baloncesto.

29. A _____ le interesa mucho la historia europea.

30. ¿Cuál estudio te interesa más a _____ ?

Worksheet 4.13 Arithmetic

➤ For practice with cardinal numbers and arithmetical functions, compute answers to the following problems and write them in the blanks to the right.

1. Siete menos cuatro son _____ .

2. Seis menos dos son _____ .

3. Seis y (más) uno son _____ .

4. Seis y dos son _____ .

5. Cinco por (multiplicado por) dos son _____ .

6. Cinco por tres son _____ .

7. Diez menos uno son _____ .

8. Diez menos nueve es _____ .

9. Siete por dos son _____ .

10. Siete y siete son _____ .

11. Ocho entre (dividido entre) dos son _____ .

12. Diez entre dos son _____ .

13. Siete menos seis es _____ .

14. Doce entre tres son _____ .

15. Cuatro por tres son _____ .

16. Once menos cinco son _____ .

17. Diez por tres son _____ .

18. Treinta entre diez son _____ .

19. Cincuenta por ciento (%) de diez son _____ .

20. Veinticinco por ciento de cuatro es _____ .

21. ¿Cuántos son once menos dos? _____ .

22. ¿Cuántos son doce entre tres? _____ .

23. Cinco por cuatro menos tres son _____ .

24. Diez por nueve menos cinco son _____ .

25. Quince es tres veces más que _____ .

26. Cinco dólares por cuatro son _____ .

27. Un día y medio son _____ horas.

28. Una hora y media son _____ minutos.

Worksheet 4.14 Prepositions

➤ Supply the necessary prepositions in the blanks. Some common prepositions include **a, de, en, entre, para, por, sobre.**

1. Yo viví en México _____ un año entero.

2. México _____ mi es un país de mucho encanto.

3. La siesta empieza _____ las dos de la tarde.

4. No observan la siesta _____ la capital.

5. Visité el istmo _____ Tehuántepec.

6. El istmo está _____ el Pacífico y el Atlántico.

7. Es la parte más estrecha _____ México.

8. También viajé _____ la ciudad antigua de Teotihuacán.

9. Me gusta ver la luna _____ las pirámides.

10. Después de Teotihuacán viajamos _____ Oaxaca.

11. Oaxaca es la tierra _____ los zapotecas.

12. Benito Juárez nació _____ las montañas de Oaxaca.

13. Vemos estatuas de Juárez _____ todas partes.

14. La estatua _____ Morelos es la más grande de México.

15. Esta estatua está _____ la isla de Janitzio.

16. La isla es muy conocida _____ los turistas.

17. Yo ahorro mi dinero _____ hacer otro viaje a México.

18. La próxima vez voy _____ ir a Guadalajara.

19. Deseo ver _____ todo la magnífica catedral.

20. Un bonito parque está _____ frente de la catedral.

21. Oigo las campanas _____ la tarde y la medianoche.

22. Cuando bajo del avión _____ México estoy contento.

23. ¿Sabes tú _____ qué me gusta tanto?

24. México ofrece algo de interés _____ cada turista.

25. ¿Lees tú mucho _____ la historia de México?

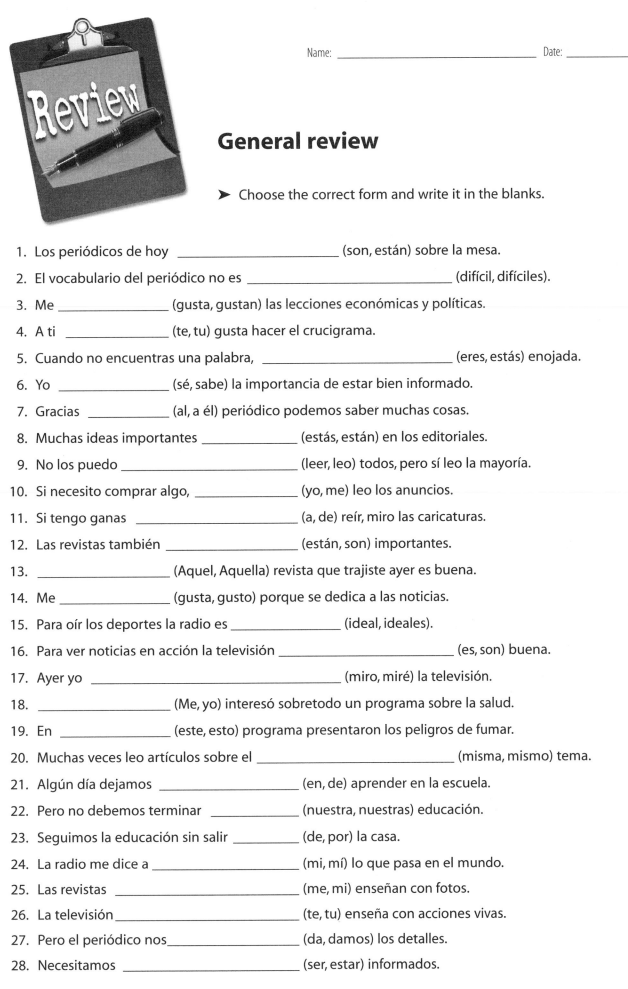

General review

➤ Choose the correct form and write it in the blanks.

1. Los periódicos de hoy _____ (son, están) sobre la mesa.

2. El vocabulario del periódico no es _____ (difícil, difíciles).

3. Me _____ (gusta, gustan) las lecciones económicas y políticas.

4. A ti _____ (te, tu) gusta hacer el crucigrama.

5. Cuando no encuentras una palabra, _____ (eres, estás) enojada.

6. Yo _____ (sé, sabe) la importancia de estar bien informado.

7. Gracias _____ (al, a él) periódico podemos saber muchas cosas.

8. Muchas ideas importantes _____ (estás, están) en los editoriales.

9. No los puedo _____ (leer, leo) todos, pero sí leo la mayoría.

10. Si necesito comprar algo, _____ (yo, me) leo los anuncios.

11. Si tengo ganas _____ (a, de) reír, miro las caricaturas.

12. Las revistas también _____ (están, son) importantes.

13. _____ (Aquel, Aquella) revista que trajiste ayer es buena.

14. Me _____ (gusta, gusto) porque se dedica a las noticias.

15. Para oír los deportes la radio es _____ (ideal, ideales).

16. Para ver noticias en acción la televisión _____ (es, son) buena.

17. Ayer yo _____ (miro, miré) la televisión.

18. _____ (Me, yo) interesó sobretodo un programa sobre la salud.

19. En _____ (este, esto) programa presentaron los peligros de fumar.

20. Muchas veces leo artículos sobre el _____ (misma, mismo) tema.

21. Algún día dejamos _____ (en, de) aprender en la escuela.

22. Pero no debemos terminar _____ (nuestra, nuestras) educación.

23. Seguimos la educación sin salir _____ (de, por) la casa.

24. La radio me dice a _____ (mi, mí) lo que pasa en el mundo.

25. Las revistas _____ (me, mi) enseñan con fotos.

26. La televisión_____ (te, tu) enseña con acciones vivas.

27. Pero el periódico nos_____ (da, damos) los detalles.

28. Necesitamos _____ (ser, estar) informados.

Worksheet 4.15 Reflexive verbs

If the same person or thing is both the subject and object of a verb, the verb is said to be reflexive. It will be preceded by a reflexive pronoun:

| **me** | *myself* | **se** | *yourself, himself, herself* | **os** | *yourselves* |
| **te** | *yourself* | **nos** | *ourselves* | **se** | *yourselves, themselves* |

Lavarse, a typical reflexive verb meaning *to wash oneself,* is conjugated as follows:

lavarse			
yo	me lavo	nosotros(as)	nos lavamos
tú	te lavas	vosotros(as)	os laváis
él, ella, usted	se lava	ellos, ellas, ustedes	se lavan

Many verbs are reflexive in Spanish but not in English.

EXAMPLES: **levantarse** *to get up*   **desayunarse** *to eat breakfast*   **escaparse** *to get away*

➤ Supply the correct reflexive pronoun in the blanks.

1. Julio _____ levanta a las seis todas las mañanas.

2. Yo tambén _____ levanto temprano.

3. Mis padres _____ levantan antes que nosotros.

4. Todos _____ acostamos temprano también.

5. Cuando _____ pone el sol, mi hermanita ya está en su cama.

6. Nosotros _____ despertamos en la madrugada.

7. Tú _____ bañas antes que los demás.

8. Yo _____ lavo las manos antes de desayunarme.

9. En mi casa, todos _____ desayunamos juntos.

10. Ellos nunca _____ cansan de comer huevos rancheros.

11. Papá _____ sienta a la cabecera de la mesa.

12. Rosina, _____ vas a enfermar si comes tanta mermelada.

13. Tú tienes razón, yo tengo que cuidar_____.

14. Rosina _____ lavó el pelo anoche.

15. Ahora ella trata de peinar _____ de un estilo diferente.

16. Mis hermanos y yo _____ preparamos para ir a la escuela.

17. Nosotros no _____ aburrimos en nuestras clases.

18. ¿Por qué _____ quedaste después de la clase ayer?

19. ¿Cómo_____ llama su maestro favorito?

Worksheet 4.16 More on reflexive verbs

➤ Supply the present tense of the verbs in parentheses in the blanks.

1. Ellos _____ (levantarse) a las seis todas las mañanas.

2. ¿Es verdad que tú _____ (llamarse) Enrique?

3. No, usted _____ (equivocarse); yo soy Roberto.

4. Ella _____ (cansarse) cuando trabaja demasiado.

5. ¿A qué hora _____ (desayunarse) tú?

6. Yo siempre _____ (desayunarse) antes de las siete.

7. Yo siempre _____ (aburrirse) mucho en las fiestas de los Ruiz.

8. Ella_____ (quedarse) en casa todos los viernes.

9. El profesor _____ (enojarse) mucho si venimos tarde a clase.

10. La profesora _____ (quedarse) después de su última clase.

11. Mis padres siempre _____ (levantarse) temprano.

12. Tú siempre _____ (peinarse) con mucho cuidado.

13. Juan dice que él _____ (aburrirse) en la clase de historia.

14. ¿Cómo_____ (llamarse) los compañeros de Arturo?

15. El profesor _____ (ponerse) los lentes para leer la lección.

16. Entonces _____ (ponerse) a escribir la tarea en la pizarra.

17. Las muchachas hoy día _____ (pintarse) mucho la cara.

18. Yo _____ (enfermarse) si como mucho helado.

19. Si Marina _____ (equivocarse) en la lección se pone nerviosa.

20. Mis padres siempre _____ (desayunarse) antes que nosotros.

21. El nuevo estudiante _____ (llamarse) Roberto Esparza.

22. Yo _____ (bañarse) casi siempre con agua fría.

23. Tú siempre _____ (ponerse) nervioso antes de un examen.

24. Los domingos no tenemos que _____ (levantarse) temprano.

25. ¿Cuándo _____ (preocuparse) tú por la contaminación?

Worksheet 4.17 More on reflexive verbs

Definite articles are used with parts of the body and articles of clothing in reflexive constructions.
Compare Spanish and English.

EXAMPLES: ENGLISH   SPANISH   LITERAL TRANSLATION

          I wash my hair   **Me lavo el pelo.**   *I wash myself the hair.*

          You put on your coat.   **Te pones el abrigo.**   *You put yourself the coat.*

➤ Supply the definite article in the blanks.

1. Tú te pones _____ guantes (m).

2. Yo me pongo _____ bufanda.

3. Ella se quita _____ abrigo.

4. Él se quita _____ chaqueta.

5. Ellos se lavan _____ manos (f).

6. Nosotros nos lavamos _____ cara.

7. Elena se pintó _____ labios.

8. Juana se quitó _____ maquillaje (m).

9. La criada se pone _____ delantal (m).

10. Los pilotos se ponen _____ uniformes (m).

11. ¿Cuándo se cepilla usted _____ dientes (m)?

12. ¿Cuándo se lava usted _____ cara?

13. La niña se ensució _____ vestido.

14. El niño se lastimó _____ rodillas.

15. Mi papá se lastimó _____ pie.

16. Yo me corté _____ dedo con el cuchillo.

17. ¿Te secas tú_____ pelo al sol?

18. ¿Cómo te mordiste _____ lengua?

19. ¿Por qué se pone el chófer _____ lentes oscuros?

20. ¿Por qué se quita el charro _____ enorme sombrero?

21. ¿Cómo te rompiste _____ impermeable (m)?

22. ¿Cuándo se va a cortar ella _____ uñas?

23. Me cepillé _____ traje antes de salir contigo.

24. Abuelito se pone _____ dentadura después delevantarse.

Worksheet 4.18 Reflexive verbs infinitive form

When a reflexive verb is assisted by one or more preceding verbs, the pronoun may precede the first verb or may be attached to the infinitive. Note also that the reflexive pronoun must have the same person and number as the subject:

EXAMPLES: REFLEXIVE CONSTRUCTIONS

Yo quiero lavar**me** el pelo.
Tú vas a quitar**te** el abrigo.
Ella piensa pintar**se** los labios.
Nosotros debemos peinar**nos** bien.
Ustedes quieren cansar**se** más.

ALTERNATE CONSTRUCTION

Yo **me** quiero lavar el pelo.
Tú **te** vas a quitar el abrigo.
Ella **se** piensa pintar los labios.
Nosotros **nos** debemos peinar bien.
Ustedes **se** quieren casar.

➤ Copy the infinitives into the blanks, then attach the correct reflexive pronouns.

1. Yo quiero _____ (levantar) temprano mañana.
2. Nosotros vamos a _____ (acostar) a las diez.
3. Ellos deben _____ (retirar) también.
4. Tú no puedes _____ (despertar) tarde.
5. Todavía puedo _____ (peinar).
6. Todos podemos _____ (equivocar) a veces.
7. Yo necesito _____ (poner) una chaqueta.
8. El debe _____ (bañar) por la mañana.
9. No quiero _____ (lastimar) en el trabajo.
10. Ella tiene ganas de _____ (desayunar).
11. Ella trata de _____ (secar) el pelo al sol.
12. Nosotros empezamos a _____ (lavar) la ropa.
13. Gloria sabe _____ (arreglar) la vida.
14. Carlos, deja de _____ (quitar) los zapatos en el cine.
15. El coronel piensa _____ (quedar) en el ejército.
16. Yo quiero _____ (ganar) la vida como policía.
17. Los jóvenes _____ (pasear) en el jardín.
18. No sé por que deben _____ (preocupar) con esto.
19. Yo empecé a _____ (enojar) con uno de los turistas.
20. Nosotros podemos _____ (bajar) del autobús.

Worksheet 4.19 Alternate reflexive construction

➤ Rewrite the sentences on p. 81, using the alternate reflexive construction.

1. _____

2. _____

3. _____

4. _____

5. _____

6. _____

7. _____

8. _____

9. _____

10. _____

11. _____

12. _____

13. _____

14. _____

15. _____

16. _____

17. _____

18. _____

19. _____

20. _____

Reflexive verbs

➤ Change the following sentences from **yo** to **él.** In the blanks to the right, write **Él** plus the corresponding form of the italicized verb.

1. Yo *me llamo* Roberto. _____

2. Yo *me lavo* las manos muchas veces al día. _____

3. Yo *me baño* todos los días. _____

4. Yo *me levan*to temprano excepto los sábados. _____

5. Yo no *me canso* fácilmente. _____

6. Yo *me pongo* la chaqueta cuando hace frío. _____

7. Yo *me cepillo* los dientes tres veces al día. _____

8. Yo *me peino* con mucho cuidado. _____

9. Yo *me desayuno* antes que mi padre. _____

10. Yo *me enojo* cuando los niños se pelean. _____

11. Yo *me pongo* ropa de lana en el invierno. _____

12. Yo *me canso* de vez en cuando. _____

13. Yo *me enfermo* raras veces. _____

14. Yo *me seco* la cara con la toalla color turquesa. _____

15. Yo *me arreglo* las uñas cada semana. _____

16. Yo *me limpio* los zapatos cuando se ensucian. _____

17. Yo no *me apuro* demasiado. _____

18. Yo *me asusto* cuando la gente maneja sin cuidado. _____

19. Yo *me pongo* nervioso si no estudio bastante. _____

20. Yo no *me afeito* con una máquina eléctrica. _____

21. Yo *me caso* después de graduarme de la universidad. _____

22. Yo no *me preocupo* sin necesidad. _____

23. Yo nunca *me aburro* en la escuela. _____

24. Yo *me quedo* en casa cuando estoy resfriado. _____

25. A propósito, yo *me llamo* Cisneros. _____

Note: Repeat orally each of the above sentences, substituting the other subject pronouns **tú, usted, él, ella, nosotros, ustedes, ellos, ellas.**

More on reflexive verbs

➤ Change the following reflexive verbs from present tense to preterite tense.

1. Yo me canso. _____

2. Ella se casa. _____

3. Tú te enojas. _____

4. Ella se baña. _____

5. Yo me preocupo. _____

6. Yo me asusto. _____

7. Ella se arregla. _____

8. Yo me arreglo. _____

9. Tú te cansas. _____

10. Él se quita las botas. _____

_____

11. Yo me desayuno. _____

12. Usted se asusta. _____

13. Tú te aburres. _____

14. Nosotros nos aburrimos. _____

_____

15. Yo me apuro. _____

16. Usted se apura. _____

17. Ella se preocupa. _____

18. Yo me enfermo. _____

19. Ellas se bañan. _____

20. Juan se queda. _____

21. Tú te retiras. _____

22. Nosotros nos levantamos. _____

_____

23. Yo me quedo. _____

24. Usted se peina. _____

25. Tú te afeitas. _____

26. Yo me afeito. _____

27. Ella se cuida. _____

28. Él se retira. _____

29. Él se apura. _____

30. Yo me aburro. _____

31. Él se enoja. _____

32. Isabel se asusta. _____

33. Pedro se casa. _____

34. Yo me peino. _____

35. Ella se mira. _____

36. Ellos se levantan. _____

_____

37. Él se desayuna. _____

38. Elena se quita el reloj. _____

_____

39. Ellas se pintan. _____

40. Yo me baño. _____

41. Él se asusta. _____

42. Usted se aburre. _____

43. Ustedes se levantan. _____

_____

44. Tú te enfermas. _____

_____

Buscapalabras geográfico

➤ The following word search puzzle contains the names of thirteen South American and Central American countries. As you find them, place their names in the blank spaces:

V	A	R	G	E	N	T	I	N	A	P
E	C	U	A	D	O	R	R	I	C	A
N	B	O	L	I	V	I	A	C	O	N
E	P	G	U	A	T	E	M	A	L	A
Z	E	C	H	I	L	E	A	R	P	M
U	R	U	G	U	A	Y	S	A	A	U
E	U	R	O	P	A	R	U	G	N	E
L	L	I	P	A	R	A	G	U	A	Y
A	C	O	L	O	M	B	I	A	M	E
D	A	S	H	O	N	D	U	R	A	S

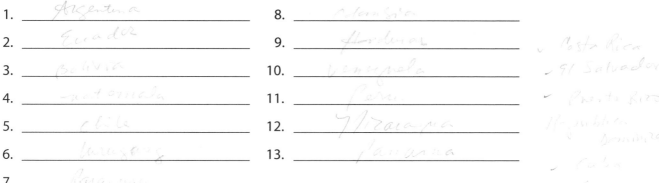

1. _Argentina_
2. _Ecuador_
3. _Bolivia_
4. _Guatemala_
5. _Chile_
6. _Uruguay_
7. _Paraguay_

8. _Colombia_
9. _Honduras_
10. _Venezuela_
11. _Perú_
12. _Nicaragua_
13. _Panamá_

✓ Costa Rica
✓ El Salvador
✓ Puerto Rico
República Dominicana
Cuba

Part 5

Contents

Worksheet 5.1 Use of infinitives

The only verb form that can follow a preposition is the infinitive. Some verbs require a particular preposition before the infinitive:

EXAMPLES:

acabar de esquiar	*to have just skied*
aprender a esquiar	*to learn to ski*
dejar de esquiar	*to stop skiing*
empezar a esquiar	*to begin to ski, to start skiing*
enseñar a esquiar	*to teach to ski*
estar para esquiar	*to be about to ski*
ir a esquiar	*to be going to ski*
pensar en esquiar	*to think about skiing*
quedar en esquiar	*to agree to ski*
soñar en esquiar	*to dream about skiing*
tratar de esquiar	*to try to ski*

➤ Supply the correct form of the verb in parentheses. Include the correct preposition if required.

1. Yo aprendí _____ (ser) maestro.

2. Yo pienso _____ (educar) a los niños.

3. Yo quiero _____ (ayudar) a mis alumnos.

4. Yo trato _____ (conocer) a cada uno.

5. Yo voy _____ (dar) un examen mañana.

6. Yo dejo _____ (criticar) demasiado.

7. Yo sé _____ (explicar) la lección.

8. Yo _____ (escribir) en la pizarra.

9. Yo empiezo _____ (identificar) las palabres difíciles.

10. Yo puedo _____ (pronunciar) cada palabra.

11. Yo sueño _____ (ver) el éxito de cada alumno.

12. Yo necesito _____ (tener) mucha paciencia.

13. Yo acabo _____ (hacer) varias preguntas.

14. Yo _____ (escuchar) a cada estudiante.

15. Me encanta _____ (educar) a los jóvenes.

Worksheet 5.2 Preterite tense of *ser* and *ir*

Ser and **ir** share the same forms in the preterite tense.

EXAMPLE: **Yo fui**   *I was* or *I went*

Both verbs are conjugated as follows:

ir			
yo	fui	nosotros(as)	fuimos
tú	fuiste	vosotros(as)	fuisteis
él, ella, usted	fue	ellos, ellas, ustedes	fueron

➤ Supply the correct preterite form of the verb in parentheses.

1. Usted _____ (ser) la persona que nos acompañó.

2. Usted _____ (ir) al cine con nosotros.

3. Yo no _____ (ser) el estudiante con quien hablaste ayer.

4. Yo no _____ (ir) a la escuela ayer.

5. ¿Cuándo _____ (ser) tú presidente del club?

6. ¿ _____ (Ir) tú a la reunión anoche?

7. Ellos _____ (ser) los culpables de la pelea.

8. Ellos _____ (ir) a tu casa para aprender.

9. ¿Por qué _____ (ser) importante la batalla de Lepanto?

10. Cervantes _____ (ir) a pelear en esa batalla.

11. Yo _____ (ir) al baile con Cristina.

12. Yo _____ (ser) su compañero y nadie más bailó con ella.

13. _____ (Ser) en enero cuando te enfermaste.

14. Tú _____ (ir) al hospital el 15 de enero.

15. ¿Ustedes _____ (ir) a ver la producción de Carmen?

16. En la ópera, nosotros _____ (ser) toreros.

17. Anteayer tú _____ (ser) muy amable conmigo.

18. Ayer yo _____ (ir) a ayudarte.

19. Tú _____ (ser) capaz de entrar sin pagar.

20. ¿Por qué _____ (ir) al circo sin dinero?

21. Roberto _____ (ser) Santa Claus en la fiesta.

22. Los niños _____ (ir) a recibir juguetes.

23. Ella _____ (ser) la muchacha que ganó ayer.

24. Nosotros _____ (ir) a su casa para felicitarla.

Worksheet 5.3 Preterite tense of *dar* and *ver*

Ver is a regular verb. Although **dar** is an **-ar** verb, it usually takes **le, les** and sometimes it takes the same endings as **ver.** (Accent marks are very seldom required of one-syllable verbs.)

dar			
yo	di	nosotros(as)	dimos
tú	diste	vosotros(as)	disteis
él, ella, usted	dio	ellos, ellas, ustedes	dieron

ver			
yo	vi	nosotros(as)	vimos
tú	viste	vosotros(as)	visteis
él, ella, usted	vio	ellos, ellas, ustedes	vieron

➤ Supply the preterite tense of the verb in parentheses.

1. Tú _____ (ver) mucha nobleza y generosidad.

2. Tú _____ (dar) un cheque a la Cruz Roja.

3. Yo _____ (ver) la infracción que cometiste.

4. Yo le _____ (dar) la pelota al otro equipo.

5. Ayer ella _____ (ver) un gato hambriento.

6. Ella le _____ (dar) de comer.

7. Los oficiales _____ (ver) los juegos olímpicos.

8. Ellos le _____ (dar) una medalla.

9. Yo _____ (ver) a varios payasos en el desfile.

10. No sabes cuánta risa me _____ (dar).

11. Nosotros _____ (ver) el robo de un coche.

12. Nosotros le _____ (dar) la información a la policía.

13. Yo _____ (ver) a una amiga en la playa.

14. Yo le _____ (dar) limonada de mi termo.

15. El maestro _____ (ver) los errores en mi trabajo.

16. Él me _____ (dar) otra página de ejercicios.

17. Yo _____ (ver) las galletas que están en la caja.

18. Ella me _____ (dar) algunas galletas a mí.

19. Tú _____ (ver) el peligro en la calle.

20. Tú me _____ (dar) un grito de aviso.

21. Nosotros no _____ (ver) el coche.

22. El claxon nos _____ (dar) mucho susto.

23. Yo _____ (ver) a muchas señoritas en tu casa ayer.

24. Sí, ellas me _____ (dar) una despedida de soltera.

Worksheet 5.4 Preterite tense of *leer* and *caer*

When the addition of a verb ending results in an **i** between vowels, change the **i** to **y**.

leer			
yo	leí	nosotros(as)	leímos
tú	leíste	vosotros(as)	leísteis
él, ella, usted	leyó	ellos, ellas, ustedes	leyeron

caer			
yo	caí	nosotros(as)	caímos
tú	caíste	vosotros(as)	caísteis
él, ella, usted	cayó	ellos, ellas, ustedes	cayeron

Note: **Caer** is often used with reflexive pronouns (**caerse**).

➤ In the blanks, supply the preterite tense of **leer**.

1. Yo _____ la noticia del accidente en el periódico.

2. María _____ la carta de su hermano con mucho interés.

3. ¿ _____ usted la carta que ella recibió la semana pasada?

4. La profesora _____ en voz alta el poema que yo escribí.

5. Tomás _____ muchos libros durante sus vacaciones.

6. Tú _____ esas dos novelas con mucho interés.

7. Todo el mundo _____ la noticia del asesinato.

8. ¿ _____ ustedes el discurso del senador en el periódico?

9. Sí, Enrique y yo lo _____ juntos anoche.

10. Antonio y su hermano _____ los libros que les regalé.

11. Tú _____ en silencio las noticias internacionales.

12. Todo el mundo _____ las noticias del terremoto.

➤ In the blanks, supply the preterite tense of **caer**.

1. La madre de Alberto se _____ en la calle ayer.

2. Tú te _____ una vez en el mismo lugar.

3. Mi compañero se resbaló y se _____ en la nieve.

4. La noticia _____ sobre el país como una bomba.

5. La anciana se resbaló y se _____ en el portal de la casa.

6. La niña se _____ en la piscina y se asustó.

7. Los dos niños se _____ de la cama durante la noche.

8. Las hojas de los árboles se _____ temprano este año.

9. Tú fácilmente _____ en la trampa.

10. Todos mis libros se _____ al suelo durante el terremoto.

11. El sombrero de Rosa se _____ en el lago.

12. Diana se _____ enferma durante el examen.

Worksheet 5.5 Preterite tense of *oír* and *traer*

Oír has the same vowel change to **y** as **leer** and **creer**. **Traer** is irregular:

oír			
yo	oí	nosotros(as)	oímos
tú	oíste	vosotros(as)	oísteis
él, ella, usted	oyó	ellos, ellas, ustedes	oyeron

traer			
yo	traje	nosotros(as)	trajimos
tú	trajiste	vosotros(as)	trajisteis
él, ella, usted	trajo	ellos, ellas, ustedes	trajeron

➤ In the blanks, supply the preterite tense of **oír.**

1. Yo no _____ el discurso del presidente ayer.

2. Por lo visto, ellos no _____ a Nicolás tocar a la puerta.

3. Tú no _____ el despertador esta mañana.

4. Yo _____ los gritos del niño.

5. Ella _____ las disculpas de José pacientemente.

6. El profesor te _____ sin mucho interés.

7. Nosotros _____ los mismos cuentos varias veces.

8. María dio un salto cuando _____ su nombre.

9. Ellos no nos _____ entrar.

10. Anoche yo _____ las noticias de las once.

11. Anoche nosotras _____ el mismo programa por radio.

12. ¿Por qué no _____ tú las campanas esta mañana?

➤ In the blanks, supply the preterite tense of **traer.**

1. Mis padres me _____ muchas cosas de México.

2. ¿Qué _____ usted de Nueva York para sus hermanas?

3. Ayer yo no _____ mi cuaderno a la clase.

4. Raquel _____ a dos amigos a la fiesta anoche.

5. El cartero no te _____ ni una sola carta esta mañana.

6. Su abuelo le _____ un tren eléctrico de Nueva York.

7. Cecilia _____ los últimos modelos de vestidos de París.

8. Tú me _____ una blusa preciosa.

9. Juan y Pedro _____ muchas curiosidades de la India.

10. Yo _____ varios regalos para las hijas del profesor.

11. ¿ _____ tú muchas cosas bonitas del Canadá?

12. Él no _____ su tarea esta mañana y el profesor se enojó.

Irregular preterite verbs

➤ In the blanks, supply the correct preterite form of the verb in parentheses.

1. Nosotros _____ (leer) la carta de Ana con tristeza.

2. Ella _____ (caerse) en la escalera.

3. La pobre _____ (ir) al hospital en ambulancia.

4. Durante la tormenta _____ (caerse) muchas ramas del olmo.

5. Yo _____ (ver) mucho daño causado por la tormenta.

6. Los relámpagos y los truenos _____ (ser) horribles.

7. Nosotros _____ (ver) tu fotografía en el periódico.

8. Yo _____ (leer) el artículo sobre la boda de ustedes.

9. Tus amigos les _____ (traer) regalos muy bonitos.

10. Yo _____ (oír) mi canción favorita por la radio.

11. Esta vez el cancionero _____ (ser) Julio Iglesias.

12. Tú y yo lo _____ (ver) hace tres años en San Diego.

13. El año pasado, yo _____ (ir) a Arizona de vacaciones.

14. Mi tía nos _____ (dar) comidas muy sabrosas en el rancho.

15. Nosotros _____ (traer) naranjas y toronjas en el coche.

16. ¿Por qué _____ (creer) tú las mentiras del vecino?

17. Yo no _____ (caerse) del caballo ni una sola vez.

18. La verdad es que él _____ (caerse) dos veces.

19. ¿Adónde _____ (ir) tú la semana pasada?

20. Yo no te _____ (ver) en ninguna parte.

21. Ellos no _____ (oír) nada de tus planes para salir tan lejos.

22. No puedo nadar. Yo no _____ (traer) mi traje de baño.

23. Yo _____ (leer) mucho sobre las playas bonitas de Acapulco.

24. Nosotros no _____ (creer) en tanta publicidad.

25. Mi padre _____ (caerse) en la fábrica donde trabaja.

26. El patrón lo _____ (traer) a casa en su camioneta.

27. El accidente no _____ (ser) serio.

28. Yo _____ (creer) en tu explicación del arte moderno.

29. Los libros me _____ (dar) otras teorías.

30. En la biblioteca ustedes _____ (leer) teorías muy distintas.

31. Tú me _____ (traer) una copia de *Lazarillo de Tormes*.

32. Yo _____ (creer) que Cervantes escribió esa obra.

33. Ahora sé que el autor _____ (ser) anónimo.

More on irregular preterite verbs

➤ Change the following subjects and verbs to the preterite tense.

1. Yo traigo _____
2. Él lee _____
3. Tú ves _____
4. Yo creo _____
5. Ellos traen _____
6. Él da _____
7. Ellas van _____
8. Ella es _____
9. Nosotros somos _____
10. Tú traes _____
11. Yo voy _____
12. Él oye _____
13. Yo me caigo _____
14. Tú lees _____
15. Él cree _____
16. Usted trae _____
17. Yo soy _____
18. Usted va _____
19. Ellos dan _____
20. Nosotros vemos _____
21. Ellos oyen _____
22. Tú te caes _____
23. Nosotros leemos _____
24. Ellos creen _____
25. Ella trae _____
26. Ustedes son _____
27. Tú vas _____
28. Ustedes dan _____
29. Juan ve _____
30. Tú oyes _____
31. José se cae _____
32. El niño lee _____
33. Usted cree _____
34. Nosotros traemos _____
35. Tú eres _____
36. María va _____
37. Los niños dan _____
38. Todo el mundo va _____
39. Nadie oye _____
40. Todos se caen _____
41. ¿Quién lee? _____
42. Nadie cree _____
43. Todos van _____
44 . Nadie va _____

Vocabulary check-up–number and gender

➤ Supply the other three forms of each noun.

MASCULINE SINGULAR	MASCULINE PLURAL	FEMININE SINGULAR	FEMININE PLURAL
1. hermano			
2. chico			
3. niño			
4. primo			
5. cuñado			
6. hijo			
7. profesor			
8. alumno			
9. dueño			
10. artista			
11. director			
12. novio			
13. cubano			
14. alemán			
15. español			
16. maestro			
17. muchacho			
18. abuelo			
19. turista			
20. actor			
21. tío			
22. inglés			
23. venezolano			
24. estudiante			
25. víctima			

General review

➤ Choose the correct form and write it in the blank.

1. Me _____ (gusta, gustan) las cuatro estaciones del año.

2. Las flores de la primavera _____ (es, son) muy bonitas.

3. La fragancia de las rosas es mi _____ (favorita, favoritas).

4. Anoche yo _____ (fui, fue) de paseo al jardín botánico.

5. Esta noche _____ (voy, voy a) ir al parque con una amiga.

6. Ella quiere patinar, pero yo no _____ (sé, sabe) patinar.

7. No le disgusta _____ (nadie, a nadie) el verano.

8. En el verano yo paso _____ (varios, varias) días en el lago.

9. Los deportes acuáticos son _____ (mi, mis) favoritos.

10. El verano _____ (traigo, trae) la temporada de la pesca.

11. Nosotros pescamos _____ (mucho, muchos) en el río.

12. Ahora _____ (estamos, somos) en el otoño.

13. En octubre las hojas empezaron a _____ (caer, caerse).

14. Ésta es la temporada también _____ (del, de el) fútbol.

15. El equipo de mi escuela siempre trata _____ (de, a) ganar.

16. Los estudiantes _____ (regresas, regresan) a la escuela.

17. A ellas _____ (le, les) gusta mucho el otoño.

18. Para _____ (me, mí) es bonito también el invierno.

19. En Indiana van a soñar _____ (con, en) una Navidad blanca.

20. Mi familia va _____ (con mí, conmigo) a las montañas.

21. Allí_____ (podemos, podemos a) esquiar.

22. _____ (Este, Aquel) hombre allá lejos esquía bien.

23. ¿A ti qué te_____ (gustas, gusta) hacer en el invierno?

24. ¿Cuál estación _____ (es, eres) tu favorita?

25. ¿Te gusta más _____ (ir, ir a) la playa o a las montañas?

26. ¿Piensas mucho _____ (en, de) las vacaciones del verano?

Worksheet 5.6 Order of object pronouns

Indirect object pronouns always precede direct object pronouns.

EXAMPLES: Juan me dio **el libro.**   Juan **me lo** dio.
             Ella nos regaló **las revistas.**   Ella **nos las** regaló.

➤ Rewrite each of the following sentences, replacing the italicized nouns with the correct form of the direct object pronoun.

1. Él me mandó *los libros.* _____

2. Ella me mandó *las revistas.* _____

3. Él nos explicó *la lección.* _____

4. Ellas te explicaron *el cuento.* _____

5. Tú me prometiste *el dinero.* _____

6. Nosotros te prometimos *los fondos.* _____

7. El cartero me trajo *la carta* esta mañana . _____

8. La camarera nos trajo *las ensaladas.* _____

9. El señor López me dio *las flores.* _____

10. Los señores Ibarra nos dieron *los dulces.* _____

11. Tú me enseñas *la gramática francesa.* _____

12. Yo te enseño *el vocabulario español.* _____

13. Ellos me entregaron *los planes.* _____

14. Ella nos entregó *el cheque de viajero.* _____

15. Mis padres me compraron *la bicicleta.* _____

16. Tu mamá te compró *el vestido nuevo* para la fiesta. _____

17. El panadero me vendió *los pasteles.* _____

18. La anciana nos vendió *las tortillas.* _____

19. Benito siempre me lleva *la ropa* a la tintorería. _____

20. Yo siempre te saco *la basura* a la calle. _____

21. Ellos nos enviaron *las maletas* al aeropuerto. _____

22. Susana me envió *la fotografía de su familia.* _____

23. ¿Quién me dejó *esta nota tonta*? _____

24. Te dejé *el recado* cerca del teléfono. _____

25. El maestro nos escribió *la fecha* en la pizarra. _____

26. Tus abuelos te escribieron *las cartas* desde Madrid. _____

Worksheet 5.7 Indirect object pronoun *se*

Both direct and indirect object pronouns begin with (*l*) in the third person. To avoid repetition of this sound, Spanish changes the indirect object pronoun (**le, les**) to **se**. The possible combinations are: **se lo, se la, se los, se las.** To clarify the indirect object pronoun **se**, the redundant pronouns [see page 67] are often used.

EXAMPLES: Juan **le dio el regalo a Carlos.**   Juan **se lo** dio **a él.**
Pablo **les dio los regalos a las chicas.**   Pablo **se los** dio **a ellas.**

➤ In the blanks, supply the verb and its indirect and direct object pronouns. The indirect object pronoun must correspond to the words in parentheses and will precede the direct object pronoun.

1. Juan las mandó (a mí)._____

2. José las mandó (a ella). _____

3. Su amigo lo trajo de Uruguay (a ella). _____

4. Tú las trajiste esta mañana (a ellos). _____

5. El profesor los explicó bien (a mí). _____

6. Ella lo dio (a Miguel). _____

7. María las prestó (a mí). _____

8. Margarita las prestó (a ellos). _____

9. Yo lo mandé la semana pasada (a ellas). _____

10. El profesor los lee en español (a nosotros). _____

11. Yo siempre lo presto (a usted). _____

12. Ellos la explicaron muy claramente (a él). _____

13. Tú la explicaste muy claramente (a mí). _____

14. Esteban la explicó muy claramente (a ella). _____

15. Yo las mandé ayer (a usted). _____

16. Yo lo di el mes pasado (a ustedes). _____

17. Él la trajo ayer (a ella). _____

18. Nosotras los prestamos el año pasado (a ellos). _____

19. El lo contó todo ayer (a mí). _____

20. Tú lo llevaste el mes pasado (a él). _____

21. Nadie lo regaló (a mí). Yo lo compré. _____

22. ¿Quién lo mandó (a usted)? _____

Worksheet 5.8 Personal pronouns with infinitives

When two verbs are used together, you will recall that the second one must be an infinitive. Object pronouns may be placed in front of the first verb (**lo quiere vender**) but are more commonly attached to the infinitive (**quiere venderlo**).

➤ In the blanks, supply the correct object pronoun, adding it to the infinitive in place of the words in italics.

1. Mi padre quiere mirar *los televisores.* _____

2. Yo quiero ver *el refrigerador.* _____

3. Él va a escoger *la alfombra.* _____

4. Tú vas a pedir *las sillas.* _____

5. Nosotros pensamos vender *el piano.* _____

6. Ustedes piensan comprar *las lámparas.* _____

7. Yo sé seleccionar *las cortinas.* _____

8. Tú sabes colgar *los retratos.* _____

9. Yo necesito probar *el sofá.* _____

10. Ella necesita obtener *la estufa.* _____

11. Ellos desean examinar *la mesa.* _____

12. Usted desea ver *el sofá-cama.* _____

13. Yo tengo que reemplazar *el cristal.* _____

14. Tú tienes que lavar *el mantel* sucio. _____

15. Nosotros planeamos cambiar *el escritorio.* _____

16. Ellas planean modernizar *la cocina.* _____

17. Nosotros tratamos de agrandar *el garage.* _____

18. Mi primo trata de construir *la casa* ideal. _____

19. Ella espera encontrar *antigüedades.* _____

20. Yo espero reparar *la radio* estereofónica. _____

21. Tú debes pintar todas *las paredes.* _____

22. Ustedes deben mezclar *las pinturas.* _____

23. Él tiene miedo de romper *los platos.* _____

24. Nosotros tenemos miedo de perder las *llaves.* _____

Worksheet 5.9 More on personal pronouns with infinitives

Both the indirect and direct object pronouns may be attached to an infinitive to form a single word. Remember that the indirect object must precede the direct object and that the vowel in the infinitive ending will have a written accent mark.

EXAMPLES: Juan quiere **darme el libro.**   Juan quiere **dármelo.**
Yo trato de **venderte las sillas.**   Yo trato de **vendértelas.**

Note: **Se** replaces **le, les** when two personal pronouns are used: **Yo quiero dárselo a ellos.**

➤ In the blanks, rewrite the verb, adding the correct indirect object pronoun, to the infinitive, in place of the words in parentheses.

1. Él no desea *mandarlo (a mí).* _____

2. Andrés no quiere *darlo (a ella).* _____

3. Tú no vas a *llevarlos (a ellos).* _____

4. Enrique puede *traerlo (a mí).* _____

5. Después de *darlo (a él),* usted puede volver a su casa. _____

6. Papá dice que está cansado de *explicarlo (a nosotros).* _____

7. ¿Puede usted *hacerlo (a mí)* ahora mismo? _____

8. ¿Por qué no quiere usted *darlo (a ella)?* _____

9. Tú vas a *leerla (a nosotros)* esta noche. _____

10. Voy a tratar de *hacerlo (a usted)* pronto. _____

11. ¿Cuándo van a *mandarlo (a ustedes)?* _____

12. Yo no puedo *traerlo (a usted)* mañana. _____

13. Tú tienes que *enviarlo (a ella)* hoy. _____

14. El no puede *traerlo (a ustedes)* antes del mediodía. _____

15. Yo estoy cansado de *decirlo (a él).* _____

16. Nosotros no podemos *prestarlo (a ellos).* _____

17. Él no está interesado en *prestarlo (a ellos).* _____

18. ¿Por qué no quiere usted *darlo (a ella)?* _____

19. Tengo que *comprarlo* hoy *(para él).* _____

20. ¿Por qué no quiere *contarlo* usted *(a mí)?* _____

21. ¿Por qué no quieres tú *decirlo (a ellos)?* _____

22. ¿Cuándo va usted a *darlo (a mí)?* _____

23. A mí no me gusta *venderlo (a ellos).* _____

24. Ellos no quieren *prestarlo (a nosotros).* _____

Worksheet 5.10 Preterite tense of *hacer* and *decir*

The verbs **hacer** and **decir** are both irregular in the preterite tense. The stem vowel of both verbs changes to **i**.

hacer			
yo	hice	nosotros(as)	hicimos
tú	hiciste	vosotros(as)	hicisteis
él, ella, usted	hizo	ellos, ellas, ustedes	hicieron

decir			
yo	dije	nosotros(as)	dijimos
tú	dijiste	vosotros(as)	dijisteis
él, ella, usted	dijo	ellos, ellas, ustedes	dijeron

➤ In the blanks, supply the preterite tense of the verb in parentheses.

1. Ayer yo _____ (hacer) la ensalada para la cena.

2. Mamá _____ (decir) que a ella le gusta.

3. Ellos _____ (hacer) demasiado ruido con sus guitarras.

4. La vecina le _____ (decir) algo a la policía.

5. Tú _____ (hacer) planes detallados para viajar por Europa.

6. Nosotros _____ (decir) que tú planeaste todo muy bien.

7. María _____ (hacer) el vestido que lleva a la fiesta.

8. Sus amigas _____ (decir) que lo hizo muy bonito.

9. ¿Quiénes _____ (hacer) estas sabrosas galletas?

10. Nosotros les _____ (decir) que las hicimos nosotros.

11. Yo _____ (hacer) todo lo posible para hablar con ellos.

12. Ellos no _____ (decir) casi nada.

13. El niño no _____ (hacer) caso a la criada.

14. La criada _____ (decir) que el niño se portó mal.

15. Ayer _____ (hacer) mucho calor.

16. Tú _____ (decir) que yo me quejé demasiado del calor.

17. El domingo yo no _____ (hacer) absolutamente nada.

18. Mis amigos _____ (decir) que yo descansé todo el día.

19. Tú _____ (hacer) bien en llamarlos en seguida por teléfono.

20. Ellos _____ (decir) que llamaste a tiempo.

21. Él _____ (hacer) sacrificios para educar a sus hijos.

22. El hijo mayor _____ (decir) que su padre se sacrificó mucho.

23. ¿Qué _____ (hacer) nosotros con nuestros ahorros?

24. Yo ya te _____ (decir) que los gastamos en el viaje al Japón.

Worksheet 5.11 Preterite tense of *querer* and *venir*

Like **hacer** and **decir,** the verbs **querer** and **venir** also change the stem vowel to **i** in the preterite:

querer			
yo	quise	nosotros(as)	quisimos
tú	quisiste	vosotros(as)	quisisteis
él, ella, usted	quiso	ellos, ellas, ustedes	quisieron

venir			
yo	vine	nosotros(as)	vinimos
tú	viniste	vosotros(as)	vinisteis
él, ella, usted	vino	ellos, ellas, ustedes	vinieron

➤ In the blanks, supply the preterite tense of the verb in parentheses.

1. Alfredo no _____ (venir) a tiempo anoche.

2. Él dijo que _____ (querer) llegar tarde.

3. Los otros _____ (venir) en el mismo autobús.

4. Yo _____ (querer) viajar en mi propio coche.

5. Anoche tú _____ (venir) a la fiesta con varios amigos.

6. Mi hermana _____ (querer) conocer a cada uno.

7. ¿Por qué no _____ (venir) a la escuela ayer?

8. Yo _____ (querer) ver el campeonato de tenis en televisión.

9. Ellos _____ (venir) temprano para ver mejor el desfile.

10. Nosotros también _____ (querer) venir temprano.

11. Mi tía _____ (venir) a casa para mostrar su camioneta nueva.

12. Nosotros_____ (querer) comprarnos una semejante.

13. El perro_____ (venir) cuando lo llamé.

14. Yo _____ (querer) darle de comer.

15. Nosotros no _____ (venir) hasta las once y media.

16. Mis papás_____ (querer) ir de compras antes de volver.

17. Los niños _____ (venir) al parque con sus padres.

18. Anita_____ (querer) jugar con sus amigas.

19. ¿Tú _____ (venir) en el tren desde Nueva York?

20. Sí, yo no _____ (querer) volar como hice el año pasado.

21. Yo _____ (venir) a tu casa anoche pero no te encontré.

22. ¿Por qué no _____ (querer) tú esperarme allí?

Worksheet 5.12 **Preterite tense of *poner* and *saber***

Poner and **saber** change their stem vowels to **u** in the preterite tense.

poner			
yo	puse	nosotros(as)	pusimos
tú	pusiste	vosotros(as)	pusisteis
él, ella, usted	puso	ellos, ellas, ustedes	pusieron

saber			
yo	supe	nosotros(as)	supimos
tú	supiste	vosotros(as)	supisteis
él, ella, usted	supo	ellos, ellas, ustedes	supieron

Saber means *to know* (*how*), but in the preterite it can mean *to find out*.

➤ In the blanks at the right, supply the preterite tense of the verb in parentheses.

1. Él _____ (poner) las flores en la mesa.

2. Yo no _____ (saber) agradecérselas.

3. El niño _____ (ponerse) la camisa al revés.

4. Carlitos no _____ (saber) ponérsela correctamente.

5. ¿Dónde _____ (poner) tú las llaves del coche?

6. ¿No _____ (saber) tú que las dejaste en la mesa?

7. José _____ (ponerse) de mal humor porque no la invitaste.

8. Nosotros no _____ (saber) su dirección.

9. La criada _____ (poner) la ropa afuera para secar.

10. Ella no _____ (saber) que tenemos una secadora eléctrica.

11. Mi hija _____ (ponerse) los zapatos blancos para salir.

12. Afortunadamente, yo _____ (saber) limpiárselos ayer.

13. ¿Por qué _____ (poner) usted tantos sellos en ese sobre?

14. Yo no _____ (saber) el franqueo correcto.

15. El año pasado tú no _____ (poner) ni un centavo en el banco.

16. ¿Cómo _____ (saber) tú eso?

17. Los niños se _____ (poner) los cinturones de seguridad.

18. Gracias a su papá, ellos _____ (saber) hacerlo.

19. El médico _____ (poner) a la víctima en el hospital.

20. ¡Qué lástima! Nosotros no _____ (saber) nada del accidente.

21. El niñito _____ (poner) el dedo pulgar en la boca.

22. Su mamá no _____ (saber) como curarle de este hábito.

Worksheet 5.13 Preterite tense of *tener* and *poder*

Tener and **poder** also change their stem vowels to **u**.

tener			
yo	tuve	nosotros(as)	tuvimos
tu	tuviste	vosotros(as)	tuvisteis
él, ella, usted	tuvo	ellos, ellas, ustedes	tuvieron

poder			
yo	pude	nosotros(as)	pudimos
tú	pudiste	vosotros(as)	pudisteis
él, ella, usted	pudo	ellos, ellas, ustedes	pudieron

➤ In the blanks, supply the preterite tense of the verb in parentheses.

1. Yo _____ (tener) que dejar un taco en mi plato.

2. Yo sólo _____ (poder) comer dos.

3. Mi tío _____ (tener) que vender su automóvil.

4. Afortunadamente, mi papá _____ (poder) comprárselo.

5. Ellos _____ (tener) la intención de visitarlos anoche.

6. Desgraciadamente, ellos no _____ (poder) hacerlo.

7. Tú _____ (tener) que comprar unas llantas nuevas.

8. Tú _____ (poder) pagarlas con tu tarjeta de crédito.

9. Mi sobrina _____ (tener) un accidente serio.

10. Por dos días no _____ (poder) andar sin muletas.

11. Nosotros no _____ (tener) tiempo para hacer la tarea.

12. Tomás y yo no _____ (poder) encontrar nuestros libros.

13. Yo no sé por que tú _____ (tener) que gritar a tu abuela.

14. Pues ella dice que no _____ (poder) oírme.

15. El chófer _____ (tener) que comprar gasolina.

16. Él _____ (poder) ver una gasolinera en la próxima esquina.

17. Nosotros _____ (tener) mucha suerte en la selva.

18. Nosotros _____ (poder) fotografiar muchos animales.

19. ¿ _____ (Tener) ustedes que trabajar el domingo?

20. _____ (Poder) ganar mucho más dinero, pero no quisimos.

21. Ayer yo _____ (tener) la oportunidad de conocer a Liliana.

22. La verdad es que no _____ (poder) pensar en nada que decirle.

Worksheet 5.14 Preterite tense of *estar* and *andar*

Estar and **andar** do not change the vowel in their stems, but they share the same irregular endings:

estar			
yo	estuve	nosotros(as)	estuvimos
tú	estuviste	vosotros(as)	estuvisteis
él, ella, usted	estuvo	ellos, ellas, ustedes	estuvieron

andar			
yo	anduve	nosotros(as)	anduvimos
tú	anduviste	vosotros(as)	anduvisteis
él, ella, usted	anduvo	ellos, ellas, ustedes	anduvieron

Note: **andar** means *to walk* and also *to go around (with).*

➤ In the blanks, supply the preterite tense of **estar.**

1. Yo _____ un mes en el hospital el año pasado.

2. ¿Dónde_____ tú anoche?

3. Nosotros _____ en casa toda la noche.

4. Juan _____ en la escuela esta tarde hasta las cinco.

5. Elena _____ muy enferma la semana pasada.

6. ¿Dónde_____ usted hace dos días?

7. ¿Dónde _____ sus amigos Manuel y Enrique anoche?

8. Creo que ellos _____ en la casa de Dolores.

9. ¿Cuándo _____ usted enfermo?

10. Las muchachas _____ de compras todo el día.

11. Tú _____ enojado conmigo por casi dos meses.

12. Yo _____ muy ocupado todo el día ayer.

➤ In the blanks, supply the preterite tense of **andar.**

1. Nosotros _____ sin zapatos en la playa ayer.

2. El niño _____ en bicicleta toda la tarde.

3. Las niñas _____ por el parque toda la tarde hoy.

4. ¿Quién _____ en mi jardín?

5. Tú estás cansada porque _____ mucho esta tarde.

6. Yo _____ en las tiendas más de tres horas ayer.

7. Nosotros _____ por todas partes en busca del perro.

8. ¿Por dónde _____ usted ayer?

9. Ellos _____ con mucho cuidado para no despertarme.

10. Tú _____ en cuatro pies para hacer reír al niño enfermo.

11. El señor Morales _____ por toda Europa cuando joven.

12. Ella se enojó porque nosotros no _____ con ella.

Irregular verbs

➤ Supply the preterite tense of the verbs in parentheses.

1. Mi madre _____ (estar) enferma todo el día ayer.

2. Yo _____ (tener) que cuidar a mis hermanitos.

3. Nosotros le _____ (traer) su medicina y sus comidas.

4. En la noche ella _____ (ponerse) mucho mejor.

5. Yo _____ (ver) a tu tía Teresa en la calle.

6. La pobre mujer _____ (caerse) en frente de un coche.

7. Gracias a Dios, el chófer _____ (poder) evitar un choque.

8. Ella _____ (decir) que va a tener más cuidado en la calle.

9. Nosotros no _____ (poder) localizar a nuestro perro.

10. Lo llamé en voz muy alta pero no _____ (venir).

11. Durante la noche lo _____ (oír) en el patio.

12. Nosotros nunca _____ (saber) por que no vino antes.

13. ¿Por qué no _____ (querer) usted ir al cine con nosotros?

14. Mi familia y yo _____ (andar) por el parque.

15. Además, ya vi la película que ustedes _____ (ir) a ver.

16. No me gusta la escena donde la niña _____ (oír) los fantasmas.

17. Yo no _____ (saber) hacer la tarea para hoy.

18. Yo traté de hacerla pero no _____ (poder).

19. ¿La _____ (hacer) tú?

20. Seguro que sí. Para mí _____ (ser) fácil.

21. Fernando _____ (traer) a sus dos hermanas a la fiesta.

22. Ellas _____ (venir) por primera vez.

23. Muchos jóvenes _____ (querer) bailar con ellas.

24. Ellas no _____ (poder) bailar con todos.

More on irregular verbs

➤ Change the subjects of the following sentences from **yo** to **él** or **ella**, and write the verb and subject in the spaces to the right.

1. Yo fui al cine anoche con Juan. _____

2. Yo traje a Elena a la fiesta anoche. _____

3. Yo vi a Enrique en la calle ayer. _____

4. Yo me caí en la calle ayer. _____

5. Yo leí esa novela el año pasado. _____

6. Yo estuve en casa de María el miércoles. _____

7. Yo hice muchas cosas ayer. _____

8. Yo dije la verdad. _____

9. Yo no quise ir al cine con ellas anoche. _____

10. Yo vine a la escuela en autobús esta mañana. _____

11. Yo puse los libros de Jorge sobre su escritorio. _____

12. Yo no supe nada de su llegada hasta ayer. _____

13. Yo no tuve tiempo para llamarle a usted. _____

14. Yo no pude asistir a clase ayer. _____

15. Yo estuve toda la tarde ayer en casa de Arturo. _____

16. Yo no oí lo que dijo el profesor. _____

17. Yo le di a José la carta de usted. _____

18. Yo no creí el cuento de Joaquín. _____

19. Yo puse las maletas en el automóvil. _____

20. Yo hice todo lo posible para llegar a tiempo. _____

21. Yo vi dos buenas películas anoche. _____

22. Yo fui al médico ayer. _____

23. Yo tuve que hacer mucha tarea ayer. _____

24. Yo traje una pelota a la playa. _____

For further practice, repeat the preceding sentences orally, changing **yo** to **tú, usted, nosotros, ellos, ustedes.**

More on irregular verbs

➤ Change the following from present to preterite tense.

1. Yo hago _____
2. Él tiene _____
3. Yo estoy _____
4. Él anda _____
5. Tú puedes ir _____
6. Yo traigo _____
7. Usted lee _____
8. Yo leo _____
9. Tú sabes _____
10. Ella se cae _____
11. Nosotros vamos _____
12. Yo quiero _____
13. Tú vienes _____
14. Yo lo digo _____
15. Él hace _____
16. Nadie lee _____
17. Ellas van _____
18. Yo oigo _____
19. Tú traes _____
20. Él pone _____
21. Yo doy _____
22. Tú eres _____

23. Yo voy _____
24. Tú tienes _____
25. Juan está _____
26. Yo ando _____
27. Nosotros vamos _____
28. Nadie está _____
29. Todos saben _____
30. Yo pongo _____
31. Tú se lo das _____
32. Ellos vienen _____
33. Él dice _____
34. Tú quieres _____
35. José quiere _____
36. Nosotros somos _____
37. María sabe _____
38. Ellos tienen _____
39. Nadie sabe _____
40. Ustedes tienen _____
41. Él puede ir _____
42. Pablo se pone _____
43. Tú haces _____
44 . Nadie va _____

General review

➤ Choose the correct form and write it in the blanks.

1. Juan y Enrique van _____ (junto, juntos) a la escuela.

2. El alumno nuevo _____ (llama, se llama) Jorge.

3. Los alumnos de esta clase _____ (son, están) muy aplicados.

4. Ellos son también muy _____ (inteligente, inteligentes).

5. El profesor López nos enseña _____ (leer, a leer) en español.

6. Anoche saludé _____ (el profesor, al profesor) en la calle.

7. El domingo yo _____ (fui, fue) al cine con Elena.

8. Ella _____ (trajiste, trajo) a su hermanito.

9. Juanito siempre tiene _____ (mucho, mucha) hambre.

10. Yo _____ (les, los) compré dulces y refrescos.

11. Además, el chico _____ (hice, hizo) mucho ruido.

12. No pienso _____ (escribirles, escribirlos) una carta.

13. ¿_____ (Estuviste, Estuvisteis) tú enferma?

14. ¿Te llevaron _____ (a ti, a tú) al hospital?

15. Te ves muy bien _____ (ayer, hoy).

16. ¿_____ (Gustaron, Te gustaron) las comidas?

17. Mi tío me _____ (dije, dijo) que saben bien.

18. Pero cree que no son _____ (suficiente, suficientes).

19. Estos señores _____ (son, están) de Brasil.

20. Tú tratas _____ (de, a) hablarles en español.

21. Ellos no _____ (pudieron, pusieron) entender lo que dijiste.

22. ¿Nunca _____ (supiste, supo) tú qué idioma hablan ellos?

23. Su lengua _____ (esta, es) semejante pero diferente.

24. A los brasileños les _____ (gusta, gustan) mucho la música.

Part 6

Contents

Worksheet 6.1 Prepositions

➤ In the blanks, supply the necessary prepositions.

1. Yo voy _____ estudiar para abogada.

2. Espero asistir _____ una universidad famosa.

3. Yo trato _____ escribir a varias universidades.

4. Yo hablo con algunas instituciones _____ teléfono.

5. Yo enseñé _____ esquiar a mi tío.

6. Mi tío conoce_____ muchos abogados.

7. Él es un juez famoso _____ la capital.

8. Yo le digo que sueño _____ ser abogado.

9. Nunca dejo _____ estudiar para serlo.

10. El abogado habla claramente y _____ voz alta.

11. ¿Le gusta _____ él leer muchos libros?

12. Él aprende _____ interpretar la constitución.

13. Creo que está _____ llover.

14. Mis estantes ya están llenos _____ libros.

15. Sueño_____ leerlos todos.

16. No dejo _____ leer.

17. Yo leo las palabras latinas_____ dificultad. No es fácil.

18. Es importante aprender _____ leerlas bien.

19. Quiero ayudar _____ la gente a resolver sus problemas.

20. La Constitución nos garantiza justicia _____ todos.

21. Juan nunca piensa _____ ayudar a los demás.

22. El abogado representa _____ los inocentes.

23. También es el representante _____ los culpables.

24. Es imporante proteger los derechos _____ los acusados.

25. No se puede vivir _____ pensar.

Worksheet 6.2 Odd word out

➤ Which word does not fit with the others? If necessary, consult the master vocabulary for any unfamiliar word.

EXAMPLE: Juan   María   Pablo   Felipe   (María)

1.	cinco	sus	siete	ocho	nueve
2.	gasto	perro	tigre	elefante	vaca
3.	guitarra	acordeón	martillo	piano	violín
4.	taxista	futbolista	violinista	entrevista	artista
5.	doctor	enfermera	cirujano	contador	médico
6.	amable	feo	simpático	cariñoso	bueno
7.	caricatura	coche	automóvil	contador	médico
8.	carpintero	carnicero	panadero	helicóptero	bombero
9.	cama	mesa	silla	estufa	derecha
10.	hombre	mujer	propina	muchacho	chica
11.	japonés	interés	español	portugués	francés
12.	pie	cabeza	oreja	piedra	ojo
13.	hablar	lugar	pescar	empezar	dar
14.	ciudad	continente	universidad	estado	país
15.	sé	sabes	sabemos	saber	sabor
16.	escuela	maestra	cuaderno	tarea	deuda
17.	de	se	en	con	sin
18.	cheque	muñeca	dinero	dólar	moneda
19.	casa	museo	biblioteca	hospital	obra
20.	título	nieto	padre	hermano	tío
21.	suelo	pared	puerta	viento	ventana
22.	tú	yo	nos	él	ustedes
23.	uniforme	jaula	sombrero	guantes	traje
24.	jaialai	tenis	fútbol	baloncesto	aparato
25.	fui	fuiste	fuego	fueron	fuimos
26.	gris	rojo	blanco	azul	joya
27.	limonada	naranja	manzana	plátano	pera
28.	postre	carne	fruta	piscina	legumbre
29.	siglo	sílaba	día	mes	año
30.	río	lago	océano	mar	llanta

Worksheet 6.3 Stem-changing -*ar* verbs

Certain verbs are identified as stem-changing (radical-changing). In some of these forms, a stressed **o** changes to **ue** and a stressed **e** changes to **ie**.

contar (ue)			
yo	cuento	nosotros(as)	contamos
tú	cuentas	vosotros(as)	contáis
él, ella, usted	cuenta	ellos, ellas, ustedes	cuentan

pensar (ie)			
yo	pienso	nosotros(as)	pensamos
tú	piensas	vosotros(as)	pensáis
él, ella, usted	piensa	ellos, ellas, ustedes	piensan

➤ In the blanks, supply the present tense of the verb in parentheses. **Contar** means to count or to tell; **contar con** means to count on. **Pensar** means to think or to plan; **pensar en** means to think about.

1. Mi padre nos _____ (contar) muchas historias de España.

2. Nosotros_____ (pensar) mucho en viajar a España.

3. Yo siempre _____ (contar) con mis amigos.

4. Yo _____ (pensar) que los amigos son importantes.

5. Tú _____ (contar) los uniformes para el equipo de fútbol.

6. Tú _____ (pensar) que falta el uniforme de alguien.

7. Si no pueden dormir, ellos _____ (contar) ovejas.

8. Ella _____ (pensar) que ellos duermen bien.

9. Nosotros no _____ (contar) con la cooperación de Ana.

10. Ustedes _____ (pensar) que ella no es sincera.

11. El sargento_____ (contar) con los soldados de su compañia.

12. Él_____ (pensar) que todos están presentes.

13. ¿Por qué _____ (contar) tú el dinero tantas veces?

14. ¿ _____ (Pensar) tú que te engañó?

15. Mi abuelo_____ (contar) las gallinas cada mañana.

16. Él_____ (pensar) que los coyotes las roban.

17. Yo les _____ (contar) las aventuras de Pancho Villa.

18. Ustedes _____ (pensar) viajar a México este verano.

19. Usted _____ (contar) las estrellas del cielo.

20. Nosotros_____ (pensar) que es imposible.

21. El muchacho _____ (contar) el dinero que ganó.

22. Yo no _____ (pensar) comprar más discos.

Worksheet 6.4 More on stem-changing *-ar* verbs

The following **-ar** verbs are also stem-changing:

acostar(se)	**(ue)**		**mostrar**	**(ue)**
almorzar	**(ue)**		**recordar**	**(ue)**
encontrar	**(ue)**		**soñar**	**(ue)**

➤ Supply the present tense of the verb in parentheses.

1. Los niños _____ (soñar) con ser astronautas.

2. Ellos _____ (encontrar) muchos artículos en las revistas.

3. Tú _____ (acostarse) a la misma hora cada noche.

4. Toda la familia _____ (almorzar) a la misma hora.

5. Yo no _____ (recordar) lo que dijo mi tío.

6. Él nos _____ (mostrar) muchos trucos que nos hacen reír.

7. Los niños _____ (soñar) con animales feroces.

8. Ellos siempre _____ (recordar) sus sueños.

9. Nosotros _____ (acostarse) tarde algunas veces.

10. Nosotros no _____ (almorzar) tarde casi nunca.

11. Ustedes no me _____ (mostrar) un coche bueno.

12. Yo no _____ (encontrar) ni uno que me gusta.

13. Tú nunca _____ (almorzar) sola.

14. Tú siempre _____ (encontrar) a una amiga con quien comer.

15. Mi papá dice que nunca _____ (soñar).

16. Yo le _____ (mostrar) un artículo sobre los sueños.

17. ¿A qué hora _____ (acostarse) tú?

18. A las diez si él _____ (recordar) hacerlo.

19. Nosotros no _____ (encontrar) nada que comer.

20. ¿Por qué no _____ (almorzar) ustedes en un restaurante?

21. ¿Con qué _____ (soñar) tú más?

22. Yo nunca _____ (recordar) mis sueños.

23. Ella nos _____ (mostrar) su vestido nuevo.

24. Ella lo usa cuando _____ (almorzar) con su novio.

Worksheet 6.5 More on stem-changing -*ar* verbs

The following **-ar** verbs are also stem-changing:

calentar	**(ie)**	**empezar**	**(ie)**
cerrar	**(ie)**	**negar(se)**	**(ie)**
comenzar	**(ie)**	**nevar**	**(ie)**
despertar(se)	**(ie)**	**sentar(se)**	**(ie)**

➤ Supply the present tense of the verb in parentheses.

1. Este horno _____ (calentar) mucho la cocina.

2. Si tú _____ (empezar) a cocinar, más vale abrir la ventana.

3. En el invierno yo _____ (sentarse) cerca de la ventana.

4. Me gusta ver el patio cuando _____ (nevar).

5. Tú _____ (despertarse) tarde muchas veces.

6. Es verdad. Yo no lo _____ (negar).

7. Mis primos _____ (comenzar) a pintar la casa.

8. ¿Por qué no _____ (cerrar) las ventanas antes de pintar?

9. Ustedes _____ (calentar) muchas tortillas.

10. Si tú _____ (sentarse), te las servimos ahora.

11. Él dice que ella se enfada mucho. Ella lo _____ (negar).

12. Él _____ (empezar) a criticarla demasiado.

13. Yo me preocupo cuando _____ (nevar) mucho durante la noche.

14. Son las diez y ya _____ (empezar) a nevar mucho.

15. ¿A qué hora _____ (cerrarse) las tiendas los viernes?

16. La mayoría _____ (comenzar) a cerrarse a las seis en punto.

17. En el verano, nosotros _____ (despertarse) muy temprano.

18. Nosotros _____ (negarse) a dormir cuando se pone el sol.

19. Yo _____ (calentar) el café un poco más.

20. Cuando _____ (nevar) afuera, prefiero el café más caliente.

21. Si hace frío, ella _____ (despertarse) durante la noche.

22. Ella se levanta y _____ (cerrar) la ventana.

23. Los González _____ (sentarse) en la primera fila del teatro.

24. El concierto _____ (comenzar) cuando se cierran las puertas.

Worksheet 6.6 Stem-changing -er verbs

Some **-er** verbs also have **o → ue** or **i → ie** stem changes:

volver (ue)			
yo	vuelvo	nosotros(as)	volvemos
tu	vuelves	vosotros(as)	volvéis
él, ella, usted	vuelves	ellos, ellas, ustedes	vuelven

perder (ie)			
yo	pierdo	nosotros(as)	perdemos
tu	pierdes	vosotros(as)	perdéis
él, ella, usted	pierde	ellos, ellas, ustedes	pierden

Other verbs in this category include **defender(se) (ie), devolver (ue), entender (ie), llover (ue), mover (ue), poder (ue), querer (ie).**

➤ Supply the present tense of the verb in parentheses.

1. Yo nunca _____ (perder) los libros de la biblioteca.

2. Yo no _____ (querer) pagar las multas.

3. El tráfico _____ (moverse) muy despacio ahora.

4. Siempre es así cuando _____ (llover) en Los Ángeles.

5. ¿Por qué no me _____ (devolver) mis discos?

6. Porque yo _____ (querer) escucharlos una vez más.

7. El acusado _____ (defender) sus derechos.

8. El abogado _____ (volver) a ayudarlo por segunda vez.

9. Abuelito _____ (perder) la dentadura cada vez que viaja.

10. Yo no _____ (entender) como puede comer sin ella.

11. Raquel _____ (volver) de Guatemala pasado mañana.

12. Nosotros _____ (poder) saludarla en el aeropuerto.

13. Te _____ (devolver) la computadora que me prestaste.

14. Yo no _____ (querer) tanta responsabilidad.

15. Ricardo me _____ (volver) a pedir dinero.

16. Él nunca te _____ (devolver) el dinero que le prestas.

17. Este tren _____ (moverse) más rápido fuera de la ciudad.

18. ¡Ojalá! Nosotros no _____ (querer) perder más tiempo.

19. El soldado _____ (defenderse) contra los rebeldes.

20. En realidad él no _____ (querer) hacerle daño a nadie.

21. Creo que nuestro equipo de fútbol _____ (perder) otra vez.

22. Si _____ (llover) no hay partido hoy.

Preterite tense

All of the following verbs are stem-changing in the present but regular in the preterite. Note, however, that verbs ending in -**zar** change the **z** to **c** in the first person singular, preterite tense.

EXAMPLES: comen**zar**   empe**zar**   almor**zar**
            comen**cé**   empe**cé**   almor**cé**

➤ Change each of the following to the preterite tense.

1. Él entiende. _____
2. Yo almuerzo. _____
3. Ella encuentra. _____
4. Tú muestras. _____
5. Yo me acuerdo. _____
6. Ellos pierden. _____
7. El día empieza. _____
8. Juan cuenta. _____
9. Nadie piensa. _____
10. Tú vuelves. _____
11. Ella pierde. _____
12. Devolvemos. _____
13. Él se sienta. _____
14. Nos sentamos. _____
15. Tú cierras. _____
16. Se despierta. _____
17. Todos cuentan. _____
18. Yo comienzo. _____
19. Se sientan. _____
20. No entiendo. _____
21. Te acuestas. _____

22. Leonora cuenta. _____
23. Ellos vuelven. _____
24. Tú entiendes. _____
25. Yo comienzo. _____
26. María piensa. _____
27. Yo pierdo. _____
28. Empezamos. _____
29. Mi tío muestra. _____
30. Él empieza. _____
31. Lola cierra. _____
32. Pablo defiende. _____
33. Yo me acuesto. _____
34. No te acuerdas. _____
35. Yo encuentro. _____
36. Elena mueve. _____
37. Nadie vuelve. _____
38. Se acuestan. _____
39. Te despiertas. _____
40. Tú entiendes. _____
41. Llueve mucho. _____
42. Tú almuerzas. _____

Worksheet 6.7 Stem-changing *-ir* verbs

Note the stem change in the present of each of the following **-ir** verbs:

consentir (ie)	**mentir (ie)**	**divertir(se) (ie)**	**sentir(se) (ie)**
convertir(se) (ie)	**preferir (ie)**	**dormir(se) (ue)**	**morir (se) (ue)**

consentir			
yo	consiento	nosotros(as)	consentimos
tú	consientes	vosotros(as)	consentís
él, ella, usted	consiente	ellos, ellas, ustedes	consienten

➤ Supply the present tense of the verb in parentheses.

1. De todas las chicas de mi clase, yo _____ (preferir) a Lola.

2. Yo casi_____ (morirse) de miedo al hablar con sus padres.

3. Yo _____ (sentirse) por fin el más afortunado de muchachos.

4. Sus padres _____ (consentir) en dejarme salir con ella.

5. Yo _____ (dormir) muy contento pensando en mi primera cita.

6. El sábado yo_____ (convertirse) en un muchacho nervioso.

7. Yo no _____ (mentir) cuando digo que estoy distraído.

8. Nosotros_____ (divertirse) mucho en la playa.

9. A los seis años Miguel es travieso y _____ (mentir) mucho.

10. A los diez años él _____ (convertirse) en un muchacho ideal.

11. Él siempre _____ (consentir) en hacer lo que dice Mamá.

12. A las nueve en punto él va a su cuarto y _____ (dormir).

13. Él _____ (divertir) a sus hermanitos y a sus amigos.

14. Si _____ (morirse) de hambre, él no se queja.

15. Más que nada _____ (preferir) ayudar a sus padres.

16. Sus padres _____ (sentirse) muy orgullosos de él.

17. El padre de Isabel _____ (consentir) en comprarle un gato.

18. Ella _____ (sentirse) muy contenta con su gatito.

19. El gato se llama Tobi. Tobi _____ (dormir) con Isabel.

20. Un día Tobi _____ (morirse), su papá le compra otro gatito, Chucho.

21. Ella dice que no echa de menos a Tobi, pero _____ (mentir).

22. Un gato no _____ (convertirse) en otro gato.

23. Al principio ella _____ (preferir) recordar a su primer gato.

24. Pero poco a poco ella _____ (divertirse) mucho con Chucho.

Worksheet 6.8 More on stem-changing -ir verbs

We have practiced with many **e → ie** and **o → ue** stem changes. A third stem change in the present, **e → i**, occurs in the following **-ir** verbs:

EXAMPLE   **conseguir   competir   despedir(se)   medir   pedir   repetir   seguir   servir   vestir(se)**

pedir			
yo	pido	nosotros(as)	pedimos
tu	pides	vosotros(as)	pedís
él, ella, usted	pide	ellos, ellas, ustedes	piden

➤ Supply the present tense of the verb in parentheses.

1. Juan y Carlos _____ (competir) en la clase de geometría.

2. Juan _____ (medir) los ángulos de varios triángulos.

3. Carlos _____ (pedir) más problemas para hacer en casa.

4. Los dos _____ (conseguir) libros avanzados sobre álgebra.

5. Juan y Carlos _____ (seguir) los ejemplos exactamente.

6. Ellos _____ (repetir) las reglas para aprenderlas bien.

7. Nosotros_____ (vestirse) con ropa vieja.

8. Mamá _____ (servir) un desayuno muy nutritivo.

9. Nosotros_____ (despedirse) de ella y salimos de casa.

10. Nosotros_____ (seguir) el sendero que sube a las montañas.

11. Nuestros mapas nos _____ (servir) para no perdernos.

12. Nosotros no _____ (competir) en llegar a la cima.

13. ¿ _____ (Medir) tú los ingredientes cuando cocinas?

14. Sí, yo siempre_____ (seguir) la receta.

15. ¿Tienes un menú favorito que _____ (repetir) mucho?

16. No, yo _____ (servir) algo nuevo cada noche.

17. ¿Qué_____ (pedir) ustedes en los restaurantes elegantes?

18. No vamos. Mi marido no quiere _____ (vestirse) con corbata.

19. Ana_____ (vestirse) y sale para su despedida de soltera.

20. En la fiesta ella _____ (conseguir) muchos regalos útiles.

21. Sus amigas_____ (servir) pastel y helado.

22. Ella _____ (repetir) para todas la fecha de su boda.

23. La celebración _____ (seguir) hasta muy tarde.

24. Cuando ellas _____ (despedir) ya es medianoche.

Stem-changing *-ir* verbs

The verbs in the following sentences change from **o → ue, e → ie** or from **e → i. Reír** (*to laugh*) and **sonreír** (*to smile*) change from **e** and **í.**

➤ Supply the present tense of the verbs in parentheses.

1. Carlos siempre _____ (dormirse) en la clase de historia.

2. Yo _____ (sentirse) muy contento en la clase de español.

3. La maestra _____ (divertir) mucho a los estudiantes.

4. Nosotros_____ (reírse) muchas veces en su clase.

5. Si hacemos un error, ella _____ (sonreírse) y nos corrige.

6. Primero que nada, la maestra siempre _____ (pedir) la tarea.

7. Si no tengo mi tarea, no le _____ (mentir) a la maestra.

8. De todas mis clases, yo _____ (preferir) ésta.

9. Buenos días, Rosa. ¿Cómo _____ (sentirse)?

10. Estoy mejor, pero no _____ (dormir) bien en este hospital.

11. ¿Te _____ (servir) ellos comidas buenas, o jugo puro?

12. Yo _____ (pedir) lo que quiero, y la enfermera me lo trae.

13. ¿Cómo _____ (seguir) la garganta? ¿Te duele todavía?

14. No, sólo me duele mucho cuando _____ (reírse).

15. Entonces yo no te _____ (repetir) el chiste que oí anoche.

16. Ay, ¿quién _____ (divertirse) en el hospital?

17. Mis hermanos _____ (competir) en la natación.

18. Yo _____ (sentir) mucho orgullo cuando ganan trofeos.

19. Ellos _____ (vestirse) en traje de baño diariamente.

20. Ellos _____ (repetir) los mismos clavados hora tras hora.

21. Por mi parte, yo no _____ (servir) para competir.

22. Yo _____ (morirme) de tanto entrenamiento.

23. Yo _____ (preferir) emplear el tiempo en estudiar.

24. Pero no _____ (mentir) al decir que les envidio su talento.

Worksheet 6.9 Preterite tense stem-changing -ir verbs

Those -ir verbs with stem changes in the present tense will also have a stem change in the third person preterite tense, both singular and plural. These changes will be from e → i or from o → u.

sentir (e→i)			
yo	sentí	nosotros(as)	sentimos
tú	sentiste	vosotros(as)	sentisteis
él, ella, usted	sintió	ellos, ellas, ustedes	sintieron

dormir (o→u)			
yo	dormí	nosotros(as)	dormimos
tú	dormiste	vosotros(as)	dormisteis
él, ella, usted	durmió	ellos, ellas, ustedes	durmieron

➤ In the blanks, supply the preterite tense of **sentir.**

1. Yo no _____ (sentirse) bien ayer.

2. Tú no _____ (sentirse) bien ayer tampoco.

3. Yo _____ (sentirse) obligado a pagar el libro que perdí.

4. La abuela _____ (sentir) mucho la ausencia de sus nietos.

5. Nosotros_____ (sentir) no poder continuar el curso.

6. Tú _____ (sentir) mucho frío anoche.

7. ¿Por qué _____ (sentirse) usted tan cansado ayer?

8. Yo _____ (sentir) mucho no estar en casa cuando Julio llamó.

9. Tomás_____ (sentirse) triste cuando nos robaron el perro.

10. Nosotros_____ (sentir) no verlos cuando fuimos a Panamá.

➤ In the blanks, supply the preterite tense of **dormir.**

1. El niño _____ (dormir) muy mal anoche.

2. Raquel _____ (dormirse) inmediatamente anoche.

3. Yo también_____ (dormirse) en seguida.

4. Tú _____ (dormir) en el tren más de tres horas.

5. El perro_____ (dormir) ayer en mi silla favorita.

6. Las niñas_____ (dormir) una siesta en la playa.

7. Tú _____ (dormir) anoche durante el programa de televisión.

8. Juan _____ (dormir) en casa de Luis la semana pasada.

9. Yo _____ (dormir) bien cuando pasé la noche en el desierto.

10. ¿Por qué no _____ (dormir) tú una siesta ayer?

Worksheet 6.10 More on preterite tense of stem-changing -*ir* verbs

In addition to **sentir e → i** and **dormir o → u** (see previous worksheet), several other verbs are stem-changing in the preterite tense:

despedirse (i)	**divertirse (i)**	**mentir (i)**	**morir (u)**	**pedir (i)**
preferir (i)	**reírse (i)**	**reñir (i)**	**repetirse (i)**	**sentir (u)**
seguir (i)	**servir (i)**	**vestirse (i)**		

➤ Supply the preterite tense of the verbs in parentheses.

1. Para el Domingo de Pascuas, mi tío _____ (vestirse) de conejo.

2. Mis hermanitos y primos _____ (divertirse) mucho.

3. Mi hermanita le _____ (pedir) huevos pintados al conejo.

4. Mis padres _____ (reírse) al ver la inocencia de los niños.

5. Después, mi madre nos _____ (servir) chocolate caliente.

6. Mis primos _____ (preferir) el Día de los Muertos.

7. Ellos _____ (vestirse) de piratas, payasos y fantasmas.

8. Algunos _____ (repetir) que les gusta espantar a la gente.

9. El vecino dijo que casi _____ (morirse) de espanto.

10. La verdad es que _____ (mentir) para divertir a los niños.

11. En el Día de los Inocentes todos _____ (mentir).

12. Todos _____ (divertirse) con las mentiras chistosas.

13. Gracias al buen humor, nosotros no _____ (reñir).

14. Las mentiras y las bromas _____ (seguir) todo el día.

15. El día siguiente todos _____ (reírse) de su inocencia.

16. Los Peregrinos _____ (despedirse) de Inglaterra.

17. Ellos _____ (seguir) rumbo a América y la libertad.

18. Fue difícil, pero ellos _____ (preferir) quedarse.

19. Muchos _____ (morir) durante el primer año.

20. Los indios les _____ (servir) de buenos amigos.

21. Ayer, el 4 de julio, nosotros _____ (sentir) mucho orgullo.

22. Yo _____ (preferir) recordar a los héroes de la Revolución.

23. Muchos _____ (morir) en la lucha por nuestra independencia.

24. También fue un día cuando todos _____ (divertirse).

25. Los cohetes _____ (servir) bien para celebrar la fecha.

Name: _____ Date: _____

Preterite tense of stem-changing *-ir* verbs

➤ Change each of the following from the present to the preterite tense.

1. Yo prefiero _____
2. Él se divierte _____
3. Él se muere _____
4. Tú pides _____
5. Él repite _____
6. Ella sirve _____
7. Yo me río _____
8. Tú te vistes _____
9. Yo me despido _____
10. Ella se siente _____
11. Yo me duermo _____
12. Ellos repiten _____
13. Eso no sirve _____
14. Ellos se ríen _____
15. Yo me visto _____
16. Nadie se divierte _____
17. Tú mientes _____
18. Ella prefiere _____
19. Él pide _____
20. Esto sirve _____
21. Todos se ríen _____
22. Tú te despides _____

23. Yo repito _____
24. Tú te duermes _____
25. Nadie prefiere _____
26. Tomás lo siente _____
27. Algunos se visten _____
28. Todos duermen _____
29. Nosotros pedimos _____
30. Ellos riñen _____
31. El profesor se ríe _____
32. Nadie se despide _____
33. Tú me lo repites _____
34. Los niños piden _____
35. ¿Quién se muere? _____
36. Nadie se viste _____
37. Eduardo se despide _____
38. Ella nunca pide _____
39. Él nunca miente _____
40. Tú prefieres _____
41. Ellos siempre piden _____
42. Tú te ríes _____
43. Ella se viste _____
44. ¿Cuál sirve? _____

General review

➤ Choose the correct form and write it in the blanks.

1. Ellos trataron _____ (de, a) llamarnos a mediodía.

2. Anoche _____ (me acuesto, me acosté) a medianoche.

3. ¿Qué hora es? _____ (Es, Son) las cinco y media.

4. Yo _____ (sé, se) que van a cenar a las siete y cuarto.

5. A mí no me gusta _____ (levantar, levantarme) antes de las ocho.

6. _____ (Este, Esto) periódico es del veinte de marzo.

7. Arturo se sienta _____ (delante, delante de) mí los domingos.

8. Anoche _____ (acosté, me acosté) después de las diez.

9. Yo encontré _____ (el, al) profesor a las dos menos cuarto.

10. Vamos a _____ (despedir, despedirnos) de los García el lunes.

11. Tú me _____ (pidio, pediste) un favor ayer por la mañana.

12. A las seis en punto la criada _____ (acostó, se acostó) al niño.

13. Jaime _____ (puso, se puso) enfermo a fines de abril.

14. Los novios _____ (se casaron, casaron) el catorce de junio.

15. Ella es la _____ (única, único) persona que vino esta tarde.

16. A la una Isabel empezó _____ (bailar, a bailar).

17. Yo tengo_____ (a, que) ver al maestro antes de las ocho.

18. Ramón _____ (estuve, estuvo) aquí a mediados de octubre.

19. Juan dijo que no vio a _____ (alguien, nadie) anteayer.

20. Pasado mañana voy _____ (a ver, ver) a mis tíos.

21. A mis padres no_____ (le, les) gusta viajar en agosto.

22. Yo me _____ (puse, puso) a estudiar a principios de mayo.

23. El primero de diciembre, él _____ (viajo, viajó) a Tejas.

24. Hoy por la mañana mi hijo _____ (vistió, se vistió) solo.

Worksheet 6.11 More on prepositions

➤ In the blanks, supply the necessary prepositions required to complete the meaning of each sentence.

1. Me encontré en la calle ayer _____ el hermano de Luis.

2. Vamos a empezar el nuevo curso _____ principios de mayo.

3. Tú vienes aquí de vez _____ cuando para ayudarnos a nosotros.

4. Yo le doy _____ comer a mi perro dos veces al día.

5. Más que nada a mí me gusta mucho montar _____ caballo.

6. El joven ingeniero se enamoró _____ ella en seguida.

7. Como _____ costumbre, tú viniste tarde a la clase esta mañana.

8. Ellos viven cerca _____ nosotros desde hace cuatro años.

9. Felipe se sienta _____ frente de mí en mi próxima clase.

10. Voy a salir hoy, a pesar _____ lo que dijo el médico ayer.

11. Ellos no pudieron localizar a Diego _____ ninguna parte.

12. Tú te llevas bien _____ todo el mundo.

13. Ellos van a tardar mucho _____ hablar español bien.

14. Ayer traté varias veces _____ llamarlo a usted.

15. Ricardo se parece mucho _____ su hermano mayor.

16. Ellos hablaron conmigo _____ teléfono tres veces ayer.

17. Este lápiz que compré en la papelería no sirve _____ nada.

18. Él va a salir _____ Nueva York el miércoles.

19. Tú vas a volver del centro _____ seguida.

20. Tengo que tomar esta medicina tres veces _____ día.

21. Este vestido que compré para la fiesta es _____ algodón.

22. Su sombrero nuevo es _____ un color oscuro.

23. El niño se echó _____ llorar en seguida.

24. Tú vienes a mi casa _____ mucha frecuencia.

Worksheet 6.12 Imperfect tense of -*ar* verbs

Spanish has two simple past tenses. The preterite tense is used for single, completed actions. The imperfect tense is used for repeated actions or those begun in the past and continuing into the present or future.

EXAMPLES:	PRETERITE	EXPLANATION
	Mi primo viajó.	*He travelled once and is not still travelling.*
	IMPERFECT	EXPLANATION
	Mi primo viajaba.	*He used to travel at various times.*
	Mi primo viajaba.	*He was travelling and still is.*
	Mi primo viajaba cuando se enfermó.	*He was travelling when he got sick.*

Regular **-ar** verbs are conjugated in the imperfect tense as follows:

hablar (*to speak*)			
yo	hablaba	nosotros(as)	hablábamos
tú	hablabas	vosotros(as)	hablabais
él, ella, usted	hablaba	ellos, ellas, ustedes	hablaban

➤ Supply the imperfect tense of the verbs in parentheses.

1. En mi niñez yo _____ (hablar) italiano.

2. Mi padre _____ (viajar) frecuentemente a la Argentina.

3. Él _____ (comprar) cosas muy bonitas allí.

4. Un día nos dijo que _____ (desear) vivir en Buenos Aires.

5. Todos los días _____ (estudiar) español.

6. Yo aprendí que burro no _____ (significar) mantequilla.

7. Mis hermanitos _____ (pelearse) mucho.

8. Mis padres _____ (tratar) de separarlos.

9. Poco a poco ellos _____ (portarse) mejor.

10. Pablo le _____ (ayudar) a Raúl con las matemáticas.

11. Raúl le _____ (enseñar) a Pablo a jugar fútbol.

12. En años recientes uno siempre _____ (acompañar) al otro.

13. El profesor nos _____ (explicar) historia muy bien.

14. Nosotros _____ (imaginarse) fácilmente la época azteca.

15. En nuestra imaginación _____ (escuchar) a Moctezuma.

16. El emperador _____ (hablar) con los conquistadores.

17. Los españoles _____ (saludar) a los indios.

18. Desgraciadamente, ellos _____ (pelear) en una horrible guerra.

Worksheet 6.13 Imperfect tense of *-er* and *-ir* verbs

In the imperfect tense, **-er** and **-ir** verbs share the same endings.

comer			
yo	comía	nonsotros(as)	comíamos
tú	comías	vosotros(as)	comíais
él, ella, usted	comía	ellos, ellas, ustedes	comían

vivir			
yo	vivía	nonsotros(as)	víviamos
tú	vivías	vosotros(as)	vivíais
él, ella, usted	vivía	ellos, ellas, ustedes	vivían

➤ Supply the imperfect tense of the verbs in parentheses.

1. Hace muchos años mis abuelos _____ (vivir) con nosotros.

2. Yo recuerdo que ellos _____ (salir) de vez en cuando.

3. Ellos _____ (asistir) mucho al cine y a los conciertos.

4. Mi abuelo nos _____ (divertir) con cuentos de su juventud.

5. Diariamente mi abuelita nos _____ (leer) espisodios de la Biblia.

6. Nosotros _____ (querer) mucho a nuestros abuelitos.

7. En la escuela mi hermana siempre_____ (recibir) buenas notas.

8. Ella _____ (aprender) muy fácilmente todo lo que estudiaba.

9. A veces yo _____ (tener) celos de ella.

10. Adelita _____ (recibir) muchos honores en la comunidad.

11. Todos _____ (decir) que ella tenía mucha inteligencia.

12. Es verdad. Ella _____ (poseer) muchas destrezas.

13. Cuando yo viajaba, yo _____ (perder) muchas cosas.

14. Yo _____ (tener) miedo de perder los boletos de vuelta.

15. A veces yo _____ (volver) a la escuela por mi cuaderno.

16. Mi memoria en aquel entonces no _____ (valer) para nada.

17. Poco a poco yo _____ (aprender) a guardar mejor mis cosas.

18. Eventualmente, yo _____ (saber) guardar bien mis cosas.

19. Nosotros _____ (coger) muchos resfriados en Nueva York.

20. La familia _____ (sufrir) mucho a causa del frío.

21. Además la nieve _____ (cubrir) las calles completamente.

22. Nosotros _____ (tener) que manejar con mucho cuidado.

23. En el invierno _____ (poner) llantas especiales.

24. Nos _____ (proteger) del sol con lentes oscuros.

25. Durante aquel año todos _____ (hacer) algo para ganar dinero.

26. Mi hermano y yo _____ (vender) periódicos y revistas.

27. Mis hermanas _____ (coser) ropa para los vecinos.

28. Mis primos _____ (preferir) trabajar en una tienda.

29. Todavía los gemelos no _____ (haber) nacido.

Imperfect tense

Because they represent continuing actions, the verbs in the following exercise are among the most commonly used in the imperfect tense. In this tense they are all regular verbs.

➤ Supply the imperfect tense of the verbs in parentheses.

1. Ellos no _____ (saber) que yo tenía un automóvil nuevo.

2. Yo _____ (creer) que Carlos estaba en casa.

3. Entonces nosotros no _____ (pensar) en casarnos.

4. Tú _____ (tener) la idea que ella hablaba español bien.

5. Yo no _____ (poder) entender por qué ella se portaba así.

6. Ellos _____ (sentir) mucho no poder ir con nosotros.

7. Yo no _____ (saber) que él escribía novelas.

8. Nosotros no _____ (poder) ver la película desde allí.

9. Tú _____ (creer) que yo viví en México por varios años.

10. Él _____ (pensar) llegar antes que nosotros.

11. ¿_____ (Saber) tú que Juan estaba en el hospital?

12. María _____ (creer) que sus compañeros estaban en el parque.

13. Yo no _____ (pensar) estudiar mis lecciones esta noche.

14. Ellos no _____ (poder) encontrar un apartamento barato.

15. Rafael _____ (saber) que Alberto tenía malas notas.

16. Tú _____ (creer) que Raquel estaba enferma desde ayer.

17. Yo _____ (esperar) ir con ustedes a las playas de Acapulco.

18. Nosotros _____ (pensar) ir a Nueva York, pero vamos a Santa Fe.

19. Yo _____ (sentirse) muy mal hasta que fui al médico.

20. Ellos le _____ (deber) dinero al tesorero del club.

21. Luis _____ (sentirse) muy apenado por su equivocación.

22. Él le _____ (deber) al Banco de Zamora más de mil dólares.

Worksheet 6.14 Imperfect tense of *ser, ir, ver*

Three important verbs are irregular in the imperfect tense:

ir			
yo	iba	nosotros(as)	íbamos
tú	ibas	vosotros(as)	ibais
él, ella, usted	iba	ellos, ellas, ustedes	iban

ser			
yo	era	nosotros(as)	éramos
tú	eras	vosotros(as)	erais
él, ella, usted	era	ellos, ellas, ustedes	eran

ver			
yo	veía	nosotros(as)	veíamos
tú	veías	vosotros(as)	veíais
él, ella, usted	veía	ellos, ellas, ustedes	veían

➤ Supply the imperfect tense of the verbs in parentheses.

1. Antes de jubilarme, yo _____ (ser) vendedor de diccionarios.

2. Yo _____ (ir) a las ciudades más grandes de cinco estados.

3. Yo _____ (ver) a los gerentes de más de cien librerías.

4. Mi prima _____ (ser) aficionada de conjuntos roqueros.

5. Elena _____ (ir) a muchos conciertos en Los Ángeles.

6. Ella _____ (ver) a todos los conjuntos más célebres.

7. Benito Juárez _____ (ser) presidente por esos años.

8. Él _____ (ir) a muchas partes para conocer mejor a la gente.

9. Él _____ (ver) como vivían en cada ciudad.

10. Nosotros _____ (ser) muy buenos amigos entonces.

11. _____ (lr) juntos a todas partes.

12. Siempre _____ (ver) las mismas películas.

13. Según mi padre, mis abuelos _____ (ser) rusos.

14. Cuando ellos _____ (ir) a América, se juraron hablar inglés.

15. Yo los _____ (ver) mucho, pero nunca oí nada de ruso.

16. Nosotros _____ (ir) anualmente al jardín zoológico.

17. Nos fascinaba un grupo de pingüinos. _____ (Ser) muy chistosos.

18. Los _____ (ver) por horas entrar y salir del agua.

19. Nuestro entrenador de fútbol _____ (ser) muy exigente.

20. Algunos _____ (ir) a los juegos con un poco de miedo.

21. A pesar de esto, nosotros lo _____ (ver) como un padre.

22. La reunión _____ (ser) a las cuatro.

23. Allí _____ (ir) también mi antigua novia.

24. Hacía mucho tiempo que no la _____ (ver).

Worksheet 6.15 *Iba a* + infinitive

Page 46 reviewed **ir a** + infinitive (*am, is, are going to*). The equivalent expression in the past tense (*was, were going to*) makes use of the imperfect tense of **ir** (page 130).

EXAMPLES: **Yo iba a estudia**r, pero dejé mi libro en la escuela.
I was going to study, but I left my book in school.

Íbamos a manejar, pero mi hermano tenía el coche.
We were going to drive, but my brother had the car.

➤ In the blanks, supply the imperfect tense of **ir a** + infinitive.

1. Yo _____
   (llamar) a Juan anoche, pero no tenía el número
   de teléfono.

2. Ellos _____
   (entregar) los paquetes ayer, pero no tuvieron
   tiempo.

3. Nosotros_____
   (acostarse) temprano anoche, pero unos amigos
   llegaron de visita.

4. Elena y yo_____
   (pasear) al parque, pero hacía mucho frío.

5. Yo _____
   (acostarse) temprano anoche, pero tenía mucho
   trabajo.

6. Nosotros_____
   (levantarse) temprano, pero teníamos mucho
   sueño.

7. Tú _____ (jugar) a las
   cartas anoche, pero Dora no se sentía bien.

8. Mi hermano _____
   (ir) a los Estados Unidos a estudiar, pero cambió
   de idea.

9. Yo _____
   (estudiar) francés el año pasado pero me
   cambié para español.

10. Tú_____
    (escribir) varias cartas anoche, pero estabas muy
    cansado.

11. Yo_____ (ir)
    a la iglesia, pero me levanté muy tarde.

12. Ellos _____
    (estudiar) medicina, pero les faltaba el dinero.

13. Nosotros _____ (ir)
    a la playa, pero llovió.

14. Ellos _____
    (casarse) en junio, pero decidieron esperar hasta
    diciembre.

15. ¿Por qué _____
    (vender) ustedes el coche que compraron el año
    pasado?

16. Él dijo que _____
    (pensar) en al asunto antes de decidir.

17. Yo le_____
    (prestar) dinero a Pedro, pero descubrí que no
    tenía suficiente.

18. Diana _____
    (cortarse) el pelo, pero su madre no la dejó.

Imperfect tense

➤ Change **yo** to **tú** in each of the following sentences, and copy the subject and verb in the spaces to the right. For additional practice (orally or by writing on separate sheets of paper), change the subject next to **él** or **ella, usted, nosotros, ustedes,** and **ellos** or **ellas.**

1. *Yo estudiaba* español con el señor García. _____

2. *Yo iba* a la escuela en autobús. _____

3. *Yo veía* al maestro en el parque con frecuencia. _____

4. *Yo era* un alumno muy aplicado. _____

5. *Yo contestaba* siempre cortésmente al profesor. _____

6. *Yo miraba* televisión todas las noches. _____

7. *Yo siempre hablaba* con ellos en español. _____

8. *Yo almorzaba* en casa todos los días. _____

9. *Yo comía* en casa de Juan con mucha frecuencia. _____

10. *Yo leía* muchas novelas durante el verano. _____

11. *Yo tenía* que devolverlas a la biblioteca. _____

12. *Yo seguía* mi horario diariamente. _____

13. *Yo me levantaba* muy temprano todas las mañanas. _____

14. *Yo siempre salía* de casa a la misma hora. _____

15. *Yo me acostaba* temprano de lunes a viernes. _____

16. *Yo siempre dormía* muy bien. _____

17. *Yo siempre me despertaba* a la misma hora. _____

18. *Yo me vestía* rápidamente para no llegar tarde. _____

19. *Yo prefería* comer en casa cada vez que podía. _____

20. *Yo jugaba* al tenis cuando vivía en Miami. _____

21. *Yo le prestaba* dinero a todo el mundo. _____

22. *Yo me reía* mucho de los chistes de Andrés. _____

Name: _____ Date: _____

More on the imperfect tense

➤ Change the verbs in the following sentences from present tense to imperfect tense. Read each new sentence and be sure that you understand its altered meaning.

1. Nosotros *viajamos* muchas veces a Europa. _____

2. Tú *andas* en los bulevares de París. _____

3. Ellos *ven* las óperas de La Scala. _____

4. Yo *asisto* a las corridas de toros de Madrid. _____
   _____

5. Ella *pinta* escenas en los Pirineos. _____

6. Ustedes *tratan* de hablar portugués. _____

7. Nosotros *compramos* relojes en Suiza. _____

8. Él *admira* las ruinas en Roma. _____

9. Mi cuñado *sube* a la Torre Eiffel. _____

10. Yo *veo* el Arco de Triunfo todos los días. _____
    _____

11. Tú *vas* a los museos de Madrid. _____

12. Ricardo *es* aficionado de la pelota. _____

13. La tía Luisa *busca* conchas en la playa. _____

14. Todos *comemos* mariscos en Galicia. _____

15. A mí me *encantan* las catedrales. _____

16. A ti te *gustan* los teatros elegantes. _____

17. Muchos hoteles *son* grandes palacios. _____

18. Los autobuses de Londres *tienen* dos plantas. _____
    _____

19. Los griegos *bailan* día y noche. _____

20. A todos les *gusta* patinar en Holanda. _____

21. Cuando *estoy* en Europa estoy contento. _____

22. ¿*Viajas* tú a Sudamérica frecuentemente? _____

More on the imperfect tense

➤ Change the verbs in the following sentences from preterite tense to imperfect tense. Read each new sentence and be sure that you understand its altered meaning.

1. Yo *manejé* el coche de mi papá. _____

2. Yo lo *hice* sin permiso de él. _____

3. El *pensó* que yo era muy joven. _____

4. Por un mes él no me *dejó* andar ni en bicicleta. _____
_____

5. En la noche yo no *pude* salir de mi cuarto. _____

6. ¡Qué sorpresa! Al mes siguiente me *prestó* su coche. _____
_____

7. *Valió* la pena pedir permiso, ¿verdad? _____

8. Mi tío me *dio* dinero para comprar dulces. _____

9. Yo *escogí* dulces de chocolate. _____

10. Yo *comí* demasiado helado también. _____

11. Además yo *fui* al mercado por galletas. _____

12. Mamá me *dijo* que yo iba a engordar. _____

13. Ella *fue* muy inteligente. _____

14. Yo t*uve* que bajar de peso. _____

15. Nosotros *esquíamos* en Colorado. _____

16. Yo *me caí* a cada rato. _____

17. Mi prima *tuvo* más suerte. _____

18. Ella *aprendió* muy rápidamente. _____

19. Pronto *conoció* a todos los entrenadores. _____
_____

20. Si hacía frío, ella no *dejó* de esquiar. _____

21. No *pudistes* imaginar la envidia que me daba. _____
_____

Name: _____ Date: _____

Vocabulary check-up

➤ Complete the following to show who sells things in different shops.

1. El _____ vende leche en la _____.

2. El _____ vende dulces en la _____.

3. El _____ vende carne en la _____.

4. El _____ vende libros en la _____.

5. El _____ vende zapatos en la _____.

6. El _____ vende pan en la_____.

7. El _____ vende joyas en la_____.

8. El _____ vende flores en la _____.

9. El _____ vende papel en la _____.

10. El _____ vende muebles en la_____.

➤ Complete the following sentences to show who works in a particular location.

1. El _____ (waiter) trabaja en el _____.

2. El _____ (barber) trabaja en la _____.

3. La _____ (doctor) trabaja en el _____.

4. El _____ (cook) trabaja en la _____.

5. El _____ (gardener) trabaja en el _____.

6. El _____ (tailor) trabaja en la _____.

7. La _____ (teacher) trabaja en la _____.

8. El _____ (programmer) trabaja en la _____.

9. La_____ (actress) trabaja en el_____.

10. El _____ (secretary) trabaja en la _____.

Buscapalabras

Palabras revueltas

➤ This word search puzzle contains all the words in the second part of each sentence in the previous worksheet. Some words will be found horizontally, and some words will be found vertically.

R	J	A	R	D	I	N	F	L	O	R	E	R	I	A	PI
E	S	C	C	A	R	N	I	C	E	R	I	A	P	S	A
S	J	O	Y	E	R	I	A	E	T	H	G	C	E	A	N
T	D	F	I	C	I	N	A	S	E	O	E	O	L	S	A
A	U	I	S	O	T	R	A	C	A	S	S	C	U	T	D
U	L	C	O	C	I	N	E	U	T	P	I	I	Q	R	E
R	C	I	P	A	P	E	L	E	R	I	A	N	U	E	R
A	E	N	A	D	E	R	I	L	O	T	I	A	E	R	I
N	R	A	N	E	R	A	Z	A	P	A	T	E	R	I	A
T	I	T	A	R	O	M	U	E	B	L	E	R	I	A	Y
E	A	C	O	M	P	U	T	A	D	O	R	A	A	L	I
L	E	C	H	E	R	I	A	L	I	B	R	E	R	I	A

Horizontal

_____
_____
_____
_____
_____
_____
_____
_____
_____

Vertical

_____
_____
_____
_____
_____
_____
_____
_____

Worksheet 6.16 Future tense

The same endings are used for all **-ar, -er,** and **-ir** verbs that are regular in the future tense. Notice that these endings are added to the entire infinitive:

	yo	tú	él/ella/ud.	nosotros	vosotros	ellos/ellas
hablar:	hablar**é**	hablar**ás**	hablar**á**	hablar**emos**	hablar**éis**	hablar**án**
comer:	comer**é**	comer**ás**	comer**á**	comer**emos**	comer**éis**	comer**án**
vivir:	vivir**é**	vivir**ás**	vivir**á**	vivir**emos**	vivir**éis**	vivir**án**

EXAMPLES: Yo te paga**ré** mañana *I shall pay you tomorrow.*
¿Cena**rás** con Ana? *Will you have dinner with Ana?*

➤ Supply the future tense of the verbs in parentheses.

1. Mañana yo _____ (estar) en San Francisco.

2. Yo _____ (trabajar) allí en un banco.

3. Yo _____ (conocer) a muchas personas.

4. En el banco yo _____ (ayudar) a mucha gente con sus ahorros.

5. También yo les_____ (prestar) el dinero.

6. El martes nosotros _____ (divertirse) mucho.

7. Mi padre, mi hermanito, y yo _____ (ir) al río.

8. Nosotros _____ (llegar) allí antes de las siete de la mañana.

9. Los tres_____ (pescar) en el río todo el día.

10. Con suerte, nosotros _____ (regresar) con muchos pescados.

11. Esta noche Isabel me _____ (acompañar) al cine.

12. Papá me_____ (dejar) usar el coche por primera vez.

13. A ella le _____ (gustar) la película porque es musical.

14. Isabel _____ (pasar) el verano en México con sus padres.

15. Ella _____ (hablar) español muy bien a su regreso.

16. Un día de éstos, mis padres _____ (comprar) una casa grande.

17. El sábado, ellos _____ (ver) más casas que se venden.

18. Sólo _____ (visitar) casas de dos plantas.

19. Ellos _____ (necesitar) cuatro dormitorios.

20. Mis dos hermanas no _____ (dormir) en la misma habitación.

21. Tú _____ (aprender) mucho en la clase de geometría.

22. Muy pronto tú _____ (resolver) los problemas más complicados.

23. Si vas a ser ingeniero, _____ (usar) la geometría diariamente.

24. Con este curso te_____ (preparar) para el cálculo.

Worksheet 6.17 More on future tense

➤ Supply the preterite and the future tense of each of the following present tense verbs. Include the subjects in each answer.

PRESENT TENSE	PRETERITE TENSE	FUTURE TENSE
1. Yo trabajo		
2. Él estudia		
3. Ellos compran		
4. Yo escribo		
5. Ella trae		
6. Yo me levanto		
7. Tú te acuestas		
8. Nosotros vamos		
9. Juan lee		
10. Usted come		
11. Él vuelve		
12. Ellos hablan		
13. María está		
14. Yo almuerzo		
15. Tú necesitas		
16. Él prepara		
17. Ella baila		
18. Yo veo		
19. Él vive		
20. Tú prefieres		
21. Él pide		
22. Ellos reciben		
23. Ella se viste		
24. Nadie oye		

Worksheet 6.18 Future tense of *caber, haber, poder, querer, saber*

All verbs have regular endings in the future tense, but a few common verbs have irregular stems. The following verbs simply drop the **e** from the stem:

caber		haber		poder		querer		saber	
cabré	cabremos	habré	habremos	podré	podremos	querré	querremos	sabré	sabremos
cabrás	(cabréis)	habrás	(habréis)	podrás	(podréis)	querrás	(querréis)	sabrás	(sabréis)
cabrá	cabrán	habrá	habrán	podrá	podrán	querrá	querrán	sabrá	sabrán

➤ Supply the future tense of the verbs in parentheses.

1. Mañana _____ (haber) mucho trabajo que hacer en casa.

2. Yo no _____ (poder) ir a la playa con ustedes.

3. Tú _____ (querer) conocer a mi tío Manuel.

4. Él_____ (saber) ayudarte con la construcción de tu casa.

5. No_____ (caber) todos en el cochecito de ustedes.

6. ¿_____ (Poder) usar nosotros la camioneta de sus papás?

7. La policía _____ (saber) proteger a los candidatos políticos.

8. _____ (Haber) suficientes policías para acompañar a cada uno.

9. Tantos abrigos no _____ (caber) en este ropero.

10. _____ (Haber) lugar para más abrigos en el ropero de arriba.

11. ¿_____ (Saber) tú comunicarte con los franco-canadienses?

12. Sí, nosotros_____ (poder) entendernos fácilmente.

13. Dos docenas de rosas no _____ (caber) en este florero.

14. _____ (Haber) un florero más grande en la cocina.

15. Mis compañeros _____ (querer) escuchar discos en la fiesta.

16. ¿Tú _____ (saber) escoger las canciones que les gustan más?

17. ¿Cuándo_____ (poder) yo probar las galletas de tu abuelita?

18. Ella _____ (querer) servirte algunas durante tu visita mañana.

19. ¿Quién _____ (saber) la dirección del consulado boliviano?

20. Seguramente _____ (haber) un directorio de consulados en el hotel.

*Haber, as an independent or principal verb, has the following forms in the present, preterite, imperfect, and future tenses: **hay, hubo, había, habrá.** As a principal verb, **haber** is the equivalent of the English *there is* or *there are.* Thus, **Hay muchos alumnos ausentes hoy.** means *There are many students absent today.* **Habrá muchos alumnos ausentes mañana.** means **There will be many students absent tomorrow.**

Worksheet 6.19 Future tense of *poner, salir, tener, venir*

All the verbs in the previous worksheet dropped the vowel of the infinitive ending. **Poner, salir, tener, and venir** replace that dropped vowel with a **d**:

	yo	tú	él, ella, usted	nosotros(as)	vosotros(as)	ellos, ellas, ustedes
poner	pondré	pondrás	pondrá	pondremos	pondréis	pondrán
salir	saldré	saldrás	saldrá	saldremos	saldréis	saldrán
tener	tendré	tendrás	tendrá	tendremos	tendréis	tendrán
valer	valdré	valdrás	valdrá	valdremos	valdréis	valdrán
venir	vendré	vendrás	vendrá	vendremos	vendréis	vendrán

➤ Supply the future tense of the verbs in parentheses.

1. Yo _____ (poner) el dinero que me diste en el banco.

2. Pronto yo _____ (tener) bastante para comprar un coche.

3. Daniel _____ (tener) su guitarra en la fiesta esta noche.

4. ¡Qué bueno! ¿A qué hora _____ (venir)?

5. Nosotros_____ (salir) juntos por primera vez.

6. Todos _____ (ponerse) ropa muy fina.

7. Ellos no están de acuerdo. ¿Cuál _____ (tener) razón?

8. Alfredo _____ (venir) más tarde. Él sabrá decidir.

9. Si vas a graduarte, _____ (tener) que ver menos televisión.

10. Después de este programa, yo _____ (ponerse) a estudiar.

11. Si no me pongo la chaqueta,_____ (tener) frío en el parque.

12. ¡Buena idea! Nosotros _____ (salir) del parque muy tarde.

13. ¿ _____ (Venir) tus abuelos a California este año?

14. ¡Sí! Ellos _____ (tener) sus boletos para fines de mayo.

15. ¿Dónde_____ (poner) ella el piano que piensa comprar?

16. Creo que ella _____ (tener) que ponerlo en la sala.

17. ¿ _____ (Salir) ustedes tarde del teatro?

18. Sí, pero nosotros _____ (venir) directamente a casa después.

19. El profesor Vidal_____ (componer) una canción.

20. El programa _____ (contener) muchas canciones originales.

21. El gobierno_____ (imponer) impuestos sobre tu sueldo.

22. Sí, pero todavía _____ (valer) la pena ganar más dinero.

Worksheet 6.20 **Future tense of** *hacer* **and** *decir*

Two other verbs are irregular in the future tense. **Hacer** and **decir** both drop the letters **c** and **e** before adding the future tense endings.

hacer			
yo	haré	nosotros(as)	haremos
tú	harás	vosotros(as)	haréis
él, ella, usted	hará	ellos, ellas, ustedes	harán

decir			
yo	diré	nosotros(as)	diremos
tú	dirás	vosotros(as)	diréis
él, ella, usted	dirá	ellos, ellas, ustedes	dirán

➤ Supply the future tense of the verbs in parentheses.

1. Yo te _____ (decir) los nombres de los candidatos.

2. Entonces yo _____ (hacer) una lista para los miembros.

3. Yo averiguaré el nombre de joven y se lo _____ (decir).

4. ¿Cuándo _____ (hacer) usted eso?

5. Si le preguntas a Juan, no te _____ (decir) la verdad.

6. Entonces, ¿qué _____ (hacer) nosotros para saberla?

7. Este dependiente nos _____ (decir) el precio.

8. ¿Qué _____ (hacer) ustedes si no tienen bastante dinero?

9. Nosotros te _____ (decir) el fin del cuento.

10. Tú me _____ (hacer) dichoso si termina felizmente.

11. ¿Me _____ (decir) usted cuándo la cena está lista?

12. Sí, además yo _____ (hacer) tu receta favorita.

13. El juez muy pronto nos _____ (decir) su decisión.

14. Creo que él la _____ (hacer) con mucha dificultad.

15. Si escuchas bien, te _____ (decir) el alfabeto griego.

16. ¿Me _____ (hacer) tú también una lista de las letras?

17. ¿Qué _____ (decir) tus padres acerca de esto?

18. No sé, pero ellos me _____ (hacer) decirles la verdad.

19. El profesor nos _____ (decir) nuestras notas el lunes.

20. ¿Por qué les _____ (hacer) esperar hasta entonces?

21. ¿Me _____ (decir) tú lo que yo necesito hacer?

22. Tú _____ (hacer) la ensalada; yo prepararé la carne.

Future tense

➤ For further practice with the future tense, change the subject of the following sentences from **yo** to **él**, and write the subject and verb in the spaces to the right. You may also practice changing the **yo** to **tú, nosotros,** and **ellos.**

1. *Yo volveré* el primero de septiembre. _____

2. *Yo hablaré.* _____

3. *Yo me quedaré* allí dos meses. _____

4. *Yo iré* a Europa en avión a principios de Marzo. _____

5. *Yo traeré* muchos regalos para mis nietos. _____

6. *Yo escribiré* esa carta antes del sábado. _____

7. *Yo saldré* alrededor del dos de agosto. _____

8. *Yo tendré* mucho que hacer pasado mañana. _____

9. *Yo sabré* muy pronto la fecha exacta de la fiesta. _____

10. *Yo haré* todo lo posible para visitar a mis amigos. _____

11. *Yo vendré* aquí a las seis y cuarto. _____

12. *Yo comeré* en un restaurante nuevo esta noche. _____

13. *Yo dejaré* los libros sobre el escritorio. _____

14. *Yo leeré* cinco novelas durante el verano. _____

15. *Yo podré* hacerlo a ratos. _____

16. *Yo diré* solamente la verdad en cuanto al robo. _____

17. *Yo estaré* de vuelta al mediodía. _____

18. *Yo me levantaré* temprano esta mañana. _____

19. *Yo seré* el mejor alumno de la clase. _____

20. *Yo estudiaré* más desde ahora en adelante. _____

21. *Yo empezaré* a estudiar francés el próximo año. _____

22. *Yo pondré* las ciruelas en una canasta. _____

23. *Yo las comeré* más tarde. _____

24. *Yo obtendré** más ciruelas mañana. _____

***Contener, detener, obtener, retener,** and **sostener** are all conjugated the same as **tener.**
The meaning of these verbs becomes clear if **-tener** is translated as *-tain.*

General review

To review regular and irregular verbs in the preterite, imperfect, and future tenses, complete the following columns. Include the subject pronoun with each entry.

PRESENT	PRETERITE	IMPERFECT	FUTURE
1. Yo pongo			
2. Él dice			
3. Ella está			
4. Yo hago			
5. Ellas comen			
6. Tú quieres			
7. Él sabe			
8. Yo vengo			
9. Ella tiene			
10. Usted sale			
11. Tú puedes			
12. Él pone			
13. Yo me acuesto			
14. Tú vas			
15. Ellos salen			
16. Nosotros somos			
17. Yo tengo			
18. Él almuerza			
19. Yo veo			
20. Él pierde			
21. Ella hace			
22. Yo vuelvo			
23. Tú estás			
24. Usted sabe			

Worksheet 6.21 More on articles

Many nouns do not end in **-o**. Furthermore, some nouns ending in **-o** are feminine; some nouns ending in **-a** are masculine. Still others use **él** in the feminine singular. Here are the rules:

1. Some words are exceptions: **la mano, el día, la foto.**
2. Nouns with the suffix **-dad, -tad, -tud, -ción** or **-ez** will be feminine (**la libertad, la realidad, la creación, la niñez**).
3. Nouns beginning with a stressed (**a**) sound, regardless of gender, will use **el** (**el arpa, el hacha, but las arpas, las hachas**).
4. Most Greek derivatives ending in **-ma, -pa, -ta** will be masculine (**el tema, el mapa, el poeta**).
5. Some nouns will change meaning according to gender (***el cometa,*** *comet;* ***la cometa,*** *kite;* ***el frente,*** *the front part;* **la frente,** *the forehead;* **el policía,** *the police officer;* **la policía,** *police force;* **el papa,** *pope;* **la papa,** *potato;* **la radio,** *radio;* **el radio,** *radium, radius*).

➤ Supply the definite article for each of the following nouns.

1. _____ hambre	17. _____ mapa
2. _____ amistad	18. _____ día
3. _____ rapidez	19. _____ actor
4. _____ hadas	20. _____ actriz
5. _____ loción	21. _____ arte
6. _____ drama	22. _____ aguas
7. _____ realidad	23. _____ poema
8. _____ manos	24. _____ ángel
9. _____ prontitud	25. _____ timidez
10. _____ agua	26. _____ acta
11. _____ condición	27. _____ lentitud
12. _____ álgebra	28. _____ posición
13. _____ ama	29. _____ pared
14. _____ lealtad	30. _____ clima
15. _____ hada	31. _____ verdad
16. _____ almeja	32. _____ amas

Worksheet 6.22 Shortened adjectives (apocope)

The following adjectives drop their final **-o** when preceding the noun they modify: **bueno, malo, uno, alguno (algún), ninguno (ningún), primero, tercero.**

The final **-a** is not dropped in the following adjectives: **buen chico, buena chica; ningún muchacho, ninguna muchacha; el tercer niño, la tercera niña.**

The adjectives **grande** and **ciento** drop the final syllable before the nouns they modify, regardless of gender:

EXAMPLES: el **gran** hombre, la **gran** mujer; **cien** toros, **cien** vacas

Some adjectives change meaning when moved from the right to the left of the modified noun:

EXAMPLES:
mujer grande	*large woman*	**camisa nueva**	*new shirt*
gran mujer	*great woman*	**nueva camisa**	*fresh shirt*
soldado pobre	*penniless soldier*	**único libro**	*only book*
pobre soldado	*unskilled soldier*	**libro único**	*unique book*

➤ Supply the proper form of the adjectives in parentheses.

1. (grande) presidente_____

2. (grande) _____ presidente

3. (bueno)_____ día

4. (bueno) _____ días

5. (primero) _____ capítulo

6. (malo) alumno _____

7. (malo) _____ muchacho

8. (nuevo) _____ cortinas

9. (limpio) agua _____

10. (ninguno) _____ nación

11. (alguno) _____ programa

12. (único) actriz _____

13. (ciento) _____ palomas

14. (alguno) _____ manera

15. (ninguno) _____ mapa

16. (grande) _____ señora

17. (tercero) _____ año

18. (tercero)_____ arte

19. (nuevo) iglesia _____

20. (alguno)_____ hombre

21. (uno) _____ chico

22. (uno) _____ chica

23. (grande)_____ reina

24. (primero) _____ rey

Worksheet 6.23 More on shortened adjectives

➤ Move the italicized adjective from the left side to the right side of the modified noun. Be able to explain any change in meaning. In the blanks, write the noun followed by the correct form of the adjective.

1. Mañana será el *primer* día de octubre. _____

2. Aquel vecino siempre fue un *mal* alumno. _____

3. El científico nació en un *gran* país. _____

4. Yo quiero ayudar a esa *pobre* mujer. _____

5. Pronto empezaremos a estudiar el *tercer* libro. _____

6. Por mi parte, no tengo un *gran* apetito. _____

7. El año pasado fue un *buen* año para nosotros. _____

8. La madre del señor Chávez es una *gran* mujer. _____

9. Él no tiene un *gran* interés en aprender francés. _____

10. Él tenía la apariencia de una *mala* persona. _____

11. Planeamos una fiesta para el *tercer* día del mes. _____

12. Mañana vamos a estudiar la *tercera* lección _____

13. Anoche ayudé a un *pobre* hombre en la calle. _____

14. Yo te aseguro que María es una *buena* muchacha. _____

15. Su hermano Guillermo también es un *buen* muchacho._____

16. El lunes fue el *primer* día de clases. _____

17. Juan no pone un *gran* interés en sus estudios. _____

18. San Francisco tiene un *buen* clima. _____

19. Los Pérez viven en el *tercer* piso del hotel. _____

20. Yo no tengo *ningún* deseo de ir a Europa. _____

21. Mentir es una *mala* costumbre. _____

22. Hoy tuvimos un *buen* día en la escuela. _____

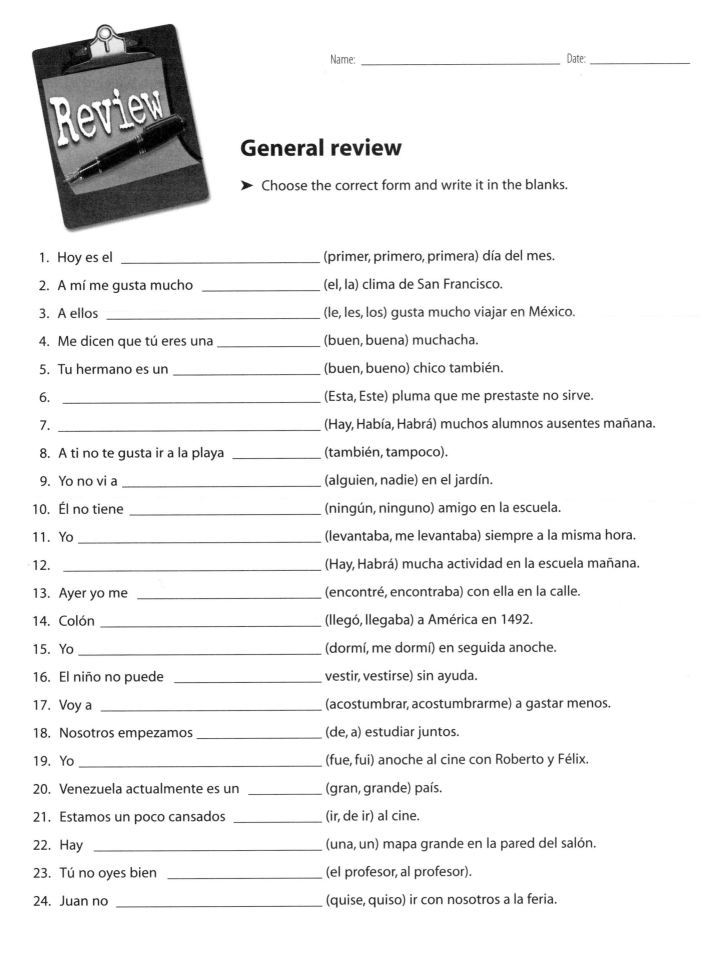

General review

➤ Choose the correct form and write it in the blanks.

1. Hoy es el _____ (primer, primero, primera) día del mes.

2. A mí me gusta mucho _____ (el, la) clima de San Francisco.

3. A ellos _____ (le, les, los) gusta mucho viajar en México.

4. Me dicen que tú eres una _____ (buen, buena) muchacha.

5. Tu hermano es un _____ (buen, bueno) chico también.

6. _____ (Esta, Este) pluma que me prestaste no sirve.

7. _____ (Hay, Había, Habrá) muchos alumnos ausentes mañana.

8. A ti no te gusta ir a la playa _____ (también, tampoco).

9. Yo no vi a _____ (alguien, nadie) en el jardín.

10. Él no tiene _____ (ningún, ninguno) amigo en la escuela.

11. Yo _____ (levantaba, me levantaba) siempre a la misma hora.

12. _____ (Hay, Habrá) mucha actividad en la escuela mañana.

13. Ayer yo me _____ (encontré, encontraba) con ella en la calle.

14. Colón _____ (llegó, llegaba) a América en 1492.

15. Yo _____ (dormí, me dormí) en seguida anoche.

16. El niño no puede _____ vestir, vestirse) sin ayuda.

17. Voy a _____ (acostumbrar, acostumbrarme) a gastar menos.

18. Nosotros empezamos _____ (de, a) estudiar juntos.

19. Yo _____ (fue, fui) anoche al cine con Roberto y Félix.

20. Venezuela actualmente es un _____ (gran, grande) país.

21. Estamos un poco cansados _____ (ir, de ir) al cine.

22. Hay _____ (una, un) mapa grande en la pared del salón.

23. Tú no oyes bien _____ (el profesor, al profesor).

24. Juan no _____ (quise, quiso) ir con nosotros a la feria.

Vocabulary check-up

➤ Choose the correct form or answer and write it in the blanks.

1. Si yo hago algo en seguida, lo hago (con dificultad, con poco interés, inmediatamente, despacio).

   _____

2. Lo opuesto de mojado es (grande, seco, ancho, pesado). _____

3. Si digo que Juan se puso enojado, eso quiere decir que Juan (se cayó, se acostó, se enojó, sonrió).

   _____

4. ¿Cuál de estas cosas se encuentra en un restaurante? (caballo, piscina, postre, nubes)._____

5. ¿Cuál de estos verbos está en el presente? (hago, puse, pudo, era)._____

6. Si usted tiene mucho calor, ¿qué hace con su chaqueta?(quitármela, ponérmela, colgarla, limpiarla)

   _____

7. Lo opuesto de ancho es (chico, grande, alto, estrecho) _____

8 ¿Quién le sirve en un restaurante? (piloto, chófer, camarero, médico) _____

9. Un sinónimo de muchacho es (joven, señor, camarero, profesor)_____

10. ¿En que estación del año hace más calor en los Estados Unidos? (primavera, verano, otoño, invierno)

    _____

11. ¿En qué estación del año hace más frío en los Estados Unidos? (primavera, verano, otoño, invierno).

    _____

12. ¿Cuál de estas palabras es masculina? (escuela, pluma, mapa, mesa) _____

13. ¿Cuál de estas palabras es femenina? (brazo, mano, ojo, cuello) _____

14. Si veo a alguien de vez en cuando, lo veo (con frecuencia, nunca, temprano por la mañana, a veces).

    _____

15. Si tengo sueño por la mañana (comer, tomar algo, dormir, levantarme). _____

16. Un sin levantarme tal vez es (siempre, quizás, seguramente, nunca). _____

17. Poco a poco quiere decir (rápidamente, al poco rato, temprano, gradualmente). _____

18. ¿Cuál de estos idiomas se habla en el Brasil? (español, francés, italiano, portugués) _____

19. El tercer mes del año (mayo, marzo, febrero, enero). _____

20. Si hoy es miércoles, que día fue ayer? (lunes, martes,sábado, domingo) _____

21. ¿Cuál de estos países se encuentra al norte de los Estados Unidos? (Venezuela, Cuba, México, Canadá)

    _____

22. ¿Si hoy es martes, que día será pasado mañana? (domingo, lunes, miércoles, jueves)

    _____

Part 7

Contents

Worksheet 7.1 Comparison of adjectives (comparative degree)

English has two ways to form the comparative of adjectives: *pleasanter* (*than*) and *more pleasant* (*than*). Spanish has only one: **más agradable (que).**

EXAMPLES: Juan es **más alto** que su hermano.   *John is taller than his brother.*
Esta calle es **más ancha** que la otra.   *This street is wider than the other.*

Spanish has four forms that are irregular:

| **bueno** | **mejor** | *better* | **grande** | **mayor** | *bigger, older* |
| **malo** | **peor** | *worse* | **pequeño** | **menor** | *smaller, younger* |

➤ In the blanks, supply the comparative degree of the adjective in parentheses, including **más, menos, que** when required. Make necessary agreements in number and gender.

1. Estas pirámides son _____ (alto) las pirámides egipcias.

2. Los cocineros franceses son _____ (moderno) los argentinos.

3. Este apartamento es _____ (caro) ciertas casas.

4. Estos ejercicios son _____ (fácil) los de ayer.

5. Nuestro clima es _____ (frío) el de Panamá.

6. Las peras son _____ (dulce) las manzanas.

7. El pudín sabe _____ (bueno) el pastel.

8. La fecha _____ (importante) la hora.

9. El gato parece _____ (grande) el perro.

10. Sus rosas son _____ (bonito) mis claveles.

11. Tú eres _____ (alta) mis otras amigas.

12. El tigre es _____ (feroz) el león.

13. Los libros son _____ (caros) los de este semestre.

14. La civilización tolteca es _____ (antiguo) la azteca.

15. Los mosquitos son _____ (pequeños) las moscas.

16. El vestido negro es _____ (popular) el rojo.

17. El coche anda _____ (rápido) el autobús.

18. Según la enfermera, tú te sientes _____ (bueno) nunca.

19. Como alumno, Felipe es _____ (aplicado) yo.

20. La margarina es _____ (saludable) la mantequilla.

21. Caracas es una ciudad _____ (importante) Maracaibo.

22. Las campanas de la iglesia son _____ (grande) las de la escuela.

Worksheet 7.2 Comparison of adjectives (superlative degree)

The superlative form of adjectives generally requires the combination of (1) definite article + (2) noun + (3) **más** + (4) adjective + (5) **de**. The noun can sometimes be omitted. With **mejor, peor, mayor,** and **menor** the word **más** is eliminated:

EXAMPLE: Juan es el **alumno más aplicado de** la clase.
          (1)   (2)   (3)   (4)   (5)
John is the most studious boy in the class.
          (1) (3)   (4) (2) (5)

POSITIVE	COMPARATIVE (+ QUE)	SUPERLATive (+ DE)
ancha	más ancha	la más ancha
altos	más altos	los más altos
buena (mala)	mejor (peor)	la mejor (peor)
grande (pequeño)	mayor (menor)	la mayor (menor)

➤ In the blanks at the right, supply the superlative degree of the adjective in parentheses. Make necessary agreements in number and gender, and use **mejor** and **mayor** wherever possible.

(Note these symbols: — add one word — — add two words   *definite article already precedes noun)

1. Este jardín es — — (hermoso) de la ciudad. _____

2. Esta estación es — — (frío) del año. _____

3. Estos ejercicios son — — (útil) de todo el libro. _____

4. Como alumno, Juan es — — (malo) de la clase. _____

5. La fiesta de esta noche va a ser — — (bueno) del año. _____

6. Tokio es la ciudad* — (poblado) del mundo. _____

7. Tú eres el alumno* — (diligente) de la clase. _____

8. Este libro es — — (práctico) de todos. _____

9. Esta reunión — — (importante) de todo el año. _____

10. Estas flores son — — (bello) de la estación. _____

11. Buenos Aires es la ciudad* — (bonito) de la Argentina. _____

12. El chocolate es el sabor* — (preferido) por los niños. _____

13. Tú eres la muchacha* — (inteligente) de la clase. _____

14. Julio es — — (bueno) profesor de la universidad. _____

15. Esta lección es — — (largo) del libro de español. _____

16. Estos edificios son — — (moderno) de Caracas. _____

17. Sudamérica tiene los animales*— (extraño) del mundo. _____

18. El Everest es el monte — (alto) de todos. _____

19. En Colombia se cosecha el café* — (sabroso) que hay. _____

20. En Egipto se cultiva — — (bueno) algodón del mundo. _____

21. Estos limones son — — (agrio) del mercado. _____

22. El tigre es el animal* — (feroz) de la selva. _____

Worksheet 7.3 More on comparison of adjectives (superlative degree)

➤ For further practice with the superlative degree of adjectives, change the italicized words to the plural.

EXAMPLE: **el traje más nuevo** to **los trajes más nuevos**

1. Compraron *la mejor casa* de la ciudad. _____

2. Estuvimos allí *el peor día* del mes. _____

3. Hicimos el ejercicio *más difícil del libro.* _____

4. Viste *la mejor película* del año. _____

5. Estudiamos en *el aula más grande* de la escuela. _____

6. Alquilaron *el apartamento más lujoso* del edificio. _____

_____

7. Viven en *la casa más hermosa* de la ciudad. _____

8. Estuve en Lima durante *el día más frío* del verano. _____

9. Tú compraste *el sombrero más bonito* de la tienda. _____

_____

10. Viajamos en *el barco más rápido* de la compañía. _____

11. Visitamos *el museo más importante* de la ciudad. _____

_____

12. Pasé allí *la peor semana* de mi vida. _____

13. Recuerdo bien *el día más feliz* de mi infancia. _____

14. Pagué en ese hotel *el precio más alto* que recuerdo. _____

_____

15. Viven en *el barrio más elegante* de la ciudad. _____

16. Visitamos *el estado más rico* del país. _____

17. Descubriste *el mejor restaurante* de la ciudad. _____

18. Estuvimos en *la ciudad más antigua* de Europa. _____

19. Cruzamos *el río más ancho* de África. _____

20. Subimos a *la montaña más alta* de México. _____

21. En Guatemala hice *la mejor compra* del viaje. _____

22. Él escribió *la mejor novela* de ese período. _____

Worksheet 7.4 More on comparison of adjectives

The expression **que** (*than*) usually follows the comparative degree, however, **que** is replaced by **de** when it precedes an expression of quantity.

EXAMPLE: **más que yo, menos que los leones,** *but* **más de diez, menos de una docena.**

➤ In the blanks, supply **de** (**del**) or **que,** whichever is correct.

1. Guadalajara es la ciudad más grande _____ Jalisco.

2. Mi cuarto tiene más ventanas _____ la sala.

3. Tú eres mucho más estudioso _____ tus primos.

4. Él habla español mejor_____ su hermano.

5. Tú tienes más _____ diez amigos en la escuela.

6. El señor es más generoso _____ los otros vecinos.

7. Tuvimos que esperar más _____ veinte minutos.

8. Ella vino más temprano _____ los otros maestros.

9. Hicieron más _____ tres viajes a Europa en un año.

10. Ésta es la época más cálida _____ año.

11. Tú estás más pálida hoy _____ nunca.

12. Hoy me siento un poco peor_____ ayer.

13. Estos ejercicios son los más fáciles _____ todo el libro.

14. Ella comió más _____ diez galletas esta tarde.

15. Tuve que esperar más _____ una hora para ver al dentista.

16. París es probablemente la ciudad más interesante _____ mundo.

17. María y Elena son las mejores alumnas _____ nuestra clase.

18. Estos ejercicios son más fáciles _____ los que acabamos de hacer.

19. Las frutas este año son mejores _____ las del año pasado.

20. Estas rosas son las más bellas _____ jardín.

21. Es el periódico más popular_____ Nicaragua.

22. Ellos son los peloteros más conocidos _____ equipo brasileño.

Worksheet 7.5 **Comparison of adverbs**

Adverbs are compared the same as adjectives (see page 150):

EXAMPLE: ADJECTIVE: Carlos es **más sincero** que Alberto.
ADVERB: Carlos habla **más** sinceramente que Alberto.

Bien and **mal** are irregular:

ADJECTIVE		ADVERB		COMPARATIVE DEGREE
bueno (*good*)	or	bien (*well*)	=	**mejor** (*better*)
malo (*bad*)	or	mal (*badly*)	=	**peor** (*worse*)

➤ In the blanks, supply the comparative form of the adverbs in parentheses.

1. Él habla español _____ (rápidamente) _____ los otros alumnos.

2. Ella puede hacer este trabajo _____ (fácilmente) _____ yo.

3. Juan habla español _____ (mal) _____ los otros miembros de su familia.

4. Le escuchamos_____ (atentamente) _____ sus propios

   amigos.

5. Hoy vinieron a la clase _____ (temprano) _____ ayer.

6. Elena baila mucho _____ (bien) _____ su hermana.

7. Tú estudias ahora_____ (diligentemente)_____ el año

   pasado.

8. Ellos entienden inglés _____ (bien) _____ español.

9. El viejo habla ahora _____ (lentamente)_____ nunca.

10. Parece que él trabaja _____ (cuidadosamente) _____ los

    otros trabajadores.

11. Yo puedo hacer estos ejercicios _____ (rápidamente) _____ antes.

12. Teresa aceptó el fracaso _____ (valientemente) _____ su hermana.

13. Los Pérez nos recibieron _____ (alegremente) de lo_____

    esperábamos.

14. Pablo habla _____ (claramente)_____ los otros estudiantes.

15. Isabel entiende inglés _____ (bien) _____ sus padres y sus tíos.

16. Ella habla inglés en la escuela _____ (frecuentemente) _____ en

    casa.

17. Su hermano sabe matemáticas _____ (bien) _____ su hermano.

18. Mi profesor explica la lección _____ (claramente) _____ el de Carmen.

Worksheet 7.6 Comparison of equality (adjectives and adverbs)

In the expressions *as* + adjective + *as* and *as* + adverb + *as*, the first *as* will be **tan** and the second *as* will be **como**.

EXAMPLE: *The cat is as big as the dog.*   El gato es **tan grande como** el perro.
   My car goes as fast as your truck.   Mi coche anda **tan rápidamente como** tu camión.
   Chicago is not as far as Miami.   Chicago no está **tan lejos como** Miami.

➤ In the blanks, supply **tan como** plus the indicated adjective or adverb. Make whatever changes are necessary in gender, number, or form.

1. Aquellas muchachas no son _____ (serio) _____ éstas.

2. Tú eres casi _____ (alto) _____ tu padre.

3. Esta calle es _____ (ancho) _____ el Paseo de la Reforma.

4. Ellos no son _____ (joven) _____ nosotros.

5. Hoy no estoy _____ (cansado) _____ ayer.

6. Tú hablas español _____ (bueno) _____ los otros alumnos.

7. Él no puede hacer ese trabajo_____ (fácil) _____ ella.

8. Elena no es_____(hermoso) _____ su hermana.

9. Los alumnos son _____ (estudioso)_____ los del año pasado.

10. Ninguna otra revista es _____ (popular) _____ ésta.

11. La hermana mayor no es_____ (inteligente) _____ la menor.

12. Nosotros no somos _____ (rico)_____ los Ramírez.

13. Los estudiantes no leen_____ (rápido) _____ el profesor.

14. Nueva York no es _____ (interesante) _____ Washington.

15. Esta iglesia no es _____ (viejo)_____ la catedral.

16. Las peras no son _____ (sabroso)_____ las manzanas.

17. Los gatos no son _____ (fiel)_____ los perros.

18. Las mujeres no son _____ (alto) _____ los hombres.

19. Esta mesa es_____ (largo) _____ ancha.

20. Este hotel es_____ (bonito) _____ el Palacio Nacional.

21. Ella no es _____ (listo) _____ ustedes creen.

22. Este sillón no es _____ (cómodo) _____ me parecía.

Worksheet 7.7 Comparison of equality (nouns)

In the expressions *as much* (noun) *as* and *as many* (noun) *as*, the first *as* will be **tanto(s)** and the second *as* will be **como**:

EXAMPLES: *My car has as many cylinders as your truck.*
Mi coche tiene **tantos** cilindros **como** tu camión.

The cookies do not need so much sugar as the candies.
Las galletas no necesitan **tanto** azúcar **como** los dulces.

➤ In the blanks, supply **tanto como** plus the necessary noun. Make **tanto** agree in number and gender with the noun which it modifies.

1. Vamos a estar en la biblioteca _____ tiempo _____ mi primo.

2. Mi primo no lee _____ libros _____ mi hermano y yo.

3. Yo tengo_____ amigos_____ mi hermana.

4. Ella no conoce a_____ estudiantes _____ antes.

5. La maestra nos da _____ exámenes _____ la del año pasado.

6. No tenemos que escribir_____ composiciones _____ antes.

7. La clase de español no tiene _____ estudiantes _____ la clase de inglés.

8. Nuestras clases no tienen _____ muchachas _____ muchachos.

9. Esta casa no tiene _____ valor_____ la de ustedes.

10. Mi nueva casa no tiene _____ cuartos_____ la suya.

11. Hoy no hace_____ calor_____ ayer.

12. Este mes no hay días _____ lluviosos_____ en abril.

13. Estos niños hacen _____ ruido _____ todos los niños.

14. Yo creo que sus juegos causan _____ ruido _____ los de nosotros.

15. No tengo _____ ahorros _____ los vecinos.

16. Tú gastas _____ dinero _____ toda mi familia.

17. Roberto no come_____ dulces _____ su esposa.

18. María come _____ legumbres _____ su marido.

19. Rosa no conoce a_____ pilotos _____ su padre.

20. Este piloto no tiene _____ horas de vuelo _____ el padre de Rosa.

21. La señora Rivera tiene _____ recetas _____ mi madre.

22. Mi madre prepara _____ comidas _____ ella.

Comparison of equality/inequality (adjectives, adverbs, nouns)

➤ Choose the correct form and write it in the blanks.

1. Yo no tomo tantas vacaciones _____ (como, que) tú.

2. Tú vas a ver las ciudades más grandes _____ (de, que) Europa.

3. La vida cuesta _____ (menos, la menos) aquí que allí.

4. Este año gastarás más dinero _____ (como, que) antes.

5. Yo pasaré más _____ (que, de) una semana en Madrid.

6. Visitaré los edificios _____ (más, los más) moriscos.

7. Los edificios son más antiguos _____ (de, que) los de Chicago.

8. Me sentiré _____ (tan, tanto) afortunado como nadie.

9. Comeré en _____ (mejores, los mejores) restaurantes europeos.

10. Este hotel es el más moderno _____ (de, en) Madrid.

11. Más que _____ (algo, nada) quiero comprar recuerdos típicos.

12. En California no hay tantas guitarras buenas como _____ (de, en) Valencia.

13. Alemania tiene más tránsito_____ (como, que) España.

14. España tiene tanto tránsito _____ (como, que) Italia.

15. Los europeos son _____ (tan, más) amables como los americanos.

16. No hay parques más bonitos _____ (de, que) los de París.

17. La industria del norte es mayor _____ (de, que) la del sur.

18. La música del sur es _____ (tan, más) bonita que la del norte.

19. Tijuana tiene más plazas de toro _____(como, que) Guadalajara.

20. Yo voy a visitar más_____ (que, de) ocho países en un mes.

21. Mi esposa leyó _____ (tantos, más) folletos sobre Lisboa como yo.

22. Saldremos para Lisboa en el avión más moderno _____ (como, que) hay.

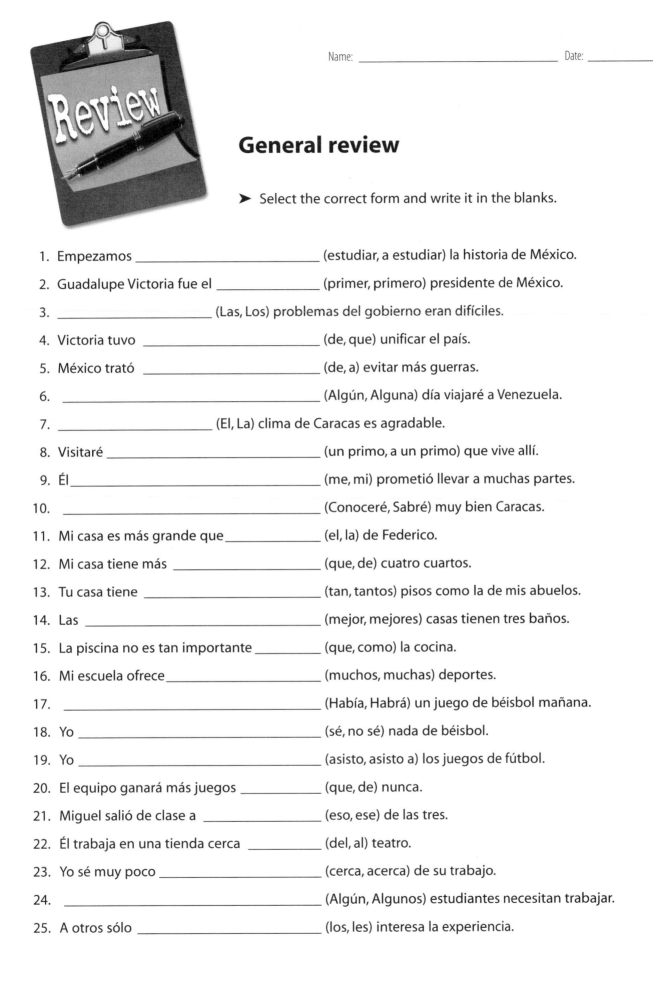

General review

➤ Select the correct form and write it in the blanks.

1. Empezamos _____ (estudiar, a estudiar) la historia de México.

2. Guadalupe Victoria fue el _____ (primer, primero) presidente de México.

3. _____ (Las, Los) problemas del gobierno eran difíciles.

4. Victoria tuvo _____ (de, que) unificar el país.

5. México trató _____ (de, a) evitar más guerras.

6. _____ (Algún, Alguna) día viajaré a Venezuela.

7. _____ (El, La) clima de Caracas es agradable.

8. Visitaré _____ (un primo, a un primo) que vive allí.

9. Él _____ (me, mi) prometió llevar a muchas partes.

10. _____ (Conoceré, Sabré) muy bien Caracas.

11. Mi casa es más grande que _____ (el, la) de Federico.

12. Mi casa tiene más _____ (que, de) cuatro cuartos.

13. Tu casa tiene _____ (tan, tantos) pisos como la de mis abuelos.

14. Las _____ (mejor, mejores) casas tienen tres baños.

15. La piscina no es tan importante _____ (que, como) la cocina.

16. Mi escuela ofrece _____ (muchos, muchas) deportes.

17. _____ (Había, Habrá) un juego de béisbol mañana.

18. Yo _____ (sé, no sé) nada de béisbol.

19. Yo _____ (asisto, asisto a) los juegos de fútbol.

20. El equipo ganará más juegos _____ (que, de) nunca.

21. Miguel salió de clase a _____ (eso, ese) de las tres.

22. Él trabaja en una tienda cerca _____ (del, al) teatro.

23. Yo sé muy poco _____ (cerca, acerca) de su trabajo.

24. _____ (Algún, Algunos) estudiantes necesitan trabajar.

25. A otros sólo _____ (los, les) interesa la experiencia.

Worksheet 7.8 The definite article

Some uses of the definite article differ from English.

ENGLISH:	*The book*		refers to a specific book
SPANISH:	**El** libro		refers to a book in general
EXAMPLES:	**La** madera es útil.		*Wood (not the wood) is useful.*
	El oro es caro.		*Gold (not the gold) is expensive.*

The definite article is used in telling time and in identifying days:

EXAMPLES:	Es **la** una.	*It is one o'clock.*
	Llegaron **el** martes.	*They arrived on Tuesday.*
	Les pagamos **los** viernes.	*We pay them on Fridays.*
(but)	La fiesta es *(fue, era, será)* viernes.	*The party is (was, will be) Friday.*

➤ In the blanks, supply the necessary article. If no article is required, simply place an X in the blank.

1. Según el calendario, hoy es_____ domingo.

2. Yo paso _____ domingos con mi familia.

3. Mi hermano siempre llega a _____ dos.

4. ¿Qué piensas hacer _____ domingo que viene?

5. Hoy me desperté a _____ cinco de la mañana.

6. No me levanté porque hoy es_____ sábado.

7. Yo nunca trabajo _____ sábados.

8. Me dormí otra vez y me despertaron a _____ ocho.

9. El despertador sonó a _____ siete y media.

10. Fue _____ lunes de la Semana Santa.

11. A _____ ocho y cuarto estaba en el coche.

12. A _____ una de la tarde empecé a pescar en el Lago Superior.

13. Más que nada me gusta _____ chocolate mexicano.

14. También me gustan _____ frijoles.

15. Yo cubro los frijoles con _____queso.

16. Así es _____ almuerzo mexicano.

17. _____ oro es un metal precioso.

18. Personalmente, prefiero _____ plata.

19. Ayer me compré un anillo de _____ plata.

20. Ayer era _____ viernes, ¿verdad?

21. La paloma es el símbolo de _____ paz.

22. La paloma es más tímida que _____ águila.

23. Parece que _____ paloma siempre tiene sueño.

24. _____ buho en cambio simboliza mucha sabiduría.

Worksheet 7.9 More on the definite article

Two other uses of the definite article that differ from English usage are:

1. The definite article is used with the names of languages, except after the verbs such as **aprender, estudiar, hablar, saber,** and after the preposition **en***:*

   EXAMPLE: El español es fácil, pero el ruso es difícil.
   Ya saben español, ahora quieren aprender francés.

2. Certain countries, cities and states require the definite article:

la Argentina	**el Canadá**	**la Florida**	**el Japón**	**el Perú**
el Brasil	**el Ecuador**	**La Habana**	**el Paraguay**	**la República Dominicana**
el Cairo	**los Estados Unidos**	**la India**	**La Paz**	**El Salvador**

➤ In the blanks, supply the definite article. Where no article is required, place an X in the blank.

1. Buenos Aires es la capital de _____ Argentina.

2. Pasaste cuatro meses en _____ Habana.

3. Vamos a hacer un viaje a _____ México.

4. Vivieron en _____ Perú muchos años.

5. Dicen que _____ español es el idioma más bello del mundo.

6. Después de aprender _____ español, tú piensas estudiar alemán.

7. Dicen que _____ inglés es más difícil de aprender que el francés.

8. _____ Brasil es el país más grande de Sudamérica.

9. Las cataratas del Niágara están en _____ Canadá.

10. Ellos vivían en Indiana; ahora viven en _____ Florida.

11. El señor Forti y su esposa siempre hablan en _____ italiano.

12. El año que viene van a hacer un viaje a _____ Italia.

13. El avión hace escala en _____ República Dominicana.

14. _____ inglés es un idioma práctico porque es muy comercial.

15. En cambio, _____ francés es el idioma diplomático.

16. _____ Japón se compone de varias islas.

17. Para muchos turistas _____ India es un país misterioso.

18. _____ Cairo es la capital de Egipto.

19. La civilización maya todavía vive en _____ Guatemala.

20. La unidad monetaria de _____ España es la peseta.

21. El sucre es la unidad monetaria en _____ Ecuador.

22. _____ chino es un idioma monosilábico.

Worksheet 7.10 More on the definite article

Three other special uses of the definite article include:

1. Before personal titles (except in direct address).

   EXAMPLE: Señora López, ¿conoce usted a **la** señora Medina?

2. To avoid repetition of an earlier word a definite article may become a pronoun.
   In English similar use is made of *that* and *those*.

   EXAMPLE: Tu novela es menos larga que **las** de Hemingway.

3. Instead of possessive adjectives (**mi, tu, su, nuestro**) with parts of the body or articles of clothing.

   EXAMPLES: El niño no quiere lavarse **las** manos.
                    Los boxeadores se pusieron **los** guantes.

➤ In the blanks, supply the necessary definite article. If no article is required, place an X in the blank.

1. Buenos días, _____ señora Noguera.

2. Buenos días. ¿Está en casa _____ señora Ríos?

3. Tu coche es muy bonito, _____ tío Luis.

4. Sí, pero _____ de tu padre es más nuevo.

5. ¿Por qué te pusiste _____ impermeable?

6. _____ tía Mercedes dice que va a llover.

7. ¿No te quitas _____ guantes antes de comer?

8. ¿Sí, y tú, no te quitas _____ sombrero?

9. ¿Prefieres las manzanas de Ohio o _____ del estado de Washington?

10. La fruta que me gusta más es _____ que crece en Washington.

11. ¿Es éste el libro que te prestó _____ senador Romero?

12. No, ya le devolví _____ del senador.

13. ¿Cómo te lastimaste _____ dedo pulgar?

14. Lo hice con el martillo. Voy a perder _____ uña.

15. Se escribieron muchos romances sobre _____ príncipe Arnaldos.

16. Me gusta más esa poesía sobre _____ de nuestro siglo.

17. ¿Te manchaste _____ vestido nuevo con café?

18. Sí, también me quemé _____ rodilla.

19. ¿Es ésta la compañera de _____ hermanos García?

20. No, _____ de ellos está arriba en el primer piso.

21. ¿Te vas a poner _____ corbata que te regalé?

22. No, esta otra se ve más apropiada que _____ que me compraste tú.

Worksheet 7.11 **Verbs ending in *-cer***

Verbs ending in **-cer** preceded by a vowel have **-zco** as the ending in the first person singular of the present indicative (**conozco, ofrezco**). **Hacer,** which uses **hago,** is a common exception. Useful **-cer** verbs include:

agradecer	*to thank*	**desaparecer**	*to disappear*	**obedecer**	*to obey*
aparecer	*to appear*	**enloquecer**	*to drive crazy*	**ofrecer**	*to offer*
carecer	*to lack*	**establecer**	*to establish*	**parecer**	*to seem*
complacer	*to please*	**fallecer**	*to die*	**parecerse a**	*to resemble*
conocer	*to know*	**merecer**	*to deserve*	**perecer**	*to perish*
crecer	*to grow*	**nacer**	*to be born*	**pertenecer**	*to belong*

➤ Supply the present tense of the verbs in parentheses.

1. Yo te _____ (agradecer) mucho este bonito libro.

2. Tú lo _____ (merecer) por ser estudioso.

3. Yo no _____ (conocer) al autor del libro.

4. Él _____ (pertenecer) al siglo pasado.

5. Yo siempre _____ (obedecer) a mis maestros.

6. Pero a veces yo _____ (enloquecerse) con tanta tarea.

7. Yo _____ (complacer) a la mayoría de ellos.

8. Me _____ (parecer) muy importante la educación.

9. Si hay trabajo, los perezosos _____ (desaparecer).

10. Piensan que nosotros _____ (nacer) para divertirnos.

11. En mi casa yo _____ (establecer) varias reglas.

12. La disciplina _____ (ofrecer) muchas ventajas.

13. Papa dice que yo _____ (parecerse) a mi abuelo.

14. Abuelito me _____ (parecer) mucho más alto.

15. Sin embargo, yo _____ (crecer) mucho cada año.

16. Yo no _____ (carecer) de buenos libros en mi casa.

17. Algunos bomberos _____ (fallecer) en su trabajo.

18. A veces sus nombres _____ (aparecer) en el periódico.

19. Yo _____ (reconocer) el peligro de su trabajo.

20. Yo les _____ (agradecer) la protección que nos dan.

Worksheet 7.12 Verbs ending in -*cir*

Verbs ending in **-cir** preceded by a vowel have **-zco** as the ending in the first person singular of the present indicative. **Decir,** which uses **digo,** is a common exception.

    EXAMPLES: yo produ**zco**, yo introdu**zco**

Some common **-cir** verbs include:

conducir	*to conduct*	**producir**	*to produce*
deducir	*to deduce*	**reducir**	*to reduce*
introducir	*to introduce*	**relucir**	*to glow, glitter*
inducir	*to induce*	**traducir**	*to translate*
lucir(se)	*to look (like); to show off*		

➤ Supply the correct present tense of the verbs in parentheses.

1. Cada idioma _____ (producir) este proverbio:

2. «No es oro todo lo que _____ (relucir).»

3. Yo _____ (traducir) la poesía española al inglés.

4. Yo _____ (producir) ahora el segundo tomo de poesías.

5. Juana _____ (lucir) su anillo de compromiso.

6. Ella _____ (introducir) el dedo en la jaula del pájaro.

7. Los testigos _____ (deducir) tu inocencia.

8. Ellos dicen que tú _____ (conducir) muy bien el autobús.

9. Los ejercicios _____ (producir) un cuerpo más sano.

10. Con ejercicio yo _____ (reducir) el riesgo de un ataque cardíaco.

11. Hace veinte años yo _____ (conducir) un taxi.

12. ¿Cómo _____ (lucir) con este sombrero?

13. ¿Cómo se _____ (traducir) el verbo *inducir*?

14. Yo lo _____ (traducir) con el verbo *to induce*.

15. Los lugares altos me _____ (producir) vértigo.

16. Yo _____ (reducir) el efecto con un medicamento.

17. Yo siempre _____ (introducir) un producto nuevo en la feria.

18. Nosotros _____ (producir) algo nuevo anualmente.

19. ¿Por qué _____ (relucir) tanto estos diamantes?

20. Yo los _____ (lucir) sólo en las grandes ocasiones.

21. Por la evidencia, yo _____ (deducir) que no eres culpable.

22. Además, ya sabes que yo siempre _____ (decir) la verdad.

Worksheet 7.13 *Conocer/saber*

Conocer and **saber** both mean *to know*. **Conocer** means to know in the sense of being familiar with a person or place—in other words, to be acquainted with. **Conocer** in the preterite tense means met. **Saber** means to know in the sense of knowing how to do something or to know as a fact.

EXAMPLES: **Conozco** Cuba.   *I know (am familiar with) Cuba.*
Conozco a Sara.   *I know (am acquainted with) Sara.*
Yo **sé** nadar.   *I know how to swim.*

➤ In the blanks, supply the correct form of **saber** or **conocer**, whichever is required for proper meaning.

1. Mis tíos _____ bien la ciudad de México.

2. ¿ _____ ellos también llegar a las pirámides?

3. Yo _____ muy bien a tu padre.

4. ¿ _____ usted que él era piloto durante la guerra?

5. Mi hermana _____ a muchos estudiantes mexicanos.

6. Es porque ella _____ hablarles en español.

7. Yo viví en Inglaterra, pero yo no _____ Irlanda.

8. ¿Tú _____ que Irlanda está muy cerca de Inglaterra?

9. Ayer yo _____ al senador de Arizona en una fiesta.

10. Yo no _____ que asistías a fiestas tan importantes.

11. Yo no _____ a aquel muchacho cerca del escritorio.

12. Yo tampoco _____ su nombre.

13. En mi juventud yo _____ muy bien el estado de Colorado.

14. Nosotros no _____ que viviste allí.

15. Mañana _____ al novio de mi hermana.

16. Tú pronto _____ la fecha de la boda.

17. ¿Cómo se llama ella? Yo no la _____.

18. Se llama Susana. Yo no _____ su apellido.

19. ¿Cómo _____ tú al director de la escuela?

20. Pues, ¿no _____ tú que mis hijos estudian aquí?

21. ¿ _____ usted quién es esta secretaria bonita?

22. Sí, la _____ bien. Es mi esposa.

Worksheet 7.14 Command form (imperative mood) – familiar

The affirmative familiar commands in the singular* (**tú**) form are the same as the third person singular of the present indicative tense: **habla, come, escribe.**

There are eight frequently used exceptions (all monosyllabic):

decir	**di**	**salir**	**sal**
hacer	**haz**	**ser**	**sé**
ir	**ve**	**tener**	**ten**
poner	**pon**	**venir**	**ven**

Although **tú** is always the subject of these verbs, it is usually omitted.

➤ Supply the singular imperative familiar command.

1. _____ (Hacer) las tareas en casa.

2. _____ (Estudiar) bien todos estos ejercicios.

3. _____ (Leer) los ejercicios en voz alta.

4. _____ (Escribir) una composición para mañana.

5. _____ (Esperar) hasta mañana.

6. _____ (Venir) lo más temprano posible.

7. _____ (Comprar) hoy los billetes.

8. _____ (Cerrar) la puerta al salir, por favor.

9. _____ (Ir) con ellos a la fiesta.

10. _____ (Prestar) este libro a Margarita, por favor.

11. _____ (Decir) siempre la verdad.

12. _____ (Poner) estas cosas en la gaveta de mi escritorio.

13. _____ (Tener) cuidado al pasar la calle.

14. _____ (Escribir) a la compañía sobre ese asunto.

15. _____ (Llevar) cuenta de los gastos de viaje.

16. No_____ (permitir) fumar a los alumnos en la escuela.

17. _____ (Comprar) otro escritorio igual para la otra oficina.

18. _____ (Tomar) un taxi si hay que llegar pronto.

19. _____ (Caminar) más despacio porque el piso está mojado.

20. _____ (Llevar) este paquete al correo.

21. Juan, _____ (poner) más atención durante mi explicación.

22. No_____ (mezclar) tus libros con los de Miguel.

* The plural affirmative familiar commands (**hablad, comed, escribid**) are not used in Latin America.

Worksheet 7.15 Command form (imperative mood) – polite

Both affirmative and negative polite commands in the singular form are based on the **usted** form in the present tense, except that the **-a** and **-e** endings trade places (use the first person singular stem of all present tense irregular verbs ending in **-o**):

PRESENT TENSE	ENDING EXCHANGE	POLITE COMMAND
usted habla	a to e	**hable**
usted come	e to a	**coma**
usted escribe	e to a	**escriba**
usted trae (traigo)	e to a	**traiga**
usted pone (pongo)	e to a	**ponga**
usted conduce (conduzco)	e to a	**conduzca**
usted es (soy)*	*Does not apply*	**sea**
usted está (estoy)*	*Does not apply*	**esté**
usted da (doy)*	*Does not apply*	**dé**
usted va (voy)*	*Does not apply*	**vaya**
usted sabe (sé)*	*Does not apply*	**sepa**

* There is no rule for the five irregular verbs whose first person singular does not end in **-o**. These five polite commands must be memorized.

➤ Supply the singular imperative polite command.

1. _____ (Ir) a la biblioteca para leer sobre los dinosaurios.

2. _____ (Comer) más despacio, mi hijo.

3. _____ (Dar) estos libros a la maestra, por favor.

4. _____ (Escribir) su nombre en su tarea o no recibirá una nota.

5. _____ (Cerrar) la puerta con llave al salir de casa.

6. _____ (Ser) siempre lo más aplicado posible en sus clases.

7. _____ (Traer) a su madre a la escuela mañana.

8. _____ (Estar) aquí el sábado a la una en punto de la tarde.

9. _____ (Poner) su chaqueta en el ropero.

10. _____ (Hablar) más alto al leer su informe.

11. _____ (Conducir) con más cuidado o chocará con otro coche.

12. _____ (Ir) a la farmacia con esta receta, por favor.

13. _____ (Salir) a tiempo para no llegar tarde a la escuela.

14. _____ (Pedir) más dinero a su patrón.

15. _____ (Decir) la verdad y no tiene que preocuparse.

16. _____ (Venir) a mi casa el domingo y hablaremos más.

17. _____ (Llevar) estos platos sucios a la cocina.

18. _____ (Vivir) más económicamente y tendrá más ahorros.

19. _____ (Volver) pronto a Los Ángeles e iremos a Disneylandia.

20. _____ (Hacer) menos ruido o nos echarán de la biblioteca.

21. _____ (Seguir) con estas lecciones y cantará como Plácido Domingo.

22. _____ (Pintar) esta casa y se verá mucho mejor.

Worksheet 7.16 Command form (imperative mood) – plural

In Latin America, familiar and polite commands are the same in the plural. Simply add **-n** to the singular polite command [see page 167]:

SINGULAR FAMILIAR	SINGULAR POLITE	PLURAL FAMILIAR AND POLITE
Habla más despacio.	Hable más despacio.	**Hablen** más despacio.
Come estas uvas.	Coma estas uvas.	**Coman** estas uvas.
Escribe menos cartas.	Escriba menos cartas.	**Escriban** menos cartas.
Ve a la tienda.	Vaya a la tienda.	**Vayan** a la tienda.
Ten cuidado.	Tenga cuidado.	**Tengan** cuidado.
Sé bueno.	Sea bueno.	**Sean** buenos.

➤ In the blanks, supply the polite plural command of the verb in parentheses.

1. _____ (Ir) a la pizarra con la tarea para hoy.

2. _____ (Escribir) las respuestas correctas.

3. _____ (Devolver) estas revistas a la biblioteca mañana.

4. _____ (Saludar) a la bibliotecaria de mi parte.

5. _____ (Venir) con nosotros al cine esta noche.

6. _____ (Traer) bastante dinero para comer después del cine.

7. _____ (Tomar) más café o té si quieren.

8. _____ (Pedir) un refresco para los niños.

9. _____ (Abrir) los libros de ejercicios en la página 72.

10. _____ (Tener) mucho cuidado al hacer estos ejercicios.

11. _____ (Vender) su automóvil al mejor precio posible.

12. _____ (Usar) el dinero para comprarse otro mejor.

13. _____ (Poner) los vasos mojados sobre la mesa.

14. _____ (Tener) cuidado. Se rompen fácilmente.

15. _____ (Recordar) que mañana es la fiesta de cumpleaños.

16. _____ (Invitar) a sus novias también. Hay lugar para todos.

17. _____ (Limpiar) bien la madera antes de pintarla.

18. _____ (Dar) una segunda mano a toda la casa.

19. _____ (Abrir) primero el regalo más grande.

20. _____ (Agradecer) a los abuelos su generosidad.

Worksheet 7.17 Command form (imperative mood) – with one object pronoun

If a direct object pronoun is used in an affirmative command, it is attached to the verb, forming a single word:

EXAMPLES: Cierra la puerta. **Ciérrala.**   Cierre la puerta. **Ciérrela.**
                Trae los libros. **Tráelo.**   Traiga los libros. **Tráigalos.**

➤ In the blanks, copy the verb (familiar and polite commands) and attach the appropriate pronoun. Be sure to add, if needed, a written accent mark.

1. Lleve *estos libros* al otro cuarto. _____

2. Espere *al señor Gómez* arriba en su oficina. _____

3. Haga *el trabajo* como le enseñé ayer. _____

4. Lea *el artículo* en voz alta. _____

5. Ponga *este cuaderno* en la gaveta de mi escritorio. _____

6. Pida *la cuenta* al regreso del mesero. _____

7. Limpie *las ventanas* antes de la fiesta del sábado. _____

8. Traiga *las maletas* a mi cuarto. _____

9. Ponga *los refrescos* sobre la mesa. _____

10. Espere a *la señora de Pérez* dentro de la tienda. _____

11. Compre *el anillo* para su novia. _____

12. Revise *la cuenta* antes de pagarla. _____

13. Eche *esta carta* al buzón. _____

14. Manda *las cartas* en seguida. _____

15. Cierra *la puerta* al salir del apartamento. _____

16. Lava *las cortinas y la persianas* otra vez. _____

17. Vende *los automóviles* lo más pronto posible. _____

18. Escriban *sus composiciones* con tinta, por favor. _____

19. Preparen *sus tareas* con más cuidado. _____

20. Compren *los billetes* en el centro. _____

21. Lleven *estas revistas* a sus amigos en la sala. _____

22. Lleven *al niño* con ustedes al circo. _____

Worksheet 7.18 Command form (imperative mood) – with two object pronouns

If a command has both an indirect and a direct object pronoun, the indirect object will always precede the direct, and both will be attached to the verb. Be sure to place written accent marks properly. If both pronouns begin with **l**, change the first pronoun to **se**:

EXAMPLES:
Traiga **el café** (a nosotros) ahora.   Tráiga**noslo** ahora.
Lea **el artículo** (a mí) en voz alta.   Léa**melo**.
Manda **esta carta** (a ella) en seguida.   Mánda**sela**.

➤ Change the noun and the words in parentheses to object pronouns and attach them properly to the verb.

1. Traiga _____ (a mí) el periódico.

2. Lleva _____ (a él) estos libros ahora.

3. Lean _____ (a mí) sus composiciones en voz alta.

4. Escriba _____ (a él) la carta esta tarde.

5. Traiga _____ (a nosotros) agua mineral con la comida.

6. Envíe _____ (a ella) el mensaje en seguida.

7. Dé _____ (a mí) esos papeles ahora mismo.

8. Devuelve _____ (a mí) esos papeles hoy, si puedes.

9. Lleven _____ (a ella) estas revistas, por favor.

10. Repita _____ (a él) la dirección de su oficina.

11. Diga _____ (a ellas) la verdad.

12. Lleve _____ (a ellos) las maletas a sus cuartos.

13. Abra _____ (para ella) este paquete.

14. Diga _____ (a nosotras) lo que ocurrió ayer.

15. Cuente _____ (a mí) su chiste favorito.

16. Venda _____ (a él) el carro en seguida.

17. Enseña _____ (a nosotros) tu vestido nuevo.

18. Cante _____ (para nosotros) su nueva canción.

19. Mande _____ (a mí) la cuenta de ellos.

20. Construya _____ (para ellos) una casa original.

21. Diga _____ (a los soldados) las órdenes del día.

22. Lee _____ (a mi tía) el telegrama que recibiste.

Worksheet 7.19 Command form (imperative mood) negative familiar/polite

Although object pronouns are attached to the end of affirmative commands, these same object pronouns precede the negative command and are detached from the verb. The same applies to reflexive pronouns. Note that the familiar verb form also changes in the negative, becoming the same as the affirmative polite command plus **-s**. The polite verb form, however, remains exactly the same in both affirmative and negative forms:

EXAMPLES:	AFFIRMATIVE	NEGATIVE	AFFIRMATIVE	NEGATIVE
	Tómelo ahora.	No lo tome ahora.	Dínoslas.	No nos las digas.
	Tómalo ahora.	No lo tomes ahora.	Levántate.	No te levantes.
	Díganoslas.	No nos las diga.	Dáselo.	No se lo des.

➤ Change the following affirmative commands to the negative form. Write the word **no**, the object pronoun(s), and the negative command in the spaces to the right.

1. Hágalos en la clase. _____

2. Llévalo a tu casa. _____

3. Escríbale la carta ahora. _____

4. Tráigame esa revista vieja. _____

5. Pónganlos sobre la mesa. _____

6. Enséñeselas a ella. _____

7. Quítese la chaqueta. _____

8. Ciérrelas antes de salir. _____

9. Pónganselos ahora. _____

10. Espérenme después de la clase. _____

11. Dígame lo que pasó. _____

12. Cuéntamelo ahora. _____

13. Véndemelos a buen precio. _____

14. Dígame la verdad. _____

15. Piénsalo antes de hacerlo. _____

16. Píntela de negro. _____

17. Enciéndamela ahora. _____

18. Inscríbete en ese curso. _____

19. Quítatelos antes de comer. _____

20. Repítesela al chófer. _____

21. Llévalo al cine esta tarde. _____

22. Désela al niño. _____

Worksheet 7.20 Adjectives without -o ending

As we know, adjectives ending in a consonant remain the same in both genders (**un libro fácil, una canción fácil, cursos fáciles**). Some adjectives that end in **-an, -ón,** or **-or** add **-a** to the feminine form.

EXAMPLES: burl**ón**   burlon**a**
             trabajad**or**   trabajador**a**
             hablad**or**   hablador**a**

Most adjectives of nationality must end in **-a** in the feminine regardless of the masculine ending.

EXAMPLES: francés   frances**a**
             español   español**a**

➤ In the blanks, supply the correct form of the adjectives in parentheses.

1. Elena es una muchacha muy _____ (trabajador).

2. Estos alumnos _____ (alemán) son muy aplicados.

3. La bandera _____ (español) es muy bonita.

4. Ella siempre tiene una expresión _____ (burlón).

5. En la bahía había muchos barcos _____ (inglés).

6. A mí me gusta mucho la lengua _____ (español).

7. En cambio, el idioma _____ (portugués) parece difícil.

8. Aquella muchacha alta es _____ (holandés).

9. La señora Chávez es muy _____ (hablador).

10. Mi hermana menor es muy _____ (juguetón).

11. La señora García es una mujer _____ (encantador).

12. En frente de nosotros vive una familia _____ (irlandés).

13. Tú tienes muchas amigas _____ (turco).

14. Los dos hermanos son muy _____ (trabajador).

15. Los dos alumnos nuevos son _____ (finlandés).

16. Mi máquina de coser es _____ (japonés).

17. La criada es muy _____ (hablador).

18. La película que vimos es _____ (francés).

19. La perrita es muy _____ (juguetón).

20. En esa tienda venden artículos _____ (español).

21. Ella es una artista _____ (escocés).

22. Dicen que la cerveza _____ (alemán) es mejor que ésta.

Buscapalabras

Buscapalabras grande

➤ Find 66 nouns by searching in all eight possible directions. Many spaces are used two or three times; nine are not used at all. See how many you can find before checking the list on the next page:

```
A  P  O  L  L  O  S  R  A  Q  U  E  T  A  C
R  U  I  D  O  A  N  I  L  O  C  A  Z  N  O
T  E  D  I  T  O  R  O  L  O  M  N  D  A  R
I  N  F  E  E  O  U  F  I  L  A  O  O  L  R
C  T  E  R  M  I  N  O  M  D  A  R  L  A  I
U  E  L  E  I  N  G  E  N  I  E  R  O  I  D
L  L  M  A  S  G  R  U  M  M  O  A  R  P  A
O  E  O  L  T  L  E  O  I  E  L  C  U  S  R
A  F  P  M  E  E  A  R  L  T  L  A  M  E  T
E  O  O  A  R  S  P  L  A  O  A  R  T  E  E
S  N  E  M  I  R  C  C  G  D  C  R  I  E  L
P  O  T  R  O  S  O  O  R  O  O  E  R  O  M
E  C  A  R  E  R  B  M  O  N  R  R  O  A  O
J  O  A  I  A  O  R  I  T  M  O  A  R  R  T
O  L  L  M  C  D  E  D  U  T  N  L  O  R  O
C  A  O  A  A  M  A  A  L  M  A  C  E  N  R
```

Worksheet 7.21 Rodeo de palabras

If you failed to circle all 66 nouns in the previous lesson, check the following list, then return to the puzzle to look for the words still missing. As each of those words is located, write its meaning in the blank to the right. If you do not know the meaning, check the master vocabulary.

alma _____

almacén _____

arpa _____

arte _____

artículo _____

boca _____

cama _____

carrera _____

carro _____

cobre _____

cola _____

colina _____

color _____

comida _____

coro _____

corrida _____

crimen _____

danza _____

dolor _____

editor _____

entrada _____

espejo _____

espía _____

fila _____

guitarra _____

idea _____

ingeniero _____

inglés _____

lana _____

letra _____

loro _____

lote _____

luto _____

mar _____

memoria _____

metal _____

método _____

milagro _____

milla _____

misterio _____

motor _____

nombre _____

norte _____

ola _____

olla _____

onza _____

oro _____

oso _____

poeta _____

pollo _____

primero _____

puente _____

raqueta _____

refrigerador _____

riel _____

río _____

rima _____

risa _____

ritmo _____

ruido _____

silla _____

taco _____

teléfono _____

tema _____

término _____

torre _____

Vocabulary

Vocabulary

This master vocabulary list contains all the words from the exercises in *Workbook in Everyday Spanish, Books 1* and *2*. For the cultural readings in *Book 2*, Spanish-English cognates have been omitted.

(A)

a, to, at
  a alguna parte, somewhere
  a causa de, because of
  a lo largo de, along
  a menudo, often
  a pesar de, in spite of
  a plenitud, fully
abdicar, to abdicate
abierto,-a, open
abogado,-a, lawyer
abrigo, shelter; coat
abrir, to open
abuela, abuelita grandmother, granny
abuelo, abuelito grandfather, gramps
abuelos, grandparents
aburrimiento, boredom
aburrir, to bore
aburrirse, to be bored
acabar, to finish
  acabar de…, to have just…
Acapulco, Mexican resort city
aceite (m), oil
  aceite de oliva, olive oil
aceituna, olive
acera, sidewalk
acerca de, about, concerning
acero, steel
acompañar, to accompany
acordarse, to remember
acordeón (m), accordion
acostar [ue], to put to bed
acostarse [ue], to go to bed
acta, certificate, statement
actitud (f), attitude
actor (m), actor
actriz (f), actress
actualidad (f), present time
actualmente, at present
actuar, to act, perform
acuático,-a, aquatic
acueducto, aqueduct
acuerdo, accord
de acuerdo con, in agreement with; according to
acusado,-a, accused

adecuado,-a, adequate
admirar, to admire
adornar, to adorn, to decorate
adquirir, to acquire
aeropuerto, airport
afán (m), zeal, eagerness
afectuoso, -a, affectionate
afeitar(se), to shave
aficionado, -a, fan (sports)
afilado, -a, sharp, sharpened
afilar, to sharpen
afinar, to tune (instrument)
afortunado,-a, lucky, fortunate
afuera, outside
agosto, August
agradecer [zc], to thank
agradecido, -a, thankful, grateful
agradar, to please
agrado, pleasure
agravio, offense, grievance
agregar, to add
agrícola, agricultural, farming
agricultor, -a, agriculturist, farmer
agrio,-a, sour
agua (f), water
  agua filtrada, filtered water
aguja, needle
ahogar(se), to drown
ahorrar, to save (money, time, *etc.*)
ahorros, savings (as in a bank)
ajedrez (m), chess
ajeno, -a, belonging to someone else; distant, detached
ajo, garlic
ajustar, to adjust
al, (a + el), to the, at the; upon
  al mediodía, at noon
  al revés, inside out
alabanza, praise
alarmar, to alarm
Albéniz (Isaac) (1860-1909), Spanish composer
alcachofa, artichoke
alcanzar, to reach (a place or point)
alcohol (m), alcohol
aldea, village
alegría, joy, merriment, gaiety

alemán,-ana, German
alfabeto, alphabet
alfiler (m), (straight) pin
alfombra, carpet
algazara, noise
álgebra (m), algebra
algodón (m), cotton
alguien, someone, somebody
algún, -una, algunos, -as, some
Alhambra (la), Moorish palace in Granada, Spain
allá, there, over there
allí, there
alma, soul
almacén, store
almanaque (m), calendar
almeja, clam
almirante (m), admiral
almorzar [ue], to eat lunch
almuerzo, lunch
alquilar, to rent
alrededor (de), around
alrededores, environs, surrounding area
altiplano, plateau
alto, -a, high; tall; stop, halt (sign)
altura, height
alumno, -a, pupil, student
Alvarado (Pedro de) (1485-1541), Spanish explorer
ama: ama de casa, housewife
amable, nice, friendly
amargo,-a, bitter
amarillo,-a, yellow
ambición (f), ambition
ambicioso,-a, ambitious
ambos,-as, both
ambulancia, ambulance
ameno, -a, pleasant, agreeable, nice
americano,-a, American
amigo,-a, friend
amistad (f), friendship
amplio, -a, wide; full, roomy
ancho,-a, wide
andar, to walk; to ride; to go
andino, -a, of the Andes (mountains)
ángel (m) angel
ángel de la guarda, guardian angel

angosto,-a, narrow
ángulo, angle
anillo, ring
anillo de compromiso, engagement ring
anoche, last night
anónimo,-a, anonymous
anteayer, the day before yesterday
antigüedad (f), antiquity; antique
antiguo, -a, antique, old
Antillas Mayores, Greater Antilles
antiséptico, antiseptic
año, year
año pasado, last year
anteojos (m, pl), (eye)glasses
anual, annual
anunciar, announce
apagar, to turn off
aparato, appliance; device; fixture
aparecer [zc], to appear
apariencia, appearance
apartamento, apartment (**departamento**
  in México)
apellidarse…, to have … as a last name
apellido, surname, last name
apenado, -a, embarrassed, grieved
apetito, appetite
aplaudir, to applaud
aplauso, applause
aplicado, -a, studious; industrious
aplicar, to apply
apoderarse, to overpower
apogeo, peak, height (of fame, power)
apreciar, to appreciate, to value
aprender, to learn
apretado, -a, tight, close
aprobación (f), approval
aprobar [ue], to approve; to pass (a test)
apropiado,-a, appropriate
apurarse, to be in a hurry
aquel, that (over there)
aquél, that one (over there)
aquí, here
Arango, Doroteo (Pancho Villa), (1878-
  1923) Mexican general
árbol (m), tree
  árbol navideño, Christmas tree
arboleda, grove of trees
arco, arch
  arco iris, rainbow
aretes (m), earrings
argentino,-a, Argentine, Argentinian
armario, closet
armonia, harmony
arpa (f), harp
arqueólogo,-a, archeologist
arquitecto, architect

arquitectónico,-a, architectural
arquitectura, architecture
artículo, article
artista, (m/f), artist
arreglar, to arrange, to regulate
arrodillarse, to kneel
arroyo, brook; gutter, stream
arroz (m), rice
  arroz con pollo, chicken with rice
arrugar (se), to wrinkle
arzobispo, archbishop
ascenso, ascent; rise
ascensor (m) elevator
asiento, seat
asignatura, school course, subject
asistir a …, to attend…
asombrar, to astonish, astound
aspiradora, vacuum cleaner, sweeper
asunto (m), affair
asustar, to frighten, startle
atacar, to attack
Atahualpa (1710-1756), Peruvian Indian
  chief
ataque cardíaco, heart attack
atentado, aggression
atentamente, sincerely
Atlántico, Atlantic (Ocean)
atlas (m), atlas
atraso, delay, slowness; under
  development
atravesar [ie], to cross
atribuir [y], to attribute
audiencia, audience; hearing
auditorio, auditorium
aula, classroom
aumentar, to augment, increase
aumento, increase
ausencia, absence
ausente, absent
autobús (m), bus
automóvil (m), automobile
autopista, freeway
autor,-a, author
auxilio, help, assistance
  primeros auxilios, first aid
avanzar, to advance
avenida, avenue
averiguar, to find out
avisar, to notify, advise
aviso, notice; warning
ayer, yesterday
ayuda, help, aid
ayudar, to help, to aid
azúcar (m), sugar
azufre (m), sulphur
azul, blue

bailar, to dance
bailarín,-ina, dancer
baile (m), dance
bajar, to lower
  bajar de peso, to lose weight, reduce
bajo, short; beneath
balar, to bleat
Balboa, Vasco Núñez de (1475-1517),
  Spanish explorer
balcón (m), balcony
baloncesto, basketball
ballet folklórico, folkloric ballet
banco, bank; bench
bandeja, tray (*charola* in México)
banderillero, bullfighter on foot with
  darts
bando, faction, party
bañar (se), to bathe (oneself)
bañista (m/f), bather, swimmer
barato,-a, cheap, inexpensive
bárbaro, -a, barbarous, barbaric
barbero, barber
barco, boat, ship
barraca, hut, cabin
barrer, to sweep
barrio, neighborhood, district
bastante, enough, sufficient
basura, trash, garbage
Batalla de Lepanto (1571), Battle on the
  Gulf of Corinth
bebé (m), baby
beber, to drink
beca, scholarship
béisbol (m), baseball
belicoso,-a, belligerent
belleza, beauty
bello,-a, beautiful
bellas artes, fine arts
Benalcázar, Sebastián de (1480- 1551), a
  Spanish conqueror of Peru
beneficio, benefit, profit
Biblia, Bible
biblioteca, library
bibliotecario,-a, librarian
bicicleta, bicycle
bien, well
bienes raíces, real estate
bilingüe, bilingual
billete (m) ticket; bill (currency) (*boleto* in
  México)
biología, biology
blanco,-a, white
Blasco Ibáñez, Vicente (1867-1928),
  Spanish novelist

blusa, blouse
boca, mouth
boda, wedding
bodega, cellar, warehouse; grocery store
Bogotá, capital of Colombia
boleto, ticket (México)
bolígrafo, ball-point pen
boliviano,-a, Bolivian
bolsillo, pocket
bomba, bomb; pump
bombero, firefighter
bombones, chocolates, candy
bondadoso, -a, good, kind
bonito,-a, pretty
borrador (m), eraser; first draft
borrar, to erase
bostezar, to yawn
botiquín (m) de emergencia, first aid kit
botín (m), button
boxeo, boxing
Brasil, Brazil
brasileño,-a, Brazilian
breve, brief, short
    en breve, in short; soon
brillante, brilliant
brincar, to jump, skip
brindis (m) toast (as with wine)
bromear, to joke
bruja, witch
brujo, sorcerer
buen (o), -a, good
Buenos Aires, capital of Argentina
bufanda, scarf
bujías, spark plugs
búho (m) owl
bulevar (m) boulevard
burlón, -ona, fond of pranks
buscapalabras (m), word-search puzzle
buscar, to look for, to search (for)
buzón (m), mail box
    echar al buzón, to mail

C

cabalgar, to ride (a horse)
caballo, horse
cabecera, head (table or bed)
cabeza, head
Cabeza de Vaca, Álvar Núñez (1500-1560), Spanish explorer
cable (m) cable; rope, line
cacahuate/cacahuete (m), peanut
cacique (m), Indian chief
cada, each
    cada vez, each (every) time

caer, to fall
    caerse, to fall down
    dejar caer, to drop, let drop
café (m) coffee; coffee shop
cajetilla, small box, pack (of cigarettes)
calculadora, calculator
cálculo, calculus; calculation
Calderón de la Barca, Pedro (1600-1681), Spanish dramatist
calendario, calendar
calentar [ie], to heat, warm up
cálido, -a, warm; hot
caliente, hot
calificar, to qualify
    calificar papeles, to grade papers
caló (m), Gypsy dialect; jargon
calor (m) heat; warmth
    tener calor, to be hot
calle (f), street
cama, bed
cámara, camera: chamber
camarero,-era, waiter/waitress
cambiar, to change, to exchange
    cambiar un cheque, to cash a check
cambio, change (money)
    en cambio, on the other hand
camelia, camellia
camello, camel
caminar, to travel, to walk
camino, road
camión (m), truck
camioneta, station wagon
camisa, shirt
campana, bell
campeón,-ona, champion
campo, field, country; camp
Canadá (m), Canada
canasta, basket
cancelar, to cancel
canción , song
cancionero, -a, collection of songs
candidato,-a, candidate
canela, cinnamon
canoa, canoe
cansado,-a tired
cansarse, to grow tired
cantante (m/f), singer
cantar, to sing
cántaro, pitcher, vessel, jug
    llover a cántaros, to rain cats and dogs
Cantinflas (Mario Moreno) (1911-1993), Mexican comic actor
cantor (m), singer
cañón (m), cannon; canyon
capaz, capable

capital capital (city); funds
capitán (m) captain
capítulo, chapter
captura, capture, seizure
carabela, caravela, old sailing ship
características, characteristics
Caracas, capital of Venezuela
carcajadas, loud laughs
    echarse a carcajadas, to burst out laughing
cárcel jail, prison
carecer [zc], to lack
cari (m), curry
caribe, of or from the Caribbean
caricatura, cartoon, caricature
cariñoso,-a, affectionate
carne (f), meat, flesh
carnicero, butcher
caro, -a, dear; expensive
carpintería, carpentry
carpintero, carpenter
carta, letter
cartera, wallet, billfold; briefcase; handbag
cartero, letter-carrier
carrera, career; race
carretera, highway
casa, house
casarse, to get married
casi, almost
caso, case; event, occurrence
    hacer caso (de), to pay attention (to)
castellano,-a, Castilian
castigar, to punish
catalán,-ana, from Cataluña, Spain; also language of the region
catarro, head cold
catástrofe , catastrophe
catedral (f), cathedral
católico,-a, Catholic
catorce, fourteen
cautela, caution
cazador (m), hunter
cazar, to hunt
cebada, barley
celebración , celebration
célebre, famous, noted
celos, jealousy
    tener celos, to be jealous
celoso,-a, jealous
cenar, to eat dinner, dine
centeno, rye
centroamericano, -a, Central- American
cepillar(se), to brush
cerca, fence, hedge
cerca (de), near, close by

cercano,-a near

cereza, cherry

Cervantes: Miguel de Cervantes Saavedra (1547-1616), Spanish author

cerrajero, locksmith

cerrar [ie], to close, shut

cerrar con llave, to lock

césped (m), grass, lawn, (*zacate* [m] in México)

cesta, basket

ceviche, appetizer of raw fish marinated (in lemon juice)

chachachá (m), chachacha (dance)

chaqueta, jacket

charca, pond, pool

charreada, Mexican display of horsemanship

charro, Mexican horseman; dancer of *jarabe tapatío*

cheque (m), check

cheque de viajero, traveler's check

chica, girl

chico, boy

chico, -a, small,

chícharos, dried peas (México)

chileno,-a, Chilean

chimpancé (m), chimpanzee

china poblana, Mexican national costume; female dancer of the *jarabe tapatío*

chino,-a, Chinese

chismear, to gossip

chiste (m), joke

chistoso, -a, funny, amusing

chocar (con), to crash (into)

chocolate (m), chocolate

chofer (m), driver

chuleta de cerdo, pork chop

churrigueresco, -a, Churrigueresque (ornate architectural style)

cicatriz (f), scar

cicatrizar, to heal

cielo, sky

cien, (one) hundred

ciencia, science

científico,-a, scientific

cierto, -a, certain; true

cigarrillos, cigarettes, (*cigarros* in México)

cilantro, coriander

cilindro, cylinder

cima, summit, top

cinc (m), zinc

cinco, five

cincuenta, fifty

cine (m), movie (theater), motion picture

cinematografía, cinematography

cinturón (m), belt

circo, circus

círculo, circle; club

circunstancia, circumstance

cirquero, circus performer

ciruela, plum

cirujano, surgeon

cita, date, appointment

ciudad, city

civilización , civilization

claro, -a, clear, light; of course!

clase (f), class

clásico,-a, classical

clavado, dive (in swimming)

clavel (m), carnation

clavo, nail (carpentry); clove (spice)

claxon (m), automobile horn

clérigo, clergyman

clima (m), climate

club (m), club

cobrar, to charge (money), to collect (a bill)

cobre (m), copper

cocer [ue], to cook, boil

cocina, kitchen, cuisine

cocinero,-a, cook

coche (m), automobile, car; baby carriage

cochecito, small car; baby carriage

cohete (m), skyrocket; firecracker

col (m), cabbage

cola, tail; glue

colección (f), collection

coleccionar, to collect

colesterol (m), cholesterol

colina, hill

colombiano,-a, Colombian

colorado, -a, red; red-faced, blushing

combate (m), combat

comedia, comedy; stage play (Spain)

comentario, commentary

cometer, to commit

cómico, -a, comic(al), funny; comedian

comida, meal; dinner, banquet

comienzo, beginning

como, as, since, because

como, cómo, how

cómodo,-a, comfortable

compañero, -a, companion, pal; associate, colleague

compasión , compassion, pity

competencia, competition

competir [i], to compete

complacer [y], to please; to accommodate

completar, to complete

cómplice (m/f), accomplice

componer, to compose

componerse (de), to be made of

composición (f), composition

compositor (m), composer

comprador (m), buyer, shopper

comprar, to buy, to purchase

comprender, to understand; to comprise

computadora, computer

comunicar, to communicate

comunidad , community

con, with

con ganas, willingly, eagerly

concierto, concert

concluir (y), to conclude

concurso, contest; race, competition

condecorar, to decorate, award (medal, honor, etc.)

condición (f), condition

condimentos, seasonings

conducir [zc], to conduct, to drive

conducta, conduct, behavior

conejo, rabbit

confianza, confidence, trust; informality

conjunto, group; rock group

conmigo, with me

conocer [zc], to be acquainted with

conocido,-a, well-known, distinguished

conquistador (m), conqueror

conseguir [i], to get, obtain

consejo, advice, counsel

considerar, to consider

consiguiente, consequent

por consiguiente, consequently

constar (de), to consist (of)

construcción (f), construction

construir [y], to construct

consulado, consulate

contar [ue], to count; to tell

contador, -ora, accountant; meter (gas, water)

contagio, contagion, infection

contener [ie], to contain

contento, -a, gay, joyful; satisfied

contestar, to answer

contienda, struggle, contest

contigo, with you (informal)

contraer matrimonio, to marry, get married

contratar, to contract, to hire

conversar, to converse, chat

convertir (se) [ie], to change, convert

cooperar, to cooperate

cooperativo,-a, cooperative
copiar, to copy
copista (m/f), copyist, copier
copla, verse; popular ballad
corbata, necktie
corcho, cork
cordial, friendly, pleasant
cordillera, mountain range
coro, chorus, choir
coronel (m), colonel
cortar, to cut; to sever
cortarse el pelo, to get a haircut
corte (f), court
Cortés, Hernán (1485- 1547),
    Spanish explorer/conqueror of
    México
cortés, courteous, polite
cortina, curtain
correcto,-a, correct
corregir [i], to correct
correo, mail
    (por) correo aéreo, (by) air mail
correr, to run
corrida de toros, bullfight
costo (de la vida), cost (of living)
corriente, current; common
coser, to sew
costarricense (m/f), Costa Rican
costumbre (f), custom, habit
cotidiano,-a, daily
crecer [zc], to grow; to increase
creciente, increasing, growing
criada, maid, servant
crímen (m) crime
criollo,-a, Creole
cristal (m), (pane of) glass
Cristóbal Colón, Christopher Columbus
criticar, to criticize
crucigrama (m), crossword puzzle
crudeza, rawness; roughness
cruzar, to cross
Cruz Roja, the Red Cross
cuaderno, notebook
cuadro, picture, painting
cual, which (one)
cualquiera, whichever
cuando, when
    de vez en cuando, from time to time
cuantioso, abundant, substantial
cuarto, room; (one) fourth
    cuarto de baño, bathroom
cuates, twins; pal (Mexico only)
cuatro, four
cubano,-a, Cuban
cubeta, pail, bucket

cubierta, covering; bedspread; ship deck;
    book jacket
cubierto, place setting; past participle of
    cubrir
cubito de hielo, ice cube
cubrir, to cover
cuchara, spoon
cuchillo, knife
cuenta, account, bill
cuerpo, body
cueva, cave
¡Cuidado!, (Be) careful!
cuidadoso,-a careful
culpable, guilty
cultivar, to cultivate, grow
cultivo, cultivation, crop
cumbre (f), top, summit
cumpleaños, birthday
cumplir, to fulfill; to comply
    cumplir años, to have a birthday
cuñada, sister-in-law
cuñado, brother-in-law
curiosidad (f), curiosity
curso, course
cuyo,-a, whose

D

daltonismo, color-blindness
damas, ladies; damas chinas, Chinese
    checkers
danza, dance
daño, harm, damage, injury
dar, to give
    dar cuerda, to wind (as a watch)
    dar gracias, to thank, express gratitude
    dar risa, to be laughable
dátil, (m) date (fruit)
dato, fact
de, of, from
    de una u otra, from (of) one or the
    other
debajo (de), under
deber, to owe; should
debido a, owing to, due to
débil, weak
decaer, decline, depress
decisión (f), decision
declamar, to declaim, to recite poetry
decorar, to decorate, trim, adorn
dedicar, to dedicate
dedo, finger
    dedo pulgar, thumb
deducir [zc], to deduce; to deduct
defender (se) [ie], to defend (oneself)

dejar, to leave, to let
dejar de, to stop (doing)
del, of the [de + el]
delantal (m), apron
deleitar, to delight; to amuse
deletreo, spelling
delito, crime, offense
demás: los demás, the rest, the others
demasiado, -a, too much (pl), too many
demostrar [ue], to demonstrate
dentadura, denture; set of teeth
dentista (m/f), dentist
dentro (de), inside
depender (de), to depend (on)
dependiente (m/f), store clerk
deporte (m), sport
deporte acuático, water sport
derecha, right (hand, direction)
    a la derecha to the right
derribar, to knock down, overthrow
desafortunado,-a, unfortunate, unlucky
desagradar, to displease
desaguar, to drain, empty
desaparecer [zc], to disappear
desastre (m), disaster
desayunar (se), to eat breakfast
descansar, to rest
descanso, rest
desconocer (zc), to not know, be
    ignorant of
describir, to describe
descubrir, to discover
descubridor, discoverer
descubrimiento, discovery
desde, since, from
    desde hace … años, … years ago
desdichado,-a, unhappy
desear, to want, to desire
desembarcar, to disembark, to land
desembocar, to flow into
desesperado,-a, desperate
desfilar, to parade, to march
desfile (m), parade
desgraciadamente, unfortunately
desgraciado,-a, unfortunate
desierto, desert
desnudo,-a, naked
desnudarse, to get undressed
despachar, to send, dispatch
despedida, farewell
despedida de soltera, bridal shower
despedirse [i] (de), to say goodbye (to)
despegar, to take off (aircraft)
despensa, pantry, larder
despertador (m), alarm clock

despertar (se) [ie], to wake up

después, after(wards)

destacar, to stand out; emphasize

destreza, skill

destruir [y], to destroy

detalle (m), detail

detenidamente, carefully

deuda, debt

devolver [ue], to return (something)

devuelto, returned, sent back (from devolver)

día (m), day

  de día, by day, in the daytime

  Día de los Inocentes, April Fool's Day (held December 28)

  Día de los Muertos, Halloween (Mexico only)

diamante (m), diamond

diariamente, daily

diapositiva, slide

Diario, daily; Daily, popular name for newspapers

dibujante (m/f), draftsman, designer, cartoonist

dibujar, to draw

diccionario, dictionary

diciembre, December

dicho, saying; -a, a forementioned (from verb decir)

dichoso, -a, happy; fortunate

dictador (m), dictator

dictar, to dictate

dieciséis, sixteen

diez, ten

difícil, difficult

dificultad (f), difficult

digno, -a, worthy; dignified

diligente, diligent; industrious

dineral (m), fortune, a lot of money (colloq.)

dinero, money

dinosaurio, dinosaur

director, -a, director, principal

disco, (phonograph) record, disc

disco compacto, compact disc

disculpa, excuse

disculpar, to excuse

discurso, discourse, speech

discusión (f), argument, discussion

discutir, to discuss; to argue

disfraz (m), costume, disguise

disgustar, to displease, to be displeasing

dislocar, to dislocate, sprain

Disneylandia, Disneyland

disparate (m), nonsense, big mistake

disponible, available

distinguir, to distinguish

distraído,-a, distracted

distribuir [y], to distribute

divertido,-a, fun

divertir [ie], to amuse

divertirse [ie], to have a good time

dividir, to divide

doblar, to double; to fold

doce, twelve

doctor,-ora, doctor

dólar (m), dollar

doler [ue], to hurt, ache, feel pain

dolor (m), pain

doméstico, -a, tame; domestic

domingo, Sunday

domingo de Pascua, Easter Sunday

don, mister (with first name)

donde, dónde, where,

dondequiera, wherever

Don Juan Tenorio, a popular Spanish drama

dormir [ue], to sleep

dos, two

dos veces, twice

dosis , dose

drama (m), drama

dramático,-a, dramatic

dramaturgo, dramatist

duda, doubt

  sin duda, without a doubt

dudoso, -a, doubtful, dubious

dueño, -a, owner, boss

duo, duet,

dulce, sweet; dessert

duplicar, to dliplicate, double

durante, during

duro, -a, hard, difficult

E

e, and (before [i] sound)

económico,-a, economical

echar, to throw, to toss, put out

  echar de menos, to miss (someone or something)

echarse a reír, to burst out laughing

edad, age; ¿Qué edad tienes? How old are you?

  Edad Media, Middle Ages

edificio, building

Edison, Thomas Alva (1847- 1931), American inventor

educado, -a, educated, refined

egipcio,-a, Egyptian

Egipto, Egypt

ejercicio, exercise

el, the (masculine)

él, he

electricidad (f) electricity

eléctrico,-a, electric

elefante (m) elephant

eliminar, to eliminate

elogiado,-a praised

ella, she

ellas, they (feminine)

ellos, they

embarcarse, to board (as a ship)

emergencia, emergency

emocionado, -a, moved; thrilled

empaquetar, to pack(age)

empeño, determination, tenacity

  casa de empeño, pawnshop

empeorar, to make worse, worsen

emperador (m), emperor

empezar [ie], to begin, start

en, in, on

  en aquel entonces, at that time, in those days

  en cambio, on the other hand

  en cuanto a …, as for …

  en ninguna parte, nowhere

  en punto, on the dot (time),

  en seguida, right away

  en voz alta, aloud, in a loud voice

enamorarse (de), to fall in love (with)

encantado,-a, charmed, enchanted, delighted

encantar, to enchant, to charm

encanto, charm, enchantment

encargarse de, to take charge of

encogerse de hombros, to shrug one's shoulders

encontrar [ue], to meet, to encounter; to find

enero, January

enfadarse, to become angry

enfermera,-o, nurse

enfermo, -a, sick, ill; sick person

enfriar, to chill, make cold

engordar, to grow fat, to gain weight

enloquecer [zc], to drive crazy

enloquecerse [zc], to go crazy

enojado,-a, angry

enojar, to anger

enojarse, to become angry

enorme, enormous

ensalada, salad

  ensalada de papas, potato salad

ensayista (m/f) essayist
ensayo, essay; rehearsal
escocés, -esa, Scottish, Scotch
enseñar, to teach; to show
ensuciarse, to soil, to get dirty
entero,-a, entire
entrar, to enter
entre, between
entregar, to deliver; to surrender
entrenador, -ora, coach, trainer
entrenamiento, training, coaching
entrenar, to train, to coach
entrevista, interview
entusiasmo, enthusiasm
envidiar, to envy, to be envious
epistolar, in the form of letters or epistles
época, period (of time), epoch
equipaje (m) luggage
equipo, team (sports); equipment
equivocación (f) error, mistake
equivocarse, to be wrong
error (m) error, mistake
escala, port of call, stopover
  hacer escala, to make a stop, lay over (in travel)
escaleras, stairs
escena, scene
esclavo,-a, slave
escoger, to choose
escolar, pertaining to school
esconder, to hide, conceal
escopeta, shotgun
escribir, to write
  escribir a máquina, to type(write)
escrito, -a, written; past participle of escribir
espacio, space
especializarse, to specialize
escritorio, desk
escuchar, to listen
escuela, school
esculpir, to sculpt
espacio, space
España, Spain
español,-ola, Spanish
espantar, to frighten
espanto, fear, fright
espantoso,-a, frightening
especialidad (f), specialty,
especializar, to specialize
espejo, mirror
esperar, to wait (for)
espía, spy
espinacas, spinach
esposa, wife

esposo, husband
esposos, husband and wife
esquiar, to ski
estable, stable, steadfast, firm
establecer [zc], to establish
estación (f), season (of year); station
estado, state
Estados Unidos, United States
estallar, to burst, explode, erupt
estante (m), (book)shelf
estaño, tin
estar, to be
  estar de acuerdo, to agree
  estar de vuelta, to be on the way back
  estar enfermo, -a, to be sick
estatal, pertaining to the state
estatua, statue
este, esta, esto, this
éste, ésta, this one
estilo, style
estómago, stomach
estornudar, to sneeze
estrecho, -a, narrow; strait (geography)
estrella, star
estudiante (m/f), student, pupil
estudiar, to study
estudioso, -a, studious; (m/f) scholar
estufa, stove
Europa, Europe
europeo,-a, European
evitar, to avoid, to evade
examen (m), exam, examination, test
excelente, excellent
excluir [y], to exclude
excursión , excursion, hike, trip
exhibición , exhibit
éxito, success
  tener éxito, to be successful
explicación (f), explanation
explicar, to explain
exportación (f), export
exposición , exhibition
expulsar, to expel
extranjero,-a, foreigner
extrañar, to seem strange; to miss, pine for
extraño,-a, strange
extraviado, -a, lost, missing

F

fábrica, factory
fácil, easy
facultad (f) de medicina, college of medicine,"med school"
fachada, façade
faja, strip, band, sash
falda, skirt; foothill
falta, lack (of); fault; error
faltar, to lack; to be missing
  faltar a clase, to be absent from class, "cut class"
fama, fame, reputation
familia, family
familiar, close relative; familiar
famoso,-a, famous
fantasma (m), ghost, phantom
fascinar, to fascinate
favorito,-a, favorite
fecundo,-a, fertile
fecha, date
felicitar, to congratulate
feliz, happy
femenino,-a, feminine
fenicio,-a, Phoenician
feo,-a, ugly
feria, fair, bazaar
feroz, ferocious, wild
ferviente, fervent, ardent
ferroviario, -a, pertaining to railroads, railway
fiebre (f), fever
fiel, faithful
fiesta, party, festival
filósofo, philosopher
filtrado,-a, filtered
finca, country estate, farm
fila, row, line
fin (m), end;
  a fines de, at the end of (date)
fingir, to feign, pretend
Finlandia, Finland
fino, -a, fine, good
firmar, to sign
físico,-a, physical
flaco,-a, thin
flamenco, pertaining to Spanish gypsies (music, dance)
flecha, arrow
flor (f), flower
florecer [zc], to flower, bloom, flourish
florero, vase
flota, fleet
fluir [y], to flow

folklórico,-a, folkloric
fomentar, to encourage, promote
fonógrafo, phonograph, record player
fondos, funds
forma, form; shape
formal, formal; reliable
formar, to form; to shape
forzado, -a, forced; strained
foto (f) photo
fotografía, photograph
fracasar, to fail, be unsuccessful
fracaso, failure
fragancia, fragrance
fragua, melting furnace
frambuesa, raspberry
francés,-esa, French
Francia, France
frase (f) sentence, phrase
frecuencia, frequency
  con frecuencia, frequently
frecuente, frequent
fregar [ie], to scrub, wash (dishes)
frenos, brakes
frente (f) , forehead
frente (m), front
  en frente de, in front of
fresco, -a, fresh, cool; cheeky, brazen
frío,-a, cold
  tener frío, to feel cold
frito,-a, fried
fruta, fruit
fuego, fire; light (flame)
  fuegos artificiales, fireworks
fuente (m), fountain; source; platter
  pluma de fuente, fountain pen
fuerte (m), fort, strong
fumador,-a, smoker
fumar, to smoke
fundador,-a, founder
fútbol (m), football
futbolista (m/f), football player
fusilar, to shoot, execute

Ⓖ

gabinete (m), cabinet; office
galardón (m), reward, prize
gallego,-a, Galician
galleta, cracker, cookie
gallina, hen
ganancia, earning, profit, gain
ganar, to gain, to earn; to win
ganarse la vida, to earn a living
ganas: tener ganas de …, to feel like…
gancho, hook; hairpin; lure

garaje (m), garage
garantizar, to guarantee
garganta, throat; gorge, ravine
gastador,-a, spender, spendthrift
gastar, to spend
gastos, expenditures, outlay
gato, -a, cat; (m) jack (lifting tool)
gaviota, (sea)gull
gelatina, gelatin
gemelos, -as, twins; (m), binoculars; cuff
  links
género, kind, class
generosidad (f), generosity
gente (f), people
geografía, geography
gerente, manager, director
gimnasia, gymnastics
ginebra, gin; **Ginebra,** Geneva, city in
  Switzerland
gitano,-a, gypsy
glándula, gland
gobernador,-ora, governor
gobierno, government
golondrina, swallow
gordo, -a, fat; (m/f), fat person
grabado, -a, recorded (as on tape)
grabar, to engrave; to record (as on tape)
gracioso, -a, funny; graceful
graduado, -a, graduate, graduated
graduarse, to graduate
gramática, grammar
gran, great, large (before a noun)
grande, large, great
grato, -a, pleasant, pleasing
gratis, free
griego,-a, Greek
grifo, faucet
gripe (f), flu, influenza
gris, gray
gritar, to shout
grito, shout, cry
grúa, derrick; tow truck
grueso, -a, thick; fat
grupo, group
guantes (m), gloves
guapo, -a, handsome; bold, brave
guardar, to save, to keep, to guard
  guardar cama, to stay in bed
  gubernativo, -a, pertaining to the
  government
guerra, war
  Guerra Civil, Civil War
guerrillero,-a, guerrilla
guisantes (m), peas
guitarra, guitar

gusano, worm
gustar, to be pleasing, to please, delight

Ⓗ

habitación (f), room, bedroom
habitante (m/f), inhabitant
hábito, habit, custom
hablador,-a, talkative
hablar, to speak
hacendado, landowner; rancher
hacer, to make, to do
  hacer caso, to pay attention
  hacer escala, to have a stop- over or lay-
  over (in travel)
hacia, toward
hacienda, (country) estate, ranch
hacha, hatchet
hada, fairy
halagar, to please, flatter
hallar (se), to find; to be located
hamaca, hammock
hambre (m), hunger
hambriento,-a, hungry
haragón, -ona, idler, loafer
hasta, until
hay, there is, there are
hazaña, feat, exploit, deed
hecho, fact; past participle of *hacer*
hegemonía, leadership, national
  dominance
helado, ice cream
helicóptero, helicopter
heredar, to inherit
heredero,-era, heir(ess)
hermana, sister
hermano, brother
hermoso,-a, beautiful
héroe (m), hero
heroína (f), heroine
hiedra/yedra, ivy
higiene (f), hygiene
hija, daughter; dear girl
hijastro, step-son
hijo, son; dear boy
hilo, thread
hipnotizar, to hypnotize
hipódromo, race track
hispanoamericano, -a, relative to a part
  of America where Spanish is spoken
hispanoparlante (m/f), Spanish speaker
historia, history, story
historiador,-a, historian
histórico, -a, historic, historical
hogar (m), home

hogareño, -a, homey, pertaining to the home
hoja, leaf; sheet (of paper)
hojalata, tin(plate)
holandés,-esa, Dutch
holgazón, -ana, lazy (person)
hombre (m), man
hombro, shoulder
　encogerse de hombros, to shrug one's shoulders
honesto, -a, honest, upright
honor (m), honor
honradez , honesty
honrado, -a, honest, trustworthy
hora, hour
hormigón (m), concrete
horno, oven
hospital (m), hospital
hotel (m), hotel
hoy, today
　hoy día, nowadays, these days
hubo, there was, there were
huelga, labor strike
huerta/huerto, garden, orchard
hueso, bone
huevos, eggs
　huevos rancheros, fried eggs with tortilla and chile sauce
huir [y], to flee
humorístico, -a, humorous, funny
hundirse, to sink

Ⓘ

ibérico,-a, Iberian
iberoamericano, -a, related to the Iberian Peninsula and America; speaker of American, Spanish or Portuguese
idéntico,-a, identical
idioma (m), language
iglesia, church
imitar, to imitate
impermeable (m), raincoat
imponente, imposing, impressive, stately
imponer, to impose
importancia, importance
importante, important
importar, to be important; to import (from abroad)
impresionar, to impress
imprimir, to print
inaugurar, to inaugurate
incluir [y], to include
incorrecto,-a, incorrect
increíble, incredible
indeseable, undesirable

indio,-a, Indian
industrializar, to industrialize
infancia, infancy
influenza, influenza, flu
influir [y], to influence
informado,-a, informed
informe (m), report
ingeniero,-a, engineer
Inglaterra, England
inglés,-esa, English
ingrediente (m), ingredient
inmigración (f), immigration
inocencia, innocence
inocente, innocent
inolvidable, unforgettable
inquilino, -a, tenant, lessee
inspeccionar, to inspect
inspirar, to inspire
instrucción, instruction
instruir [y], to instruct
insuficiente, insufficient
insufrible, unbearable
inteligente, intelligent
intentar, to attempt, try
interés (m), interest
interesante, interesting
interesar, to interest
intérprete (m/f) interpreter
interrogar, to interrogate
interrumpido,-a, interrupted
interrumpir, to interrupt
invención (f) invention
invento, invention
inventor (m), inventor
invierno, winter
inversión (f), investment
invertir [i], to invest; to invert
investigar, to investigate
ir, to go
irse, to leave
Irlanda, Ireland
Isabel, Elizabeth
isla, island
istmo, isthmus
Italia, Italy
italiano,-a, Italian
izquierda, left

Ⓙ

jaialai (m), Basque ball game
jaleo, spree, racket, fuss
jamás, never
Japón, Japan
japonés,-esa, Japanese
jarabe tapatío, Mexican Hat Dance

jardín (m), garden
jardinero, gardener
jaula, cage
jefatura, leadership; headquarters
jinete (m/f), rider, horseman
jirafa, giraffe
jota, Spanish dance; letter [j]
joven (m/f), young, young person
joya, jewel
joyería, jewelry
joyero, jeweler
jubilarse, to retire (from working)
juego, game
juez (m), judge
jugada, play (sports)
jugador (m) player; gambler
juglar (m), minstrel
jugo, juice
juguete (m) toy
juguetón,-ona, playful
julio, July
junio, June
junto a, next to
juntos, together
juventud (f) youth

Ⓚ

kilo, kilogram
kilómetro (cuadrado), (square) kilometer

Ⓛ

la, the (fem. article); you, her, it (pronoun)
La Habana, Havana (Cuba)
labio, lip
laboratorio, laboratory
labrado, carved; wrought
labriego, -a, farmhand, peasant
ladrar, to bark
ladrón,-ona, thief
lago, lake
lámpara, lamp
lana, wool
lanzador (m), pitcher (baseball)
lanzar, to throw, fling, pitch, hurl
La Paz, seat of government of Bolivia
lápiz (m), pencil
largo,-a, long
las, the (fem. article); you, them (pronoun)
lastimado, -a, injured, hurt
lastimar, to injure, hurt
lastimarse, to get hurt
latino, -a, Latin; (person) who speaks a Romance language
lavado,-a, washed

lavadora, washing machine (clothes or dishes)
lavandera, laundress
lavar, to wash
lazar, to lasso, rope
Lazarillo de Tormes, anonymous Spanish picaresque novel
lealta , loyalty
lección (f) lesson
lectura, reading
leche (f), milk
leer, to read
legumbres (f), vegetables
lejos (de), far (from)
lengua, tongue; language
  lengua extranjera, foreign language
  lenguas romances, Romance languages
lentes (m), lenses, eyeglasses
lentitud (t) slowness
león,-ona, lion
Lepanto, Corinthian Gulf battle site where Cervantes was wounded (1571)
letra, letter (of alphabet); lyrics (of a song)
levantarse, to get up, to rise
ley (f), law
libertad (f) , liberty
libra, pound (measurement)
librería, bookstore
libro, book
licencia, license
liderato, leadership
lienzo de charreadas, field where charros perform
ligero, -a, light (in weight); swift
limón (m), lemon, lime (in Latin America and Spain)
limonada, lemonade
limpiar, to clean
limpio,-a, clean
lindo,-a, pretty
línea, line; stripe; queue
lío, mess, snarl
Lisboa, Lisbon (Portugal)
lista, list; menu
listo, -a, ready; clever
llamar, to call
llamarse, to be named
llano, plain
llano, -a, level, smooth, even
llanta, tire (vehicle)
llave (f), key (for locking); faucet
llegar, to arrive
llenar, to fill
lleno,-a, full
llevar, to carry

llover [ue], to rain
llover a cántaros, to rain cats and dogs
lluvia -as, rain
lluvioso, -a, rainy
lo, it
  lo opuesto, the opposite
lobo, wolf
localizar, to locate
Londres, London, capital of England
loción, lotion
lograr, to manage (to)
Lope de Vega, Félix (1562-1635), Spanish dramatist
loro, parrot
los, the (masc. article); you, them (pronouns)
lote (m), lot (plot of land)
  lote de estacionamiento, parking lot
lotería, lottery
loza, china, crockery
lucir [zc], to shine; to show off
lucha, struggle
luchar, to struggle, to fight, to wrestle
lugar (m), place
  tener lugar, to take place
lujoso,-a, luxurious
luna, moon
lunes (m), Monday
luto, mourning
  estar de luto, to be in mourning
luz , light
  luz eléctrica, electric light

Ⓜ

macizo, -a, solid, pure (metals)
madera, wood, lumber
madre (f), mother
Madrid, capital of Spain
madrileño, -a, of or from Madrid
madrugada, dawn, daybreak
madrugar, to get up early
maestría, mastery; teacher's degree
maestro,-a, teacher
maíz, (m), corn
majadería, silliness
majestad (f), majesty
malagueño, -a, of or from Málaga (Spain)
maleta, suitcase
(La) Malinche or **Doña Marina,** Aztec woman interpreter and companion of Cortés
mamá, mother
mandar, to send
manecilla, hand (clock or watch)
manejar, to drive; to govern

manera, manner, means; method, mode
manganeso, manganese
manifestación, demonstration, rally
mano (f), hand
mantel (m), tablecloth
mantequilla, butter
manzana, apple
mañana, tomorrow
mapa (m), map
máquina, machine
  máquina de coser, sewing machine
  máquina de escribir, typewriter
mar (m), sea
margarina, margarine
mariachi (m), mariachi, Mexican musical group
marinero, sailor
mariscos, shellfish
martes (m), Tuesday
Martí, José, (1853- 1895), Cuban poet and liberator
martillo, hammer
marzo, March
Marruecos, Morocco
más, more
masa, dough
masculino,-a, masculine
masticar, to chew
matador (m), matador; killer
matar, to kill
matemáticas, mathematics
materia, (school) subject; material, stuff
matrimonio, marriage; married couple
maullar, meow (cat)
máximo,-a, maximum
mayo, May
mayor, older; larger; greater
mayoría, majority
me, directly or indirectly involving me
mecánico, mechanic
mecánico,-a, mechanical
medalla, medal
mediados: a mediados de, in the middle of (time)
medianoche (f), midnight
mediante, by means of
medicamento, medication
medicina, medicine
médico, physician, doctor
medio,-a, half
mediodía (m), noon
medir [i], to measure
mejor, better, best
mellizo,-a, twin
memorizar, to memorize

mencionar, to mention
menor, younger; smaller
  el menor, la menor, the youngest
menos, minus, less, least
mensaje (m), message
mentira, lie, falsehood
menudo, -a, tiny, very slim
  a menudo, often
menú (m), menu
mercado, market
mermelada, marmalade
mes (m), month
mesa, table
meseta, plateau
mestizo,-a, half-breed
meta, goal
mexicano,-a, Mexican
mezcla, mixture, blend
mezclar, to mix
mezquita, mosque
mi, my
mí, me (as object of prepositon)
microbio, microbe
miedo, fear
  tener miedo, to be afraid
miembro (m/f), member
mientras, while
miércoles (m), Wednesday
militar, military
millonario,-a, millionaire
mío,-a, mine
mirador (m), vantage-point, lookout
minuto, minute
mirar, to look (at)
Misisipi (m), Mississippi
mismo,-a, same
misterioso,-a, mysterious
mitad , half
Moctezuma, Aztec emperor
moda, style, fashion
modelo (m/f), model
mojarse, to get wet
mojado,-a, wet
moneda, coin
mono, -a, monkey; cute; pretty
monosilábico,-a, monosyllabic
montaña, mountain
Montañas Rocosas, Rocky Mountains
montar, to mount
  montar a caballo, to ride a horse
morder [ue], to bite
Morelos: José María Morelos y Pavón
  (1765-1815), Mexican general
moreno, -a, dark, brunet(te)

morir(se) [ue], to die
morisco,-a, Moorish
moro, -a, Moor; Moorish
mosca, housefly
mostrar, to show, demonstrate
motocicleta, motorcycle
motor (m), motor
muchacha, girl
muchacho, boy
mucho,-a, much
mudéjar, Moorish style of architecture
mudo, -a, unable to speak
mueble (m), furniture
mujer (f) woman
muelle (m), wharf, quay; spring (as in a
  watch)
muerto, -a, dead; past participle of morir
multa, fine
multar, to fine
mundial, worldwide
mundo, world
muñeca, doll; wrist
museo, museum
música, music
músico, musician
mulsulmán,-ana, Moslem
muy, very

(N)

nacer [zc], to be born
nación (f), nation
Naciones Unidas, United Nations
nada, nothing
nadador,-a, swimmer
nadar, to swim
nadie, nobody
naranja, orange
naranjada, orangeade
nariz (f), nose
natación (f), swimming
naufragio, shipwreck
navaja de afeitar, shaving razor
navegar, to navigate, to sail
Navidad (f), Christmas
navideño, -a, pertaining to Christmas
neblina, mist
necesidad (f), necessity
necesitar, to need
negar [ie], deny
negarse a [ie], to refuse to
negro,-a, black
nervioso,-a, nervous
netamente, purely, clearly

nevar [ie], to snow
ni, nor
  ni la mitad, not even half
nicaragüense, of or from Nicaragua
nieta, granddaughter
nieto, grandson
nietos, grandchildren
nieve (f), snow
ningún, -una, no, not one
ninguno,-a, none
niña, girl
niño, boy
nobleza, nobility; goodness
noche (f), evening, night
  de noche, in the evening, at night
  esta noche, tonight
Nochebuena, Christmas Eve
nombre (m), name, noun
nada, nothing
noreste, northeast
nos, directly or indirectly involving us;
  ourselves
nosotros, we, us
nosotras (f), we, us
nota, note; grade (school)
noticia, news item; notice
noventa, ninety
novio, -a, sweetheart; bridegroom; bride
núcleo, nucleus
nuestro,-a, our(s)
Nueva York, New York
nueve, nine
nuevecito, -a, brand new
nuevo,-a, new
Nueva Jersey, New Jersey
nuez (f), nut, walnut; Adam's apple
número, number
numeroso,-a, numerous
nunca, never
nutrición (f), nutrition
nutritivo,-a, nutritious

(O)

o, or
ó, or (between Arabic numerals, as in 2 ó 3)
obligado, -a, obliged, forced to
obra, work, work of art
ocasionar, to cause, produce
océano Pacífico, Pacific Ocean
ochenta, eighty
ocho, eight
octava, octave
octavo,-a, eighth

octubre, October
ocupado, -a, busy, occupied
ocurrir, to occur
odiar, to hate
oferta, offer; sale, bargain
ofrecer, to offer
oído, (inner) ear; heard (from oir)
ojalá, impersonal expletive to express hope or wish
ojo, eye
ola, wave
olimpiadas, olympics
olímpico,-a, olympic
olmeca, Olmec (Mexican Indian civilization)
olla, pot
once, eleven
onza, ounce
ópera, opera
opinión , opinion
oportunidad , opportunity
optómetra (m/f), optometrist
oración , sentence, phrase; prayer
ordenar, to order
oreja, (outer) ear
orgullo, pride
orgulloso, a, proud
oriente (m), Orient, east
origen (m), origin, source
orilla, shore, bank; edge
oro, gold
orquesta, orchestra
ortografía, spelling
oscuro,-a, dark
oso, bear
otoño, autumn
otra vez, again, another time
otro,-a, other, another

(P)

paciencia, patience
Pacífico, Pacific (Ocean)
padre (m), father
Padre Hidalgo, "Father of Mexican Independence" (1753-1811)
padres, parents (both mother and father)
paella, Spanish national dish (shellfish, chicken and rice)
pagar, to pay
página, page
país (m), country, nation
paisaje (m), landscape, countryside, scenery
pala, shovel
palabra, word
palacio, palace

Palacio de Bellas Artes, Palace of Fine Arts
paloma, dove
pampa, Argentine plain
pan (m), bread
panadería, bakery
panadero, baker
panameño,-a, Panamanian
panecillo, dinner roll, small loaf of bread
pantalla, movie screen
papa, potato (original Indian name)
papá , (m), papa, dad
papel (m), paper
paquete (m), package
par (m), pair
para, for; in order to
parecer [zc], to seem
parecerse [zc] (a), to resemble
pared (f), wall
pariente (m/f), relative (family)
parque (m), park
parte (f), part
    en ninguna parte, nowhere
participar, to participate
particular, private; personal
parrafo, paragraph
pasado manana, the day after tomorrow
pasajero,-a, passenger
pasaporte (m), passport
pasar, to pass, spend (time), to go
pasear, to walk, stroll
paseo, walk, stroll
    dar un paseo, to take a walk
    de paseo, strolling, out for a walk
    Paseo de la Reforma, major Mexico City boulevard
pastel (m), pie, pastry; cake
pasteurizar, to pasteurize
patata, potato (Spain)
patín (m), skate
patinar, to skate
pato,-a, duck
patrimonio, inheritance, heritage
patriótico,-a, patriotic
patrón, -ona, boss, employer; (m); pattern
pavo,-a, turkey
(guajolote/guajalote in México)
payaso, clown
paz (f), peace
peatín (m), pedestrian
pedazo, piece, fragment
pedir [i], to ask (for)
pegar, to hit, strike; to glue, stick
peinar (se), to comb (oneself)
pelear (se), to fight, to quarrel
película, film

peligro, danger
peligroso,-a, dangerous
pelota, ball
pelotero, ball player
peluquería, beauty salon, hairdresser's shop
pensar [ie] (en), to think (about)
peor, worse, worst
pequeño, -a, small, little
pera, pear (fruit)
perder [ie], to lose; to misplace
perderse [ie], to get lost
perdón, pardon
perecer [zc], to perish
peregrino,-a, pilgrim
perezoso,-a, lazy
perfeccionar, to improve
perfume (m), perfume
período, period
periódico, newspaper
periodista (m/f), reporter, journalist
permiso, permission
permanecer [zc], to remain, to stay
pero, but, yet
persa (m/f), Persian
perseguir [i], to persecute
persiana, louver door or window, Venetian blind
persona (f), person
pertenecer [zc], to belong
perteneciente a, belonging to, pertaining to
peruano,-a, Peruvian
perro,-a, dog
pesado,-a heavy
pesca, fishing; catch
pescado, fish (out of water)
pescador (m), fisherman
pescar, to fish
pesebre (m), manger, crib
peseta, monetary unit of Spain
peso, weight
peso, monetary unit of México, Bolivia, Colombia, Cuba, and Dominican Republic
pez (m), fish (alive)
pianista (m/f), pianist
piano, piano
piano de cola, grand piano
picador (m), mounted lancer in bullfight
Picasso, Pablo Ruiz (1881- 1973), Spanish painter
pie (m), foot; a pie, on foot
    de pie, standing
piedra, stone
pieza, piece, one of several parts

pillete (m), young rascal
pingüino, penguin
pintar, to paint
  pintarse, to apply makeup
pintor, -a, painter
pintoresco, -a, picturesque
pintura, painting; paint
pionero, -a, pioneer
pirámide, pyramid
pirata (m), pirate
Pirineos, Pyrenees Mountains
piscina, swimming pool
piso, floor
pista, track; runway
pista de hielo, ice rink
pizarra, chalk board
Pizarro, Francisco (1475- 1541), Spanish
  explorer of Perú
placer (m), pleasure
plan (m), plan
planchar, to iron, press
planear, to plan
plano, map, street map; plan of a building
planta, plant
  planta baja, ground floor
plantar, to plant
plata, silver
plátano, banana
plática, informal talk, chat
plato, plate, dish
playa, beach
plaza, square
plaza de toros, bullring
plenitud (f), fullness, abundance
plomero, plumber
plomo, lead (metal)
pluma, feather; pen
población population; town
poblado, town, village
pobre, poor
pobreza, poverty
poco, little (in amount)
  poco a poco, little by little
  poco, -a, little (in amount)
podio, podium
poesía, poetry
poeta (m/f), poet
policía (m), police officer
  policía (f), police force
político, -a, politician; political
pollito, chick
pollo, chicken
Ponce de León, Juan (1460- 1521),
  Spanish explorer
ponche (m), punch (beverage)

poner, to put, place
  poner atención, to pay attention
  ponerse, to put on (as clothing)
  ponerse a, to begin to
  ponerse, to become
por, by, for, through
  por consiguiente, consequently
  por lo visto, apparently
  por primera vez, for the first time
  por todas partes, everywhere
  por qué, why
porque, because
portafolio, portfolio
portarse, to behave
portugués,-esa, Portuguese
poseer, to possess
posguerra, postwar
posición (f), position
postre (m) dessert
práctica, practice
practicar, to practice
práctico,-a, practical
pradera, meadow, prairie
precaución (f), caution, precaution
precioso, -a, precious; beautiful
pregunta, question
preguntar, to ask (a question)
prender, to light, to turn on
preocuparse, to be concerned, worried
preparar, to prepare
  prepararse, to get ready
presentar, to present; to introduce
presentir, to have a foreboding, suspect
préstamo, loan
prestar, to lend
prevención (f), prevention
primavera, spring
primo,-a, cousin
primer(o),-a, first
primeros auxilios, first aid
primordial, basic, essential
princesa (f), princess
príncipe (m), prince
principios: a principios de, at the
  beginning of
problema (m), problem
producción (f), production
producir [zc], to produce
profesión (f), profession
profundo, -a, deep, profound
programa (m), program
prohibir, to prohibit
prometer, to promise
pronombre (m), pronoun
prontitud (f), promptness

pronto, soon; quickly
pronunciación , pronunciation
pronunciar, to pronounce
propina, tip (gratuity)
propio, -a, own, one's own
próspero,-a, prosperous
protección , protection
protector,-a, protective
proteger, to protect
provenzal, Provençal, language
proverbio (m), proverb
próximo, -a, next, near
psicólogo,-a, psychologist
publicar, to publish, publicize
pudín (m), pudding
pueblo, town; people
puente, bridge
puerta, door
puertorriqueño, -a, Puerto Rican
puesto, post, position (as in **pulmonía**,
  pneumonia
puño, fist; cuff
pupitre (m), desk (of a student)
purificar, to purify

Q

que, that, which, than
qué, what
quedarse, to remain, to be left
quejarse, to complain
quejas, complaints
quemar, to burn
quemarse, to get burned
querer [ie], to want, to wish; to love
queso, cheese
quien, quién, who
quienquiera, whoever
quince, fifteen
quitar, to take away or off
quitarse, to remove, take off
Quito, capital of Ecuador
quizá, quizás, perhaps, maybe

R

rabo (m), tail
radicar (en), to live (in) (a town or city)
radio (m), radium, radius
  radio (f), radio)
rama, branch (of a tree)
ramo, bunch, bouquet; branch, field (of
  endeavor)
ranchero, -a, rancher, farmer; from the
  ranch
rápidamente, rapidly

rapidez, speed, rapidity
rápido, -a, rapid, fast
rascacielos (m), skyscraper
rasurador (m) razor
raza, race (of people)
razón (f), reason
  tener razón, to be right
realizar, to realize, make happen
rebelde (m/f), rebel
rebuznar, to bray
recado, message
receta, recipe
recibir, to receive
recién casados, newlyweds
recién llegado, newcomer
recién pintado, -a, just painted, "fresh paint"
recio, -a, strong, stout
recipiente (m), vessel
recoger, to gather
recomendar [ie], to recommend
recordar [ue], to recall, to remember
recreo, recreation, recess
recuerdo, memory; souvenir
red (f), net
redactor,-a, editor
redondo, -a, round, spherical
reducir [zc], to reduce
reemplazar [zc], to replace
referencia, reference
reformar, to reform; to renovate
refresco, refreshment
refrigerador (m), refrigerator
regadío, irrigation, irrigated land
regalo, gift, present
regar [ie], to water, irrigate
regatear, to haggle, to bargain
región (f), region, area
regla, rule; ruler
regresar, to go back
regular, to regulate
reina, queen
reinado, reign
reino, kingdom
reír(se), to laugh
  reírse de, to make fun of, laugh at
relámpago, lightning
relinchar, to neigh, whinny
reloj (m), clock, watch
relucir [zc], to shimmer, to sparkle
remar, to row
remediar, to remedy, repair
remendar [ie], to mend
remolcar [ue], to tow
renancimiento, Renaissance; rebirth

reparar, to repair
repartir, to distribute, divide, share
reportar, to report
reporte (m) report
República Dominicana, Dominican Republic
resbalar, to skid
resfriado, resfrío, cold, chill
residente (m/f), resident
resolver [ue], to resolve, solve
respaldar, to back, support
respeto, respect
responsabilidad (f), responsibility
respuesta, answer
restaurante (m), restaurant
retirarse, to retire, withdraw
retraso, delay
reunión meeting, gathering
revista, magazine
revolución (f) revolution
rezar, to pray
rico,-a, rich
riel (m), rail
riesgo, risk
rima, rhyme
rincón (m), corner, nook
río, river
risa, laughter
ritmo, rhythm
rizar, to curl
robar, to steal, to rob
robo, robbery, theft
rodeado,-a, surrounded
rodilla, knee
rojo,-a, red
Roma, Rome, capital of Italy
romance, coming from Latin (language)
romántico,-a, romantic
romper, to break
roncar, to snore
ropa, clothes, clothing
ropero, closet
roquero, -a, rock artist or musician
roto, -a, broken, torn
rubio,-a, blond(e)
ruido, noise
ruidoso,-a, noisy
rumbo a, in the direction of, headed toward
ruso,-a, Russian
ruta, route

S

sábado, Saturday
sábana, sheet (bedding)
sabana, savanna, treeless plain
saber, to know
sabor (m), flavor
sabroso, -a, flavorful, tasty
sacar, to take (out of)
  sacar fotos, to take photographs
sacerdote (m), priest
sacudir, to shake, to dust
sal, salt
sala, living room
salir, to leave, go out
salón (m), large room
salsa (f), sauce, (m) kind of dance
salto, leap
salud (f), health
saludar, to greet
salvavidas (m/f), life-preserver, lifeguard
samba, popular dance in Brazil
San Juan, capital of Puerto Rico
sanar, to cure, recover
Sancho Panza, servant to Don Quixote
sano,-a, healthy
saquear, to ransack, sack
sarampión (m), measles
sastre (m) tailor
sátira, satire
satisfacer, to satisfy
secadora, dryer (clothes, hair)
secar, to dry
sección (f), section
secretaria, secretary
segundo,-a, second
secundario,-a, secondary
sed (f), thirst
seda, silk
seguridad (f), security
seis, six
selección (f), selection
seleccionar, to select
selva, jungle
selvático, pertaining to wilderness or jungle
sembrar [ie], to sow, to plant
semejante, similar
semestre (m), semester
senador,-a, senator
sendero, path
sentado, -a, seated, sitting
señalar, to signal, point out
señor, (m), mister, sir; man
señora, Mrs.; woman; lady

señorita, miss; young woman; young lady
sentir(se) [ie], to feel
separar, to separate
septiembre (m), September
sequedad (f), dryness
sequía, dry spell, drought
serio,-a, serious
servilleta, napkin
serrucho, saw; kingfish
sesenta, sixty
setenta, seventy
seudónimo, pseudonym
si, if, whether
sí, yes
sidra, sparkling cider
siempre, always
siesta, nap, afternoon snooze
  dormir una siesta, to take a nap
siete, seven
siglo, century
  Siglo de Oro, Golden Age [of Spanish literature]
significar, to mean, to signify
sílaba, syllable
silla, chair, seat
sillón (m), easy chair, armchair
simpático, -a, nice, likable
sin, without
  sin duda, undoubtedly, without a doubt
sincero,-a, sincere
sinfónico,-a, symphonic
sino, but (used for contradicting)
sinónimo, synonym;-a, synonymous
síntoma (m), symptom
soberanía, sovereignty
sobre, over, above; (m) envelope
sobrepasar, to surpass
sobre todo, above all
sobretodo, overcoat
sobrio, -a, moderate, temperate, sober
sofá (m), sofa
solamente, only
soldado, soldier
solo,-a, alone
sólo, only (shortened form of *solamente*)
soltero,-a, unmarried
sombrero, hat
sombrilla, parasol, umbrella
sonrisa, smile
soñar [ue] (con), to dream (about)
sopa, soup
sordo,-a, deaf
sorprendente, surprising
sorprender, to surprise
sortija, ring; ringlet of hair, curl

sospecha, suspicion
sospechar, to suspect
sospechoso, -a, suspicious; suspect
sótano, cellar
Soto, Hernando de (1500-1542), Spanish explorer
su, his, her, your, their
subdirector, vice principal, assistant director
subir, to go up, ascend
suceder, to happen, occur; to succeed (a king)
suceso, event, happening
sucio,-a, dirty
Sudamérica, South America
sueco,-a, Swedish
suegra, mother-in-law
suegro, father-in-law
sueldo, salary
suelo, floor; soil
sueño, dream; sleep
  tener sueño, to be sleepy
suerte, luck
suéter (m), sweater
suficiente, sufficient, enough
sufrir, to suffer
Suiza, Switzerland
sumar, to add
suntuoso, -a, sumptuous, lavish
superficie (f), surface
supermercado, supermarket
suplir, to supplement; provide
sur (m), south
surgir, to arise, emerge, appear
sustantivo, substantive, noun or pronoun
susto, fright, scare
suyo, -a, his, hers, yours, theirs

(T)

tabaco, tobacco; cigar
tabla, board, plank
también, also, too
tampoco, neither
tan, so, as
tanto, -a, so much, as much
tantos, -as, so many, as many
tarde, late; (f) afternoon
tarea, task, assignment
tarjeta, card
tarjeta de crédito, credit card
taxi (m), taxi
taxista (m/f), taxi driver
taza, cup
te, to you

té (m), tea
teatro, theater
técnico, -a, technical; (m/f), technician
tela, cloth, fabric
telefonear, to telephone
telefónico, pertaining to telephones
teléfono, telephone
telegrama (m), telegram
teleguía, TV program guide
televisión (f), television
televisor (m), televison set
tema (m), theme, subject
temblor (m), earthquake; quiver, tremor
tempestad (f), storm, tempest
templado, -a, moderate, temperate; lukewarm
temporada, season
  temporada de pesca (caza), fishing (hunting) season
  temporada de lluvias, rainy season
temprano, early (in the day)
tener, to have; to hold
  tener calor, to be hot
  tener éxito, to be successful
  tener frío, to be cold
  tener hambre, to be hungry
  tener lugar, to take place
  tener miedo, to be afraid
  tener razón, to be right
  tener sed, to be thirsty
  tener sueño, to be sleepy
tenis (m), tennis
tenista (m/f), tennis player
teoria, theory
Tenochtitlán, capital of the Aztec Empire
Teotihuacán, cultural and religious center of the Aztec Empire
tercer(o),-a, third
termo (m), thermos
ternura, tenderness
terremoto, earthquake
terreño, plot of land
tesorero,-a, treasurer
testificar, to testify
testigo (m/f), witness
testigo ocular, eyewitness
tía, aunt
tiempo, time; weather
  hace buen tiempo, it's good weather
  tiempo libre, free time
tienda, store; tent
tigre (m), tiger
tijeras, scissors
timbre (m), electric bell; stamp
timidez , shyness

tímido,-a, timid, shy
tinta, ink
tintorería, dry cleaners
tío, uncle
típico,-a, typical
tirantes (m), suspenders
título, title; diploma
tiza, chalk
toalla, towel
tocar, to touch; to play (instrument)
  tocar a la puerta, to knock on the door
todo,-a, all
tolteca (m/f), Toltec, Toltec Indian
tomar, to take; to drink
tomate [jitomate in México], tomato
tonto,-a, foolish
torero, bullfighter
tormenta, storm
torneo, tournament
toro, bull
  corrida de toros, bullfight
toronja, grapefruit
tortilla, tortilla (Mexico); omelet
torre, tower
tos (f), cough, coughing
toser, to cough
trabajar, to work
trabajo, work
tradición (f), tradition
traer, to bring
tráfico, traffic, commerce
traidor,-a, traitor
traje, (m) suit (of clothes)
  traje de baño, bathing suit
tranquilo, -a, tranquil, calm
transistor (m), transistor
tránsito, traffic
tranvía, (m), streetcar
tras, behind, after
tratar, to treat
tratar de, to try to
travesía, crossing, voyage
travieso,-a, mischievous
treinta, thirty
  treinta y uno, thirty-one
trenza, braid (hair)
tres, three
triángulo, triangle
trigo, wheat
trío, trio

tripulación (f), crew (of a ship)
triste, sad
tristeza, sadness
triunfo, triumph
trofeo, trophy
trono, throne
tropa, troop
truco, trick
trueno, thunder
tu, your
tú, you (familiar)
turco -a, Turk; Turkish
turista (m/f), tourist
turquesa, turquoise (gem)
tuyo,-a, yours

U

u, or (before [u] sound)
últimamente, lastly, finally; lately
último, -a, last (in line or number)
ultramarino,-a, overseas
un, -a, a, an, one
Unamuno, Miguel de (1864-1936),
  Spanish novelist and poet
unidad (f), unity, unit
  unidad monetaria, monetary unit
unificar, to unify
uniforme (m), uniform
universidad (f), university
uno, one
uña, fingernail
usar, to use
uso, use; usage; wear and tear
usted, -es, you (formal)
útil, useful
utilizar, to use, utilize
uva, grape

V

vacío, -a, empty; (m), void, vacuum
vacunar, to vaccinate
valentía, courage, valor
valer, to be worth
  valer la pena, to be worth the trouble
  or effort
valiente, brave
valioso, -a, valuable, useful, worthwhile
valor (m), value; courage

vals (m), waltz
vapor (m), steam, vapor; steamship
vaquero, cowboy
varios,-as, various
vasco/vascongado,-a, Basque
vascuence (m), Basque (language)
vaso, glass (for drinking)
vecino,-a, neighbor
vehículo, vehicle
veinte, twenty
veintinueve, twenty-nine
velocidad (f), speed, velocity
venado, deer, stag; venison
venda, bandage
vendedor, -a, salesperson, vendor
vender, to sell
venezolano,-a, Venezuelan
vengar, to avenge
venir [ie], to come
venta, sale; selling
ventana, window
ver, to see, to look
verano, summer
verbo, verb
verdad (f), truth
verdadero,-a, true
verde, green
verduras, greens, vegetables
vergüenza, shame; shyness
  tener vergüenza, to be embarrassed, to
  be shy
vértigo, vertigo,dizziness
vestido, dress
vez (f), time, instance
  de vez en cuando, from time to time
  diez veces, ten times
  en vez de, instead of
  otra vez, again
  por primera vez, for the first time
  una vez, once
viajar, to travel
viaje (m), trip, journey
viajero,-a, traveler
víctima (m/f), victim
vida, life
viejo,-a, old
viento, wind
viernes, Friday
violín (m), violin
violinista (m/f), violinist

virreinato, viceroyalty
visitante (m/f), visitor
visitar, to visit
vitaminas, vitamins
vivir, to live
volar [ue], to fly
volver [ue], to return (from somewhere)
vosotras (f), you (plural familiar)
vosotros, you (plural familiar)
voto, vote
voz (f), voice
  en voz baja, in a soft voice
  voz pasiva, passive voice
vuelo, flight
vuelta, return
  boleto de vuelta, return trip ticket
  boleto de ida y vuelta, round-trip ticket
  de vuelta, on the way back
vuelto, change (money); past participle of
  volver

y, and
yeso, plaster; chalk
yo, I
yodo, iodine
yuca, cassava
yucateco, -a, of or from Yucatán, México

zapatería, shoe store
zapatero, maker or seller of shoes
zapato, shoe
zarzuela, Spanish operetta
zoológico, zoo